ARTILLERY OF HEAVEN

Figure 1. Syria Mission Field in the mid-nineteenth century. Source: Isaac Bird, *Bible Work in Bible Lands; or, Events in the History of the Syria Mission* (Philadelphia: Presbyterian Board of Publication, 1872), frontispiece.

ARTILLERY OF HEAVEN

American Missionaries and the Failed Conversion of the Middle East

USSAMA MAKDISI

Cornell University Press
Ithaca and London

A volume in the series

The United States in the World

Edited by Mark Philip Bradley and Paul A. Kramer

First published 2008 by Cornell University Press
First printing, Cornell Paperbacks, 2009

Printed in the United States of America

Library of Congress Cataloging-in-Publication Data

Makdisi, Ussama Samir, 1968–
    Artillery of heaven : American missionaries and the failed conquest of the Middle East / Ussama Makdisi.
        p. cm. — (The United States in the world)
    Includes bibliographical references and index.
    ISBN 978-0-8014-4621-4 (cloth : alk. paper)
    ISBN 978-0-8014-7575-7 (pbk. : alk. paper)
    1. Shidyaq, As'ad, 1798–1830.   2. American Board of Commissioners for Foreign Missions.   3. Missions, American—Lebanon—History—19th century.   4. Missions, American—Middle East—History—19th century.   5. Religious pluralism—Middle East—History—19th century.   6. Maronites—Lebanon—History—19th century.   7. Christianity and other religions—Islam.   8. Islam—Relations—Christianity.   I. Title.   II. Series.
    BV3210.L4M35 2008
    266'.0237305692—dc22   2007029232

Cloth printing   10 9 8 7 6 5 4 3 2 1
Paperback printing   10 9 8 7 6 5 4 3 2

For Elora

and in memory of Edward and Rosemarie

Contents

Acknowledgments

This is a book of many debts. Its inspiration came from a comment made by my late uncle Edward Said in one of his books several years ago, when he chided me, and my generation of scholars from the Middle East, for coming all the way to America to study the Arab world. I always thought that the criticism was not quite fair, although it was fairly meant, for Edward, more than anyone else I have known, wrote passionately and sincerely for the humanistic study of self and other. I truly regret that neither he, nor my aunt and fellow historian Rosemarie Said Zahlan, lived long enough to read these lines.

There are other scholars who have followed this project from its inception: Bernard Heyberger, Ray Mouawad, and George Sabra have all been extraordinarily generous with their time and criticism. I acknowledge the assistance of the staff of the following institutions: the Houghton Library at Harvard, Andover Theological Library, the Archives and Special Collections of the Yale Divinity School Library (especially Joan Duffy) and Yale University Library, the Archives and Special Collections of Mount Holyoke College and Williams College (especially Sylvia Kennick Brown), the Special Collections of the Leyburn Library at Washington and Lee University, the Rauner Special Collections Library at Dartmouth College, the Boston Athenaeum Library (especially Stephen Z. Nonack), the British Library, the Congregational Library in Boston, the Başbakanlık Archives in Istanbul, the Historical Archives of the Propaganda Fide in Vatican City (and the assistance provided by Youssef Mouawad, Monsignor Nicolas Thevenin, and Father Camillus Johnpillai to facilitate my access there), the Near East School of Theology in Beirut, the Jafet Library of the American University of Beirut (especially Asma Fathallah), and the Archives of the Maronite Patriarchate at Bkirke, Lebanon (especially Sami Salameh). I have also been greatly aided by the staff in the Department of History and at Fondren Library at Rice University, especially Anna Youssefi and Anna Shparberg. I thank Père Nasser Gemayel for sharing with me some of his personal collection relating to the Asʿad Shidyaq affair and Rev. Habib Badr of the National Evangelical Church of Beirut for his encouragement. I acknowledge as well the support provided by the American Council of Learned Societies, the Center for Behavioral Research at the American University of Beirut and its director Samir Khalaf, Harvard University's Center for Middle Eastern Studies, the Harvard Divinity School, the Fares Center for Eastern Mediterranean Studies at Tufts University and its director Leila Fawaz, and the Office of the Dean of Humanities at Rice University.

My friends and colleagues at Rice and elsewhere have been helpful with their many criticisms and suggestions and their assistance. There are too many to thank, and so here I acknowledge only those who have read or helped with parts of this book, including Asli Gur, Evan Haefeli, Nadia Naz Janjua, Ilham Khuri Makdisi, Michael Maas, Scott McGill, Carl Pearson, Mark Pegg, Dana Robert, Paula Sanders, Heather Sharkey, Paul Silverstein, Himmet Taşkömür, Kerry Ward, and Lora Wildenthal, and those who read entire drafts, including Allison Sneider, Peter Sluglett, Alan Mikhail, Bruce Masters, Peter C. Caldwell, Niels Hooper, Jeremy Salt, Paul Kramer, Mark Bradley, the anonymous readers of both the University of California Press and Cornell University Press, and the graduate students in history at Rice, Laura Renee Chandler, Gale Kenny, and especially David Getman, who provided outstanding help as a research assistant. I am grateful to the brilliant work of my editor at Cornell University Press, Alison Kalett, who has vigilantly seen this book into its final form.

I owe deep thanks to my mother, Jean Said Makdisi, who read multiple drafts; to my father, Samir Makdisi; and to my brothers Karim and Saree. I owe infinite gratitude to my wife, Elora Shehabuddin, who has put up—

and occasionally not—with my rambling and my prose. Finally, for the welcome distraction they provided, I am thankful for my son, Sinan, and daughter, Nur, whose respective entries into this world coincided with the beginning and end of this project.

ARTILLERY OF HEAVEN

Introduction

This story, at first glance, appears to be a simple missionary tale. At its center is a young man inspired by foreign missionaries to renew his faith in God. Though persecuted by his former coreligionists, he dies true to his new beliefs. Here is a reminder of the enduring power of faith, a narrative as old as Christianity itself. Yet at the same time it is a testament to the consequential involvement of America in the world.

What follows is the story of a foundational encounter between Americans and Arabs. It traces the arrival of the first American Protestant missionaries to the Arab provinces of the Ottoman Empire, and the ensuing persecution and death of one of their earliest converts. This is a history in need of telling because it illuminates the beginnings of an evolving, complex relationship between America and the Arab world that goes back further than most people realize. It is also an opportunity to explain why and how a cultural clash involving Americans and Arabs unfolded and, equally important, how the encounter between them changed the actors and cultures on both sides. What began as a spiritual American crusade overseas led to unanticipated consequences, not least (but not solely, either) a liberalism that can be credited neither to Americans or Arabs alone but to a transnational history that demands a new kind of narrative.

Some of the basic facts of this history are clear. The convert's name was Asʿad Shidyaq. He belonged not to the Muslim majority of the vast multi-religious and multiethnic Ottoman Empire, whose seat was in Istanbul, but to the Eastern Christian community of the Maronites, who submitted ecclesiastically to the Roman Catholic Church. The Ottoman Empire stretched from North Africa, through the Middle East, and into the Balkans, binding together various provinces and peoples, among whom were Arabs, Armenians, Greeks, and Turks, under the dynastic rule of the Muslim Ottomans. Islam, as a religion, was given primacy. But Christians, including Maronites, who traced their church back to the seventh century, as well as Armenians, Syrian Orthodox, Greek Orthodox, Catholics, and Jews were granted full religious autonomy and liberty to make sense of their own place in this diverse yet unequal world.

Asʿad Shidyaq came from a prominent family in a land we today call Lebanon. Then as now, it lay some six hundred miles distant from Istanbul, and some five thousand miles from Boston, home of the American Board of Commissioners for Foreign Missions (ABCFM), the largest and most influential foreign missionary society in the nineteenth-century United States. From Boston, missionaries of the ABCFM had set out in 1819 to reclaim the lands of the Bible and to evangelize its Muslim, Christian, and Jewish inhabitants.

Asʿad's full name, Asʿad ibn Yusuf ibn Mansur al-Shidyaq ibn Jaʿfar ibn Fahd ibn Shahin ibn Jaʿfar ibn Raʿd ibn Fahd ibn Raʿd al-Hasruni, hints at the established place that the Maronite community occupied on the fringes of the sultan's dominions, and therefore calls attention to the scandal of his conversion to a Protestant faith which at the time had no native community and consequently no legal standing in the empire. Born in 1798, he was very well educated by the standards of his day and initially was groomed for the priesthood. He embraced American evangelical principles sometime in 1825, however, and desired to proclaim them publicly to his people. He was immediately harassed and then persecuted by his church in the name of its perpetual religious orthodoxy and its age-old fealty to the Roman Catholic Church. Forcibly detained in a remote monastery in 1826, he sought to escape several times. Finally, he was tortured, and was stripped of his Christian name. He was reviled as *Rab Shayul,* or Lord of Hell, by the patriarch of the Maronite Church. He died, it is thought, in abject confinement sometime in 1830, physically and metaphorically annihilated by his erstwhile community, abandoned by the local princes, unknown and insignificant to a distant sultan far too preoccupied with the aftermath of a massive Greek revolt to be bothered by the drama unfolding in a remote corner of his empire. But he was hailed by the American missionaries as their celebrated martyr and as a vindication of their mission.

For the missionaries, the life and death of As'ad Shidyaq was emblematic of a historic clash that pitted an assertive evangelical American Christianity against what it regarded as one of its most implacable foes, Islam, as well as the degenerate and effete Oriental Christianity that suffered under its yoke. From America the missionaries had come to save those whom they described as the religiously "mingled" peoples of the East. Their awareness of what they believed to be the waning power of Islam, and what they regarded as the corruption of Eastern Christian churches, galvanized the missionaries. They believed themselves to be at the vanguard of the liberation of the world and the heirs to the Protestant Reformation. Indeed, for all their time spent in the Bible lands, for all their detailed accounts of the manners and customs of the local peoples, and for all their efforts to master Arabic, men such as Jonas King, Isaac Bird, Eli Smith, and Henry Harris Jessup, to name only four of the most prominent American missionaries whom we shall encounter in the following pages, faithfully adhered to the pedagogical hierarchy evoked by the original seal of the ABCFM: a seminaked native kneeling down before, and accepting a Bible from, a white male missionary who is pointing to a heavenly dove.[1]

Such a transaction, in turn, revealed how tightly the scriptural commission to go and make disciples of all nations was tied to historical, racial, and cultural assumptions that emanated from a more recent American past. Although the stance and outline of the native in the ABCFM seal resembled the slave from the famous abolitionist seal of the British Committee for the Abolition of the Slave Trade, he was bound by no chains. The transaction, moreover, directly recalled, and in an important sense expanded, the narrative of the original seal of Massachusetts Bay Colony, which showed an Indian looking toward a star and uttering the Macedonian cry, "Come Over and Help Us." It recalled as well legendary names such as John Eliot and David Brainerd, pioneering missionaries to American Indians.[2] And it recalled, along with this, a sense of obligation, or what the nineteenth-century evangelical community in the United States regarded as the selfless but largely unrequited compassion that men like Eliot and Brainerd had felt for the heathen. By definition almost, it underscored a history of unfulfilled expectations, of two centuries of disappointing evangelical labor to Indians, of relentless expansion, settlements, wars, massacres, of vexed Indian-white relations that constituted the stain of American mission work.

Figure 2. Original seal of the American Board of Commissioners for Foreign Missions. Source: ABC 85.9 (10). By permission of the Houghton Library, Harvard University and Wider Church Ministries of the United Church of Christ.

That this stain was not indelible was the hope of American missionaries who emerged out of an early-nineteenth-century landscape shaped by a revolution, by revivals of faith, and by millennialist aspirations in a new nation. They regarded themselves as the true "artillery of heaven," divinely inspired men and women who could unilaterally reshape the face of the world, confident of victory as time flew forward to its much-anticipated end. Their militancy reflected their idealism, their denigration of other religions and cultures, the magnitude of their self-appointed errand to the world. Above all, they embodied a reinvigorated sense of mission born from the crucible of white conquest and Indian defeat in the New World.

༄

The parable of As'ad Shidyaq is in this sense an American tragedy. It tells of a young life extinguished in a futile quest to graft a bold but uncompromising American puritanism on an implacably multireligious world. This book investigates the dialectic of failure and renewal of mission work in both an expanding American republic and the Ottoman Empire, and the opportunities that overseas mission work improbably opened. It attests to the way in which nineteenth-century American missionaries universalized the scope and mandate of what had been a distinctly American missionary experience among Indians. Shaped by their ambivalent embrace of certain white triumph over the Indians in North America, they responded to the difficult realities of a new Ottoman frontier they had opened but could not dominate. The dynamic saw a venerable missionary strand of American history collide with, and gradually relent before, the imperatives of a different, Ottoman Arab time and place.

More than anything else, this cultural clash occurred at the meeting point of two powerful currents of history. The former was represented by an expansive American missionary movement for which unconstrained individual freedom of conscience had to lead inevitably to an evangelical Protestantism, and no accommodation with other religions could long be tolerated. The latter emerged out of an Ottoman Arab orthodoxy that regarded the mutual recognition of different religious communities as a guarantee of order and harmony in a profoundly unequal multireligious Islamic society.

Far from being a story of tolerance and intolerance, or of modernity and tradition, or of an ahistorical American imperialism and Arab resistance, the first American missionary encounter with the Arab world very much represented the contradiction and struggle between two different and fundamentally antithetical readings of the world. One reflected a determination to refashion that world on evangelical terms at a time of ascendant Anglo-American power; the other, a violent refusal to accept these terms.

۞

The archival and analytic frame for understanding this dynamic intersection of cultures rests on a juxtaposition of American missionary interpretations and narrations of the Shidyaq affair and a trove of Arabic documents, from the construction of an idealized Maronite Church history under Islamic rule that justified the persecution of Asʿad Shidyaq, to a convert's Arabic testimony of faith, to the increasingly illegible scribblings of a prison diary, to a final, unsigned confession of Catholic faith. The significance of Asʿad Shidyaq's story and of the several conflicting and evolving narrations of his fate lies primarily in their ability to illuminate the historical and historiographic richness that complicates an otherwise simple history of a convert's life and death, and of course a simplistic thesis of a clash between American and Arab civilizations.

This balance of perspectives and archives, and the bringing together of the many hitherto divergent national and local historiographies they represent, is a key contribution of this book. It is also a reflection of what is so glaringly absent in the missionary and nationalist historiographies of American–Middle Eastern relations, which have tended to focus on only one side of this encounter, usually the American. Collectively, missionaries and the historians who followed them have missed what is conceptually most distinctive about the origins of a sustained U.S. engagement with the Middle East: the plural nature of the encounter itself and the diversity of its sources. An appreciation of both of these factors should make historians radically reconsider how they approach this history and, consequently, how they describe it.

The account offered by this book thus speaks not about a clash of cultures, and still less of civilizations, so much as a cultural encounter that pitted *one* group of Americans against *one* group of Ottoman subjects *in a specific time and place*.[3] The precision is deliberate and is meant to stress what I hope will become apparent by the end of this book. The missionaries, despite their pretension to the contrary, no more represented all of Christian America than the Maronites opposing them represented the entirety of the East. Although the American missionaries from the outset identified him as an "Arab," Asʿad Shidyaq was not properly speaking an Arab in any nationalist or racialist sense. Arabic was, however, his mother tongue; he lived in the Arab provinces of the Ottoman Empire, and he helped lay the basis for what is presently known as the Arab Protestant community. Therefore to the extent that this book also refers to him as an Arab and locates him in the Arab world, it does so with full awareness of the contingency and diversity of these terms. Acknowledging certain fundamental differences between contemporary American and Arab cultures, and between particular readings of the world, should not validate monolithic representations of religion or culture or nation, nor should it obscure the continuous transformations that make them living, and hence relevant, realities. Too often, alas, it has.

இ

From the outset, a brittle narrative of American mission work has imposed itself on a rich history of confrontation and collaboration across cultures. It has juxtaposed the indispensability of missionaries with the irrelevance of actual native history and agency. The missionary genre, to be sure, is old, and is not, in its basic proposition of the unilateral nature and direction of mission work, unique to America or its missionaries. Classic evangelical missionary publications such as the Englishman William Carey's 1792 *Enquiry into the Obligations of Christians* found a strong echo in the Americans Gordon Hall and Samuel Newall's 1818 *Conversion of the World*.[4] The latter volume, passionately and militantly written in seventy-six pages by two American

Board missionaries, exemplifies a fundamental conceit of mission histories. From a presumably Christian center, missionaries saw themselves enlightening the darker areas of the world. For the chroniclers of mission, the setting might just as well have been the Sandwich Islands as Syria; the Maronite As ͨad Shidyaq might just as well have been the Cherokee Catherine Brown, and the Ottoman sultan, the Hawaiian queen Keopuolani.

More recent historians of American religious or diplomatic history have consistently reproduced, in admittedly less evangelical terms, the perspective and structure of classic missionary memorials, charting the unilinear path of missionaries from dynamic West to stagnant East, from light into darkness, from white to nonwhite, from historiographically important to less important, and thus have continued to overlook the actual histories and archives of non-Western societies.[5] The seminary education of the American missionaries to Palestine and Syria inspired them to keep extensive personal diaries as an integral expression of their faith. Their missionary training, moreover, encouraged them to provide more general descriptive and ethnographic accounts to record the variety of human conditions that they, as missionaries, would encounter in their quest to convert the world's heathen before the imminent end of time. These missionaries left a paper trail that humanizes their world. In the hands of empathetic scholars, missionary men and women have become dramatic historical actors rather than stock figures.

The abundance of missionary sources has facilitated an almost effortless embrace of a missionary perspective, but it does not entirely explain American historians' failure to adopt a fuller account of mission. There have been, to be sure, scores of hagiographies, celebrations, and, more recently, critical evaluations of American mission work. But there has been little concerted effort to appreciate the foreignness of missionary encounters. The distinct parochialism of this historiography reflects the fact that missionaries and questions of conversion do not occupy the same salient intellectual space for the nineteenth-century United States as they do for the British Empire, be it colonial British America or later in non-American parts of the empire.[6] Work on nineteenth-century American missions has tended to be hagiographic or missiological, or at best focused on a critical analysis of the nationalist and gendered implications of mission, but rarely, if ever, on the actual objects of mission. To appreciate the complexity of American missions, however, it is imperative to distinguish between the larger history of mission and the narrower travails of missionaries, and between a transnational history and a less ambitious national story.[7]

Because these two aspects of mission have been so frequently conflated, the history of American foreign missions, indeed, the history of America overseas, has in a crucial sense not yet been written. American historians working on U.S. interactions with foreign places and peoples have traditionally not been interested in seriously studying the worlds beyond American shores, let alone qualified to evoke them.[8] Although two centuries ago American missionaries abroad struggled to learn foreign languages and master foreign cultures, American scholars have largely confined themselves to telling a U.S. story overseas, positive or negative, as if all that mattered was the "American" aspect of this story.[9] Obscure histories, however, can illuminate those we think we know.[10] Ottoman Arab lands "discovered" by the missionaries were not simply the setting for a preordained or predetermined narrative but an active stage on which strands of American and Arab history, with all their passions and prejudices, were played out.[11]

ᵜ

Arab historians have been, if anything, at an even greater loss than their American counterparts when dealing with the question of missions. The answer to one form of historiographic myopia is not, or at least not only, to write from a so-called native perspective, to switch vantage points, to valorize local resistance, or to retreat into orthodoxy. It is certainly not to *deny* stories such as those of Asʿad Shidyaq, as the Maronite Church has done, or ignore it, as Lebanese historians have done, simply because they contain inconvenient or embarrassing truths. For far too long secular Arab historians have shied away from religiously sensitive topics in the interests of a putative national unity, allowing the void to be filled with scholarship obsessed with the idea of perpetual hostility between Christian and Jewish minorities and an oppressive monolithic Muslim majority.[12]

To be sure, there remain a plethora of stories to tell, histories to reveal, and narratives to be created about the countless "native helpers," "hopeful converts," and "bigoted fanatics" who constitute the largely anonymous local color of missionary portraits. To piece together the forgotten humanity at the heart of the missionary world—the converts and their societies—in as much complexity as possible is certainly an important endeavor, and surely more easily done for the literate modern Middle East than for the broken remnants of pre-Columbian America subjected to unmitigated Western colonialism. That it has not been done is testimony to the fact that the missionaries to the Levant are recalled by scholars more for their later, more secular educational work associated with the Syrian Protestant College (today the American University of Beirut) and Robert College (today Istanbul's Bosphorus University) than for their initial overtly evangelical enterprise. But it is also due to the fact that the study of missionaries has until very recently been out of favor among historians of the region, who have focused instead on rehabilitating the historiographic reputation of the nineteenth-century Ottoman state, which missionaries, Catholic as well as Protestant, did much to sully. It is telling indeed that the last major work on American missionaries to the Levant was written in 1966 by the Arab historian A. L. Tibawi.[13] To the extent that missionaries and converts have maintained a historiographic presence, it is due to the work of historians interested in tracing the Ottoman response and resistance to Western cultural imperialism.[14]

꧁

Missionaries, of course, have been particularly vulnerable to the charge of cultural imperialism—whether in British India, Africa, or the West Indies, Spanish America, Puritan New England, or the Ottoman Empire. The remarkable similarity of their writings on "the" heathen, whatever the locale, and their routine denigration of foreign cultures and their determination to restructure them, have made them an obvious target for satirists and novelists from Mark Twain and Herman Melville to Chinua Achebe and Amin Maalouf. Missionaries have been stigmatized by their relationship with colonialism, and by decolonization, whose logic depended on the essential juxtaposition of colonized over colonizer, and above all on a notion of a monolithic native culture subverted by missionaries but redeemed and represented by nationalist leaders. But decolonization, rather than giving voice to natives, simply took it away from the missionaries.

To emphasize resistance and to reduce the missionaries in the Ottoman Empire to mere "cultural imperialists" is to misconstrue the resiliency of the Ottoman Arab world and the originality of cultural spaces created by the intersection of American and Ottoman histories. The Ottomans, after all, were not Tzvetan Todorov's Aztecs, and the Americans were not traveling in the company of conquistadors. Later in the century, perhaps, when missionaries worked more directly in collaboration with Western colonial powers in the region, particularly in British-occupied Egypt or in French-occupied Lebanon, the charge of cultural imperialism becomes more tenable, but certainly not at the outset of the mission, when first two, then four men wandered across Mount Lebanon, Syria, and Palestine for several years, pleading and preaching the Word of God in a multireligious empire still confident, if no longer certain, of its ability to withstand Western encroachment.

To denounce missionaries as cultural imperialists is also to misunderstand the often ambivalent location missionaries occupied within their own societies as well as in foreign fields.[15] And it is to ignore the polyvalent registers of native worlds and the deliberate choice made by many individuals such as As'ad Shidyaq to associate with foreign missionaries. That his life and death unfolded at the margins of two worlds—overseas from the American view and in rural Mount Lebanon from the Ottoman view—among Protestant missionaries and Maronite Christians should make us appreciate how cultures are always in context. Nowhere were the Protestant missionaries more "American" than when they came into contact with an obviously foreign Ottoman society, even as they were identified locally as "English" because of the language they spoke and because of the protection they enjoyed from British representatives. And even as they allowed this fiction to stand because of a lack of U.S. diplomatic presence for the first decade of their work, in few other places could these Americans have represented the antebellum United States in so evangelical and so uncontested a manner. The Maronite Christians, in turn, represented *a* face of a vast Muslim empire. Their struggle against foreign heretics reveals the extent to which Maronites were integrated into a highly stratified world of Ottoman Lebanon that accommodated religious difference and privileged rank over religion and elites over commoners.[16]

࿇

The point here is not to dismiss out of hand the association of nineteenth-century American missionaries with imperialism but to study the relationship more profoundly. There is no need to deny what is obvious: as much as the term "cultural imperialism" paints an admittedly broad stroke, the term has resonated for the simple reason that Western, including American, missionaries did overwhelmingly justify the subordination, if not always the ethnic cleansing or extermination, of native peoples during a genocidal nineteenth century.

The history of Anglo-American mission work is, if anything, to a large extent the history of cultural imperialism manqué. An endeavor in which one group genuinely believes in, and seeks to spread, its own superior religion and way of life obligates the transformation of others. This is not necessarily cultural imperialism. In North America, however, Anglo-American mission work was from its inception implicated in settler colonialism, which both made possible and consistently upset the most benevolent mission projects among Indians, from John Eliot's Puritan beginnings to the ABCFM's own substantial commitment to proselytize Indians in the southeastern United States. Such a vexed relationship with power at home inevitably framed the perceptions and expectations of foreign fields such as the Levant, where American political control was notably absent.[17] The methodologies and ideals of early American evangelism to the Islamic world were inevitably refracted through the experience of archetypal mission work to the Indian heathen. Overseas was a space uncluttered by the incorrigible violence of American settler colonialism, which forced Indians consistently to give way to white expansion. The Bible lands were a proving ground for American redemption, ostensibly free of the entanglements and corruptions of American colonialism and Western empire, where Americans could glory in a language of benevolence that was rapidly running its course with Indians at home. Cultural imperialism, in short, rather than being an epithet in this book, describes a process that has several genealogies and articulations, frustrations, and failures. Rather than concluding a discussion, it signals the beginning of a long-overdue dialogue between Americans and Arabs.

இ

This book traces several overlapping imperial, colonial, and local conversations, some of considerably longer duration than others. Part I serves as a prelude to the main narrative. It outlines the origins and contours of an aggressive settler-colonial American discourse, famously encapsulated by the early-eighteenth-century Puritan divine Cotton Mather in his monumental *Magnalia Christi Americana,* which opposed Puritan to Indian and paradoxically both encouraged and confounded missions. It also explores the simultaneous elaboration halfway across the world of a defensive Maronite ecclesiastical discourse which firmly subordinated the Maronite Church to the Roman Catholic Church, in the epic *Tarikh al-Azmina,* or *A History of the Ages,* by the father of the Latinized Maronite Church, Istifan Duwayhi, in the seventeenth century. Both Mather and Duwayhi constructed mythologies of purity, but from radically different perspectives: the former recorded the creation of an uncompromising *new* society that was meant to augur worldwide Christian expansion; the latter defended an *ancient* church that had long since reconciled itself to coexistence in an impure multireligious world. The coincidental evocations of profoundly different Christian worlds by two remarkable (and remarkably different) figures helped set the stage for the early-nineteenth-century Shidyaq affair as a clash between those who saw themselves as the inheritors and defenders, respectively, of these seemingly irreconcilable Christian cultures.

Although it emphasizes an enduring American predicament of missions to the Indian heathen on the one hand, and elaborates on the nature of Maronite orthodoxy in the shadow of Ottoman Muslim rule on the other, this prelude also serves to underscore the disjuncture between nineteenth-century American missionaries and their colonial predecessors, as well as that between the Maronite Church in the seventeenth and the nineteenth centuries. John Eliot did not lead inevitably to Pliny Fisk and Levi Parsons, but a fuller comprehension of the latter two depends, in many respects, on an understanding of the former.

Part II charts the specific history of the American Board itself and the arrival of its missionaries in biblical lands they had read about intently but did not know in any actual sense. Here I outline how American missionaries were confronted by people who refused to conform to their millennial fantasy or to their location in a missionary world that regarded the inhabitants of the Ottoman Empire in a substantially similar way to that in which it regarded the American Indian "heathen." At the same time, however, the Maronite Church was stunned by the decision of several individuals, most notably Asʿad Shidyaq, to embrace sincerely the missionaries and their message of salvation. This section also explores the implications of Asʿad Shidyaq's puritanism, detailing his physical fate by drawing on a variety of sources, especially his own writings. It reveals how the missionaries, matched almost text for text by Eastern churches, imperial authorities, and Asʿad's own copious Arabic writings, quickly and defiantly constructed a martyrology of Shidyaq that presumed to transform a stunning defeat into an evangelical victory.

Out of this crucible both Americans and Maronites grudgingly came to recognize their inability to win total victory over each other at a time of rapid and turbulent transformation of the Ottoman Empire. Part III accordingly follows the divergent ways in which American missionaries and their converts re-narrated the life of Shidyaq against a backdrop of imperial Ottoman reform. The official Ottoman recognition of Protestantism in 1850, the historic proclamation in 1856 of the equality of Muslim and non-Muslim subjects in the eyes of a self-professed "civilized" sultan, and the extraordinary scenes of sectarian violence in Mount Lebanon and Damascus in 1860 which culminated in the massacres of Christian subjects forced both missionaries and their converts to reevaluate the significance of Asʿad Shidyaqʾs persecution in an age of manifest Western hegemony.

More specifically, Part III investigates how the American missionary memorialization of Asʿad Shidyaq after 1860 was noticeably less millennialist and more self-consciously modern than the first reports issued about a native "brother in Christ." It was also far more racist, in line with a hardening Anglo-American perspective marked by the Indian Mutiny of 1857 and confirmed by the curtailing of American Board missionary work among the Indians in North America.[18] Asʿad Shidyaqʾs persecution was reconfigured as the prelude to what the Americans regarded as an inevitable "Eastern" fanaticism and massacres of 1860, an indication of a native condition unable to grasp on its own the benevolent outstretched missionary hand. Even as more educated, more articulate, and more confident individuals emerged from the nascent native Protestant community, most, but significantly not all, missionaries firmly adhered to a more pronounced racial hierarchy. This hierarchy increasingly idealized America, orientalized the East, and presumed to speak for the natives in a conversation about mission conducted mainly with American critics and supporters rather than with the people the missionaries had ostensibly come to save. Perhaps most noticeably, late-nineteenth-century missionaries professed far more knowledge about other faiths than, and in a manner unthinkable to, the first generation of American missionaries to the East. Yet by characterizing Islam and the unevangelized Orient as inherently unfit for modern life, they exhibited a new determination to conclude what they regarded as a historic struggle between Christianity and Islam.

The implications and irony of this evolution in missionary culture becomes readily apparent, and can only be fully appreciated, when we discover the parallel, neglected Arabic rehabilitation of Asʿad Shidyaq which broke with missionary and Maronite orthodoxies and their mutually exclusive narratives of purity. The author of this mid-century vindication of Shidyaq was a veritable child of the missionary encounter, Butrus al-Bustani, also a Maronite convert to Protestantism who embodied the possibilities and predicaments of a new, less cloistered nineteenth century. At a moment when severe sectarian tensions beset his country, Bustani elaborated a locally rooted ecumenical humanism and a secularized evangelical sensibility. He explicitly called for, and worked toward, a new form of coexistence based on equality, one that was derived from an embrace of the region's religious diversity but was transformed through a dialogue of East and West, Muslim and Christian.

The ecumenical humanism so evident in Bustani underscored its absence among later-nineteenth-century American missionaries, which in turn brings us back to the larger historiographic intervention this book makes. The documents that defined this encounter, that conserve its history, and that make possible its narration in the pages that follow have to be read *relationally,* and not simply against the grain. In vain will one scour the missionary archives in search of some original template for Bustani's ecumenism; by the same token, one will not find such expression in the records of the Ottoman state, the *sharia* court registers, or Maronite Church documents of the time. Although he adapted a missionary vernacular of barbarism and heathenism and helped reify notions of East and West, there were no "national" roots or origins—American or Arab—for his discourse of tolerance and his adumbration of an Arab cultural renaissance. His quintessentially nineteenth-century outlook was not something borrowed or imported, nor did it emerge unshaped by the experience of mission. Rather, it was a testament to the fact that what had been framed initially as a clash of cultures irreconcilably and perpetually arrayed against each another had ultimately produced new possibilities for dialogue within and across cultures.

This is a story, in the final analysis, that is not simply about the productive failures of American cultural imperialism; it is also about the failure of an anti-missionary orthodoxy. The struggle between antithetical readings of the world, each born of a specific and exclusive fantasy of purity, cost Asʿad Shidyaq his life. But it also eventually produced a liberal attempt to reconcile cultures anticipated by neither. The rich histories of missions and the worlds upon which they acted must be rescued from the unimaginative nationalist and sectarian polemics that taint all those associated with missions with the stigma of foreignness. By the same token, the unpredictable outcome of the intersection of competing histories, cultures, and contexts must not be too quickly credited to missions, or grasped as evidence of the benevolence of missionaries, as if they were shrewd investors in underrated native futures.[19] There is no such thing, ultimately, as the "fundamental egalitarianism" of the Christian message or the simple "imperialism" of American missionaries.[20] There were Christians, there were (mixed) messages, and there were (eventually) new discourses of equality: but the relationships among all these were neither obvious nor fundamental, and certainly not straightforward.

A new historical imagination is needed to uncover the entangled histories of a missionary encounter that began on the eve of modernity.[21] It is patently clear that historians of both America and the modern Middle East have been far too steeped in their respective disciplinary traditions to narrate an episode that is at once American and Arab, and that by its nature demands a historiographic openness that neither tradition has afforded.

The only way to tell a story of a cross-cultural encounter involving Americans and Arabs is to enlarge dramatically the conventional scope of inquiry. It is to see how relevant histories unfolded simultaneously, if distinctly and unevenly, in the Ottoman Empire and the United States, to compare historical process with historical process, and to understand the implications of their juxtaposition brought about by the missionary intrusion into the Ottoman Empire. It is literally to unravel history's different strands first woven together by American missionaries in so fervent a manner. This book represents a first attempt to do so.

Part I

PRELUDE

Chapter 1

Mather's America

John Eliot was the preeminent Puritan missionary of his time. When the American Board decided to name a mission station to the Choctaw Indians in the southeastern United States after Eliot in 1818, it was because his name evoked for them the promise of unfulfilled benevolence to the heathen. He was among the few missionaries in the country's colonial past to whom the American Board could point; he was, in their eyes, an example of what a new Christian nation might yet become: powerful yet charitable toward the remaining Indians of the United States, expansive yet racially inclusive, and above all singularly evangelical. In laying claim to Eliot's name, nineteenth-century American Protestants recalled and sought to rework an earlier incarnation of the famed missionary at the hands of the Puritan divine Cotton Mather. Mather made Eliot the subject of a prominent memorial in his *Magnalia Christi Americana,* an epic of conquest and Christianity in New England published at the turn of the eighteenth century.[1]

Taken together, Mather's hagiography of his fellow Puritan and his account of Indians encapsulated some of the enduring problems—indeed, paradoxes—of American mission work that nineteenth-century missionaries hoped to resolve. The most obvious of these was the overwhelming fact of settler colonialism, the aggressive expansion of English settlement that in its Puritan form in New England both promoted and undermined missions. Mission work served, crucially, at once as an atonement for the gross violence of the colonial experiment and a reflection of its presumed benevolent spirit.

The second problem very much stemmed from the gross disparity of power between whites and Indians which sustained and frustrated missionaries; the missionaries attempted to maintain what they saw as a noble *Protestant* mission, with its attendant notion of literacy, voluntary conversion, and choice, amidst the ongoing intimidation and subjugation of Indians. The sincere belief among missionaries that faith must not be compelled was matched by their obviously hierarchical and largely unaccountable relationship to their native converts. Although they witnessed steady displacement of Indians at the hands of settlers, and recognized, and sometimes even lamented, the inherent violence of the settler colonialism of which they were a part, Puritan missionaries clung to the notion that their labors were less coercive and more spiritual than what they viewed formulaically as "Papist" missions. They not only recorded Indian voices but easily redacted them as well into mission apologetics whose audience was not Indian but white: sympathizers with mission on the one hand and skeptics on the other.

The third problem was the contradiction between purity of self and the purification of Indians; what missionaries such as Eliot idealized as a patriarchal relationship between Puritan evangelical fathers and converted Indian babes in Christ remained for the vast majority of their Puritan and non-Puritan compatriots an antithetical relationship between Christian survival and heathen savagery. As a result, Puritan missions, and their ideal of a universal Christian community, foundered amidst a gradual, grudging Puritan toleration of non-Puritans and an increasingly adamant rejection of coexistence with the unadulterated heathen. The meager harvest of souls produced in turn equal measures of disappointment and reflection. From this colonial context emerged the defining and exculpatory tropes of American mission work: the barbarous native, the unscrupulous settler, and the benevolent missionary.

৳

Cotton Mather's *Magnalia Christi Americana* chronicled and celebrated an American Puritan world coming into being. It told a story of how Puritans became "the owners and masters of the country," and about how the native Indians had willingly and inevitably acquiesced in their own subjugation.[2]

Here, as Mather saw it, was a self-consciously new society that wished to subordinate worldliness to the immutable but interpretable Word of God. It was a society whose impulse was powerfully simple: to eradicate impurity where possible and to shun it where not; hence an arduous voyage to the "desarts of America," a disavowal of the corruption of the Catholic and Anglican churches, a total reliance on the truth of the Scriptures, a continuation of the European reformation through the agency of churches "very like unto those that were in the first ages of Christianity," and consequently a fervent desire to set up a truly pious community of visible saints who would brook no heresy, no idolatry, and no error.[3]

Far from the current stereotype of witch-burning Puritans, a fundamental aspect of the Puritan idea lay in the notion that true Christian faith had to be voluntarily embraced, not compelled. By the same token, a Puritan orthodoxy in New England was determined to stamp its imprint on what was a clearly heterogeneous world which included, besides "wild beasts and beastlike men" (as John Winthrop described Indians in 1642), many immigrants who were not committed Puritans.[4] Nobody, therefore, was allowed to settle in Massachusetts without the express consent of the colony's magistrates, themselves elected only by full members of a Puritan church who had demonstrated evidence of their own regeneration; all were required to observe the Sabbath and attend church services, of which only the Congregational form was tolerated. Heretical books were burned. Roger Williams was famously banished in 1635; Quakers were persecuted, Baptists shunned, and Jesuits banned. Indians, however, were allowed to settle near the English in order to further their conversion, but only if, the General Court declared, they shall "there live Civilly and Orderly."[5]

🐍

Mather described Eliot's mission in the third book of *Magnalia* under the title "The Triumphs of the Reformed Religion in America." He tellingly situated Eliot's mission to *surviving* Indians of New England following decades of settlement, warfare, and disease. Mather had already recounted in the first book of *Magnalia* a story of how a "chosen Generation" arrived in a "howling wilderness" in New England that had been "wonderfully prepared" by the Hand of God to receive its new inhabitants. "The Indians in these parts," he wrote, "had newly, even about a year or two before, been visited with such a prodigious pestilence, as carried away not a *tenth*, but *nine parts* of *ten*, (yea, 'tis said, *nineteen* of *twenty*) among them: so that the woods were almost cleared of those pernicious creatures, to make room for a *better growth*."[6] Divine inspiration and assistance was supplemented, Mather admitted, by "our English guns," which further terrified "ignorant Indians."[7]

Even as Mather set Eliot's life within the framework of a larger story about the welcome destruction of uncivilized Indians, he also elevated Eliot as a genuine model of missionary piety to these same Indians. To a Puritan outlook in which Indians were in many ways beyond the pale of what Puritans considered an apostolic church order and society, Mather's history of Eliot constituted an important corrective. Despite the solemn and original aspirations and pretensions of the first generation to "win and incite the natives of that country to the knowledge and obedience of the only true God and Saviour of mankind," few Indians were converted.[8] The colony of Massachusetts Bay, whose seal famously depicted an Indian calling out to the Puritans to "Come Over and Help Us," had witnessed only fitful missionary efforts. If facts on the ground had already raced ahead of ideals, here was a story that allowed these ideals to keep pace with, and even steal a march on, the facts. Here, finally, was a missionary's place in the story of the kindling of an allegedly pure and primitive Christianity in America. Here, finally, was an American Moses to take his place alongside an American Joshua in Mather's *Magnalia*.

Eliot was a Moses in two senses for Mather. First he helped deliver his own English people out of bondage, and *then* he became a lawgiver to another, quite different Indian people whom Mather referred to as "the veriest *ruines of mankind* which are to be found any where upon the face of the earth."[9] He was instrumental in leading the Puritans from persecution in England into the promised land of America, where he helped propagate a new way of life under a church government in New England. Eliot, Mather wrote, "came to New-England in the month of November, A.D. 1631, among those blessed old planters which laid the foundations of a remarkable country, devoted unto the exercise of the Protestant religion, in its purest and highest reformation." So important for Mather was this sense of rupture with an immediate past that he made it a point to insist that he could not "presently recover" the name of Eliot's "place of his nativity" and that, moreover, it was unimportant to do so, for it had been superseded by a new society in a new world that Eliot had helped found.[10] Eliot became a model of piety, humility, family religion, and mortification for a *new* American society; he wore simple clothes and loathed long hair; and he was deadened, Mather insisted, to the pleasures of this world. Eliot was first a Christian, then a minister to fellow Puritans, and finally an evangelist to the Indians, a sequence that highlighted the difference between a minister's relationship with his own congregation and a missionary's relationship to an isolated and subordinated people. According to Mather, Eliot was the embodiment of charity, for in his view it was charity that had inspired the evangelist to lead the Indians collectively and completely away from the devil's "ancient possessions."[11]

ᘞ

Almost all histories of John Eliot, and certainly those that Mather drew upon to paint his portrait of the selfless missionary, begin with him reaching out to Massachusett Indians eager to learn about Christianity.[12] Pamphlets published in London by advocates of Eliot's work such as *The Day-Breaking, if not the Sun-Rising of the Gospell with the Indians in New-England* in 1647 tell how Eliot and three companions, after a four-mile ride from Roxbury, arrived at the Indian encampment at Nonantum on 28 October 1646. They describe how the Puritan Eliot dutifully informed an Indian leader called Waban and his followers about the joys of heaven and the terrors of hell, how he patiently explained to them the meaning of the Ten Commandments. In Waban's wigwam, Eliot reminded the Indians how wicked they were in their current state. He offered them hope of salvation if only they were to pray to the Christian God. The enduring significance of this narrative lay less in its ability to tell a true story—the details of this particular episode at Nonantum may have occurred precisely as Eliot recounted them—than in its ability to glorify his missionary work as the epitome of a benevolent Puritanism without apparent rebuttal from any Indian source. It is not that the Indians were utterly silenced but rather that their voices were heard heavily mediated by those more powerful.[13]

God may have directly inspired Eliot, as Mather suggested, to take on the burden of civilizing and Christianizing so wretched a people as the Indians of Massachusetts, but the missionary labored in a context in which much of Indian culture had already been dislocated and destroyed by the English, their way of life already severely compromised by the arrival of so many settlers and by the undeniable fact of one English victory after another. In 1644, before Eliot began his proselytizing, five sachems (tribal chiefs) of the Massachusett tribe submitted themselves, their people, and their lands to the Puritan colony. They also committed themselves to allow Puritan missionaries to preach to them and their followers. Two years later the Massachusetts Bay Colony forbade Indians from worshipping their own gods.[14] And in 1658 the colony established a superintendent over all Indians under its authority, one who could sit as a judge, install his own officials, issue decrees and instructions, and order penalties for not "promoting and practicing morality, civility, industry, and diligence."[15]

Relentless foreign encroachment upon Indian lands, and disease, warfare, and massacres, made submission and conversion attractive to many Indians, but by no means a majority.[16] As one Indian put it in an account of his conversion transcribed by Eliot and published in 1660, he initially prayed "because I saw the *English* took much ground, and I thought if I prayed, the *English* would not take away my ground."[17] By 1674 there were some 2,300 Indians living in praying towns in Massachusetts Bay, Plymouth, Martha's Vineyard, and Nantucket out of an Algonquian-speaking population of 20,000 in southern New England, who themselves were overshadowed by the 60,000 English colonists.[18]

Unlike most of these English colonists, Eliot firmly believed that the successful evangelization of the Indians was both possible and necessary. While he flirted with the idea that the Indians of the New World were the descendants of Old Testament Israelite tribes, he pitied those described as "these poore Natives the dregs of mankinde and the saddest spectacles of misery of meere men upon earth."[19] More fundamentally, he insisted that the conversion of Indians demanded their secular civilization under English tutelage. Eliot believed that Christianity was not possible "whilst they live so unfixed, confused, and ungoverned a life, uncivilized, and unsubdued to labor and order."[20]

Eliot was thus instrumental in confining Christian Indians to "praying towns"—incarnations of Eliot's vision of erecting a pure "Christian commonwealth" in which the converts and their missionary benefactors would "fly to the Scriptures for every Law, Rule, Direction, Form or what ever we do."[21] Customs, rituals, and beliefs at odds with Puritan sensibilities, from wearing long hair to killing lice between the teeth and from dress to form of settlement, were either forbidden or strongly discouraged. As Mather pointed out proudly, "Our Eliot was no Mahometan."[22] The apostle to the Indians would not, Mather believed, allow for the dissolute toleration that epitomized Islam. Thus the "civilized" Indian town at Natick was modeled by Eliot after an English village. It boasted a meetinghouse, a fort, and straight streets along which converted Indians displayed their utter dependence on their Puritan masters, from the clothes they wore to the ideas of private property they accepted, the God they worshipped and the way they worshipped him, and above all their utter and direct submission to the authority of Eliot and the Massachusetts Bay Colony.

In 1653 Eliot published the testimonies of twenty-six conversion narratives in *Tears of Repentance: Or, A further Narrative of the Progress of the Gospel Amongst the Indians in New England*. Its main purpose was to convince a skeptical Puritan community of the viability of evangelized Indians in a Puritan world; its main effect, however, was to illuminate a fundamental problem of accountability inherent in missionary work to those considered uncivilized in the colonial world of New England—one that would find an echo in the nineteenth-century Levant.

Whereas a Congregational minister such as Eliot was given his authority by his English congregation in Roxbury, which paid his salary and provided him the pulpit, so that he was accountable to it for his actions, Eliot the missionary was accountable not to the converts but to the New England Company, founded by the English parliament in 1649, which sustained his labor. He maintained an altogether authoritarian relationship with those he considered uncivilized. Eliot himself confessed as much when he likened himself to Moses, writing, "That which I first aymed at was to declare & deliver unto them the Law of God, to civilize them, [which] course the Lord took by *Moses,* to give the Law to that rude company because of transgression, *Gal.* 3.19. to convince, bridle, restrain, and civilize them, and also to humble them."[23] Whereas a Protestant minister often *cajoled* his congregation into more sincere piety, a Protestant missionary essentially *dictated* to his Indian converts the forms of Christian behavior. He drew up laws for the evangelized Indians; he instituted rituals of public confession and humiliation; he was instrumental in creating a new world which many of these converts apparently sought to embrace. Individual conversion, supposedly autonomous and unforced, remained firmly bound up in much wider Indian cultural and religious tutelage and formal political vassalage immediately presided over by Eliot and other Puritans.

For Eliot it could not be otherwise, so great were the obstacles in the face of his missionary project. The Indians spoke little English and could not, for the most part, read their own language, which Eliot had transcribed. Although Eliot oversaw the translation of the full Bible into Massachusett in 1663, just over a decade later he could count only 119 baptized natives, and only 74 of them in full communion with covenanted churches.[24] These disappointing figures were nevertheless easily rationalized. Mather, for instance, asserted that Eliot's mission was based on consent, genuine expressions of piety, and real understandings of faith. He believed in his English rendition of an encounter between the patient Puritan missionary and the grateful but deeply depraved native. And he depended on an explicit contrast with the Roman Catholic mission of English Puritan imagination.[25]

As Mather put it in *Magnalia,* the Roman Catholics turned out multitudes of converts but not, in his estimation, genuine Christians, since they were not instructed with the "*whole Bible.*" Referring to Las Casas's catalogue of "tragical cruelties," and dismissing "Roman Catholick *avarice,* and *falsity,* and *cruelty*" because Spanish priests proselytized only in areas from which they could extract silver, he noted that the "New-Englanders could expect nothing from their Indians." Eliot as a missionary and the Puritans as a community sacrificed for those they might otherwise have easily destroyed, enslaved, or dispossessed.[26]

Benevolence, in a word, was the other side of raw power. "The good people of New-England have carried it with so much tenderness towards the tawny creatures among whom we live," Mather wrote, "that they would not own so much as one foot of land in the country, without a fair *purchase* and *consent* from the natives that laid claim unto it; albeit, we had a royal charter from the King of Great-Britain to protect us in our settlement upon this continent."[27] In his view, a proper estimation of Puritan charity derived not just from its stark opposition to alleged Roman Catholic avarice but from undeniable Puritan cultural, legal, and military superiority over the Indians. Eliot was worthy of admiration because he was actually concerned with redeeming Indians, who, Mather wrote, understood no arts, built no homes, wore no clothes, had no physicians, built no ships, and had no language worth studying or religion worth reforming. "This," Mather notoriously added, "was the miserable people which our Eliot propounded unto himself to teach and save! And he had a double work incumbent upon him; he was to make men of them, ere, he could hope to see them saints; they must be *civilized* ere they could be *Christianized.*"[28]

ළ

The missionary ideal of a universal, if hierarchical, Christian community decisively lost out to the Puritans' preoccupation with their own salvation and security and with their colonizing imperative for land. The ambivalence of the former magnified the obviousness of the latter. Missionaries such as Eliot sought to protect Indians from the depredations and hostility of English settlers.[29] His effort to create an Indian version of a Puritan church was finally rewarded in 1660 when an Indian church at Natick was recognized by Puritan elders. All along, Eliot wanted to believe that the mission was reaping its much anticipated harvest: "all the Massachusetts," he had one Indian convert tell a kinsman in his fictional *Indian Dialogues* of 1671, "pray" to God.[30] But he was also troubled by what he knew was at the heart of the conflict between Indians and Puritans. In his 1671 preamble to the same *Dialogues,* Eliot urged the commissioners of the United Colonies "that in all your respective colonies you would take care that due accommodation of lands and waters may be allowed them [the Indians], whereupon townships and churches may be (in after ages) able to subsist; and suffer not the English to strip them of all their lands, in places fit for the sustenance of the life of man."[31]

Eliot's paradigm of American missionary work was finally shattered by the outbreak of King Philip's War in 1675. In much the same way that an earlier failure at Roanoke had led to the dispelling of certain illusions about good Indians eagerly awaiting English help *and* the elaboration of new racist discourses about the idle Indian, so too did King Philip's War finally disillusion those few Puritans who had only half-believed that Indians desperately sought salvation.[32] The war was itself catastrophic. The ferocity and scale of Indian attacks led by the Wampanoag leader Metacom, or King Philip, who wanted to put an end to English encroachment on Indian land, were unanticipated. The destruction of so many settler outposts and towns was unprecedented. This fed a general and indiscriminate Puritan fury against all Indians, even though many Christian Indians had fought alongside the English forces.[33] The vituperation with which Indians, regardless of religion or tribe, were assailed and condemned as a result of the war also reflected the ingrained assumptions about Indian indolence and inferiority and Puritan superiority and benevolence.

Their uninvited benevolence spurned and their missionary illusions exposed, most Puritans were outraged at the perceived perfidy of the many Indians who had taken up arms against them. While unevangelized Indians were enslaved and killed, the Christian Indians in some fourteen praying towns were collectively deported to Deer Island. Following this war, which the historian Francis Jennings has described as the "Second Puritan Conquest," any semblance of a powerful, autonomous Indian presence in New England came to an end.[34] While the Puritan "Apostle" John Eliot had recognized that the unfair treatment of Indians and unchecked settler desire for land had precipitated King Philip's War, the general animosity toward Indians at the end of the war discredited the work of such men. It also sharply curtailed the first chapter of a distinctly American missionary endeavor that

had sought to reconcile the brutal imperatives of Puritan settler colonialism with the more benign ideals of establishing a biracial, if effectively segregated, Christian commonwealth. As Eliot watched his world collapse
around him, he was reduced to pleading pathetically with the magistrates of
Massachusetts Bay. He urged them in 1675 not to abandon the ideal of native conversion and salvation, even of those Indians captured in the ongoing war. "If they deserve to die," Eliot begged, "it is far better to be put to
death under godly governors, who will take religious care that means may
be used, that they may die penitently."[35]

ᆭ

Mather, writing about these events many years later, was far more unequivocal than Eliot in his condemnation of the Indians. He placed the entire episode of King Philip's War in unsentimental perspective. "It is
observable," he wrote, "that several of those nations which thus refused the
gospel, quickly afterwards were so *devil-driven* as to begin an unjust and
bloody war upon the English, which issued in their speedy and utter extirpation from the face of God's earth. It was particularly remarked in Philip,
the ring-leader of the most calamitous war that ever they made upon us;
our Eliot made a tender of the everlasting salvation to that king; but the
monster entertained it with contempt and anger." Clearly relishing the
memory of the providential victory over the natives, Mather continued:
"The world has heard what a terrible ruine soon came upon that monarch
and upon all his people. It was not long before the hand which now writes,
upon a certain occasion, took off the jaw from the exposed *skull* of that
blasphemous leviathan."[36]

This confession of contempt for a vanquished foe underscored the Puritan certainty of cultural, religious, and racial superiority and, after 1676,
victory over Indians. The Puritans' total mastery over the natives contrasted
with their own uneasy and formally servile relationship as subjects to an
English sovereign. The refusal to accommodate religious and cultural differences with Indians was made more apparent by the process of accommodation to the political and social realities of New England which Mather
himself witnessed and personified. From a strict and uncompromising
Calvinist orthodoxy, many Puritans had moved in 1662 to accept the Half-
Way Covenant.[37] The commonwealth, which had explicitly rejected religious toleration and had compelled public conformity in both civil and
ecclesiastical spheres as an inherent aspect of a voluntary compact entered

into by all those who chose to settle in an exemplary and godly English colony, was itself forced by the crown to change course. Mather eventually recognized that doctrinal differences within the English community in New England could be accommodated if not reconciled. Royal decree abrogated the Massachusetts charter and put paid to the idea of an isolationist Puritan commonwealth in 1684.[38] The new charter of 1691, with a Bill for the General Rights and Liberties, severed the relationship between ecclesiastical and civil society and granted freedom of worship to all Christians except Catholics. At the ordination of the Baptist minister Elisha Callender in 1718, for example, Mather told Baptists that "*Liberty of Conscience* is the Native Right of Mankind." And in 1725 he apologized to the Quakers by admitting that he "abhors *and* laments *the abominable* Persecution *which you have suffered in former Days.*"[39]

While Mather *may* have grown more contrite with regard to the persecution of people he belatedly recognized as fellow Englishmen (so long as they continued to pay religious taxes to support the established churches), he exhibited little remorse for the treatment of natives. More than the Eliot he so admired, Mather captured the paradox of American mission work. He wanted to save Indians, but he detested them. He had, after all, been appointed by the New England Company in 1685 as a commissioner to oversee the evangelization of Indians, a position he held for three decades.[40] Yet he wrote vituperatively of Indians. When he reflected on the failure of mission, there was little doubt where he placed the opprobrium. He acknowledged, as had Eliot before him, that there were "profane" and "debauched" English individuals, unscrupulous settlers who took advantage of the Indians, who defrauded them, and who plied them with alcohol. But ultimately he blamed the Indians themselves for their own wretchedness.[41] The memory of wars with the Indians was perhaps too encompassing, the captivity narratives of English people held for ransom too etched in his mind, and the apparition of defiant Indians too revolting for Mather to be able to put things in any other perspective.

Looking back across the astonishing transformation of the landscape of America across the seventeenth century from heathen to Christian hands, and the tremendous violence attendant upon such a transformation, Mather considered Eliot's charity toward the Indians striking not merely for what it promised and represented at the time, but because it seemed, in retrospect, to be futile. Mather acknowledged that Eliot was involved in a "great affair," but he also confessed that "I know not wither that of an evangelist . . . be not an office that should be continued in our days."[42] After all was said and done, the remnants of the Christian Indians were in Mather's eyes still "poor, mean, ragged, starved, contemptible, and miserable."[43]

When Mather published *India Christiana* in Boston in 1721, just a few years before his death, he betrayed his weariness of a missionary project that he had for so long promoted. In his account of the state of evangelical affairs with the Indians, he reiterated his praise for the indefatigable, indeed wondrous, work of John Eliot, who tried to "*Humanize* these Miserable *Animals.*" But he also frankly admitted the lack of progress in missionary activity. "*'Tis a Day of Small Things,*" he wrote, adding that the Indians had not been nearly as civilized and as Christianized as he would have hoped. "Indeed," he added finally, as if coming to terms with the significance of a failing movement, "I despair of any very Great Matters to be done" until the Jews were returned "unto their Land, and Converted unto their GOD." Until then, he said, "Let us be doing what we can!"[44]

Although the failure of the missionary movement was evident to Mather, he did not see this as an indictment of the entire Puritan enterprise. Eliot, in his view, had made a most generous offer of civility and Christianity to the Indians; they had maliciously and stupidly spurned his offer, and it was they who suffered the consequences. Failure was thus ascribed almost entirely to the Indians' obstinacy and violence, to their virtual inhumanity, to their lack of civility, to their addiction to temporal power and alcohol, even to God's unfathomable design for human regeneration.

☙

In washing his hands of the Indians, Mather did more than rescue Eliot's reputation. He preserved a sense of an inherently benevolent history from the implications of an uncompromising settler colonialism that left little room for missionary activity, and even less for Indians. He also anticipated the American Board's nineteenth-century rejuvenation of the spirit of Eliot and later missionaries such as David Brainerd. Like Mather, the American Board would be able to glorify Eliot and still justify the conquest of America. But they had different understandings of their inheritance. Whereas Mather would boast about the destruction of recalcitrant Indians, his early-nineteenth-century missionary heirs lamented the broken promises to the heathen of America. They did not see themselves locked in an existential battle for survival in the manner imagined by Puritans such as Mather. For them, the Indians were no longer, in any significant sense, a danger. Whereas Mather embellished what he saw as the sublime piety of his father's generation and pondered the failings of his own, the early American Board and its missionaries were supremely confident that theirs was an age that could redeem a nation through its work in the world.

The possibility of changing the world, a theme so evident in postrevolutionary American mission work, emanated from an experience of having imperfectly changed America. The unconquered world, however, contained what the American experience did not have: millions of heathen, including those Indians who lived within the borders of the United States, whose civilization might yet go hand in hand with their Christianization. It offered to vindicate the ideals of mission in an arena untainted, or so nineteenth-century missionaries had to believe, by the realities of settler colonialism which had both made and unmade John Eliot's mission to the Indians. The unconquered world presented a stage on which an original American mission narrative, and an original American promise of salvation at the frontiers of Christendom, might be reenacted, and this time fulfilled. As in the first essay, paradoxes would manifest themselves, and mission work would be torn between the salvation of self and others, between notions of conversion and contexts of compulsion, between evangelical hierarchy and brotherhood. To these would be added another paradox that compounded a language of Christian universalism with a narrower nineteenth-century vernacular of American nationalism.

Chapter 2

"The Grammar of Heresy":
Coexistence in an Ottoman Arab World

Nowhere, perhaps, was Mather's epic chronicle of the conquest of America more interestingly counterpoised than in the equally epic history of the ages written by the patriarch of the ancient Maronite Church, Istifan Duwayhi. If Mather's was a world defined by Christian conquest, Duwayhi's was defined by Christian survival. That is to say, the patriarch of the Maronites read the world very much from the position of one whose community had already fought its heresies, maintained its ecclesiastical order even as it slipped under the shadow of Muslim domination following the Arab conquest of Syria in the seventh century, and as a result had long since come to terms with the implications of a history in which it was no longer master, but to which it was, through its brilliant patriarch's eyes, very much a witness.

Duwayhi's *Tarikh al-azmina—A History of the Ages*—elaborated Mather's own pithy, if obviously prejudiced, denunciation of a tolerant Islam.[1] It was a history that illuminated the recesses of a past almost entirely unknown to Mather, or for that matter to the American missionaries who would later descend upon the Holy Land. From the outset this chronicle, originally written by Duwayhi in Karshuni (Arabic written in a Syriac script), dated in the Muslim *hijri* calendar, and sent to the Vatican in the late seventeenth century, vividly portrayed the vicissitudes of a Muslim world that encompassed Orthodox Christians, Syrian Christians, Latin Christians, Armenians, and Copts, as well as Jews, Shiʿa Muslims, and other heterodox communities such as the Druzes. It was a world that was also inhabited by European missionaries and, of course, by Maronite Christians, into whose community Duwayhi was born in 1630 and over which he presided as its greatest patriarch from 1670 until his death in 1704. This Muslim world was defined most basically by a recognition that different faiths were bound to coexist and, crucially, by a knowledge that the interactions of these different faiths had varied greatly from dynasty to dynasty, city to city, and century to century. The common anchor of this world was a recognition of and acceptance by all communities that they dwelled as subjects of an Ottoman Muslim sultan whose dynasty avowedly reigned, if not always ruled, in accordance with the laws and ideals of Islam.

🕮

The Ottoman Turks conquered Constantinople in 1453, and in 1516 they also triumphed over their Mamluk foes in Egypt and Syria. They inherited from the Byzantines an imperial capital and the seat of the Greek Orthodox patriarchate. They granted the Greek Orthodox patriarchal courts jurisdiction over marriage, divorce, wills, and inheritance, and all civil cases between Orthodox Christians, although litigants always had the option of resorting to an Islamic court. They did the same for the Jewish and Armenian communities of the empire. From the Mamluks they seized Arab provinces, which included the famous cities of Aleppo, Damascus, Cairo, Jerusalem, Mecca, and Medina, and also their Arabic-speaking populations.[2]

For reasons of both faith and expediency, the Muslim Ottomans tolerated all Christian communities as separate but unequal. Muslim preeminence did not deny the importance of the earlier, albeit in the Muslim view incomplete, revelations of Judaism and Christianity. The Ottomans therefore acknowledged the scriptural basis in the Quran for Muslim tolerance of those Christians and Jews as *ahl al-kitab,* or "People of the Book," but also considered them *dhimmis,* protected subjects who were required to a pay a poll tax, or *jizya,* and to submit to Muslim sovereignty. The Ottomans upheld the terms of the "Pact of ʿUmar," which refers to an apocryphal treaty that the caliph ʿUmar was said to have made in the seventh century with the inhabitants of Jerusalem but which is more likely a distillation of treaties and arrangements made in later periods. It mandated fiscal, architectural, and eventually sartorial distinctions to differentiate communities from one another. These distinctions affirmed the precedence of Islam and Muslims in all public spaces in return for protecting Christian and Jewish communities and allowing them to preserve their own laws and customs. Christians were not allowed to ring church bells, learn the Quran, teach it to their children, convert any Muslim, or blaspheme against Islam. They were prevented from using certain titles, carrying swords, and wearing white turbans, which were reserved exclusively for Muslims. They were instead ordered to wear distinctive belts. The *dhimmis* were also not to build houses higher than those of Muslims or to erect new churches.[3]

Taken together the Islamic texts, sayings, decrees, and judicial rulings that sought to regulate the unequal relationship between Muslims and non-Muslims had one seemingly clear thrust: to demarcate by dint of a set of commonly recognized disadvantages the subordinate place that non-Muslims would have in a Muslim world. Rather than conformity, as was the case with the Puritans, the emphasis was on difference. Cultural imperialism, which was so pronounced an aspect of English dealings with Indians, was notably absent. The Ottomans legitimated their rule in the Arab lands, the heartland of Islam, by upholding established Muslim imperial traditions already in place; they did not impose their language on their Arab subjects or expect them to alter their way of life fundamentally. Unlike the Indians, who were perceived as savage and in many respects satanic by Puritans, Arab Christians were recognized by Muslim authorities as belonging to a common tradition. By and large, there was no imperial policy to force conversions to Islam, with the notable exception of the famous levies of Christian boys from the Balkans who were groomed to join the ranks of the imperial Ottoman elite. Because of such attitudes, they also allowed foreign Catholic, and later Protestant, missionaries to proselytize, but only among subordinated non-Muslims. They thus sustained a mosaic of communities, often antagonistic in faith, but bound together in an imperial landscape that generally precluded any possibility of ethnic or religious cohesiveness.

Tolerance was an ineluctable expression of imperial policy. It was a unilateral dispensation rather than a way of life, and its impulse was to discriminate in the literal sense of the term between Muslim and non-Muslim in order to uphold an imperial logic that defined the Ottoman Empire as an *already achieved* Islamic order.[4] Ottoman jurists, bureaucrats, and rulers in Istanbul had to contend with a constant stream of complaints and petitions mostly from urban Muslim and non-Muslim subjects across the empire seeking to clarify and make the most of how and where—never if—Christian and Jew belonged to this Muslim polity.

Like all previous Muslim rulers, the Ottomans waxed and waned in their religious enthusiasm; the stipulations of the Pact of ʿUmar were alternatively abridged and elaborated, enforced and ignored over time.[5] Ottoman imperial decisions, in any event, were heavily mediated, and often overturned for better or worse by local circumstances across the empire.[6] An entire community of crypto-Christians known as the "white Maronites," so called because they wore white turbans reserved for Muslims while secretly maintaining their Christian faith, were allowed by the Ottoman governor of Tripoli in 1608 to embrace their former faiths openly, without fear of persecution; yet in 1697 another Maronite was impaled in Tripoli for his alleged apostasy despite the fact that the Grand Mufti of the empire had ruled unequivocally that his initial conversion to Islam had been undertaken by force and therefore was null and void.[7] While jurists were always careful to couch their rulings within the highly elaborated framework of Islamic law defined by the Grand Mufti ensconced in Istanbul, for the most part they and their Ottoman sovereign ignored the fact that in rural Mount Lebanon, as in many other fringe areas of the empire, the Pact of ʿUmar was honored mostly in the breach.

🕮

The mountainous region that Western pilgrims and missionaries referred to as Mount Lebanon, parts of which were variously attached to the imperial provinces of Damascus, Tripoli, and after 1660 Sidon, was in fact governed by a number of different, and often heterodox, families. The diversity of ethnicity and religion of these families reflected the turbulent crosscurrents of a region repeatedly invaded, occupied, and settled by one great army or another.

That almost all the local dynasties in Mount Lebanon itself were known to be Shiʿa, Druze, or Christian did not unduly trouble the Ottomans. They simply demanded, and usually received, an annual display of obeisance from the emirs, who in turn pledged to remit a variety of taxes and to maintain public order in their respective domains. Whenever these emirs were not able to produce the required sums, or, as was the case with the Shiʿa Hamade or Druze Maʿn emirs for much of the sixteenth and early seventeenth centuries, whenever they rebelled against imperial authority, the Ottomans unleashed a punitive expedition that typically underscored the heterodox nature of the "accursed sinners."[8] Occasionally these expeditions could and did alter the balance of local power. More often than not, however, once

Ottoman order was reestablished, the imperial governors invariably forgave, and in a crucial sense forgot, or put into abeyance, not only the transgressions but also the supposedly immutable infidelity that defined the transgression.

This form of politics, this rhythm of rebellion and reconciliation, this constant masking and unmasking of heresy was not merely pragmatic. Even as it acknowledged the military and economic limits of a state unable to govern rugged mountainous regions directly, it also reflected an Ottoman imperial social order that privileged rank as much as it did religion. There was more than one language of discrimination in the empire: the constant shift from strident condemnations of the villainous, accursed, miscreant, and heretical Druzes to pompous praise for these same Druze emirs, in other words, was a reflection not simply of the vagaries of imperial strategy but also of the consistency of an elaborate hierarchical imperial culture that cut right across religious lines.[9]

A shared knowledge between imperial governors and local chieftains made politics work: it did not and could not march inexorably forward toward resolution of heresy except fleetingly. It indicated how there was often (but not always) the possibility of the "accursed sinner" receiving pardon, of the rebel being rehabilitated, and thus reverting to the status quo ante; how rigid texts—sultanic decrees, military orders, religious disabilities—were often superseded, but never entirely supplanted, by the dynamic worlds these texts sought to discipline and order; how, in other words, an unstable equilibrium between obedience and rebellion, orthodoxy and heresy, was constantly managed, upset, and restored by both imperial fiat and local maneuver. This cycle of politics allowed the Ottoman state to function locally while it allowed the local leaders to inhabit an imperial body. It brought the Ottoman Empire into Mount Lebanon as much as it made Mount Lebanon an integral part of the Ottoman Empire.

The vast majority of conflicts in the seventeenth century that the Maronite patriarch Istifan Duwayhi witnessed and recorded, for example, were not of a religious nature but of a far more banal variety, such as a ferocious competition between notables and imperial officials over who would have the privilege of extracting revenue due the Ottoman treasury from often hard-pressed common cultivators. The social order in Mount Lebanon was thus marked far less by religious discrimination or by the terms of the Pact of ʿUmar than by a rigorously upheld distinction between the elites and commoners of every village. This division between high and low, between supposedly knowledgeable elites and ignorant commoners, defined all arenas of political, religious, and social life in Mount Lebanon. The very hierarchy of the Maronite Church, and the role that important families played in filling its most coveted ranks, underscored this point. In the two generations previous to Duwayhi's, his family produced no fewer than eight bishops and two patriarchs. Duwayhi himself was sent to Rome by Patriarch Jirjis ʿAmira, whose mother was a Duwayhi, and his election to the patriarchate in 1670, while eventually officially confirmed by the pope in Rome, first had to be found acceptable by the powerful Maronite shaykh Abi Nawfal al-Khazin, whose family came to dominate the church hierarchy in the eighteenth century. The elected patriarch had to go in person to the lord's house in order to receive his sanction.[10] An accommodation of religious difference presupposed a strict and unalterable segregation between different classes of society, each of which was expected to defer to and obey that above it and so on up to the Ottoman sultan himself, who, in theory at least, benevolently ruled over a vast multireligious empire. Heterodox Mount Lebanon, in other words, crystallized the most basic aspects of Muslim tolerance at the same time that it tempered its harsher prescriptions.

☙

It was the rural topography of Mount Lebanon, with its deep valleys and rugged mountains, that first attracted Maronite Christians to it in significant numbers in the tenth century. The Maronites belong to the Aramaic branch of Syrian Christians, together with the Syrian Orthodox Christians, or Jacobites, named after the sixth-century founder of their church, Jacob Baradaeus. They trace their origin to the fifth-century hermit Marun (hence the term "Maronite"), whose disciples founded the eponymous monastery of Dayr Marun on the banks of the Orontes River near the Syrian town of Hama. In a period of intense and often violent Christological controversies that rent the Christian communities of Syria, the monks of Dayr Marun embraced the monothelitic formula initially proposed in 638 by the Byzantine emperor Heraclius in an effort to reconcile dissenting Jacobites to the Byzantine church. While the latter maintained that Christ was simultaneously man and God (and thus had two natures united in one person), the former insisted that Christ was God become man and thus had one divine nature which simply took on human form. (The Jacobites were hence accused of being Monophysites.) Emperor Heraclius outlined a compromise doctrine which maintained that Christ had two natures but one will, a doctrine that became known as Monothelitism, but which appeased neither the Byzantine church nor the Jacobites. This compromise was in turn condemned as an outright heresy in 680 by the Sixth Ecumenical Council of Constantinople. The monks of Dayr Marun, however, clung to the monothelitic formula. They thus laid the basis for later Roman Catholic suspicion of Maronite deviance and its converse, a strident Maronite denial of such deviance, and an equally strident affirmation of the perpetual orthodoxy of the Maronite Church.[11]

Following the Arab conquest of Syria, which effectively separated the See of Antioch from Byzantine control and led eventually to the Arabization of the various Christian communities under Muslim rule, the Maronites elected their own independent patriarch, Yuhanna Marun, to the vacant See of Antioch. They then began to follow the course of the Orontes River, settling in the upper reaches of Mount Lebanon to escape persecution from a weakened but still potent Byzantine Empire. At the same time that Muslims came to predominate in the coastal cities of Tripoli, Beirut, and Sidon, the Maronites expanded their monastic tradition in austere hermitages and monasteries along the valley of the Qadisha (a Syriac word meaning "holy") River, which coursed its way from the high mountains of Lebanon, near the last remaining ancient, and reputedly biblical, cedars, down to the city of Tripoli, where, under the distinctly Arabic name of Abu ʿAli, it empties into the Mediterranean.[12]

By the time Istifan Duwayhi wrote his *Tarikh al-Azmina* in the late seventeenth century, the Maronites had long been stigmatized by both Latin and Orthodox Christianity for their supposed embrace of heretical beliefs, and for their isolation from the main currents of Christianity. Roman pontiffs took advantage of the Crusades to try and wean them away from the "error" of their beliefs and their proximity to Islam. In 1180 the Maronites formally submitted to Rome, whereupon Franciscan missionaries were dispatched time and again to investigate and reform Maronite ritual in line with Latin practice. Among the most famous of these Franciscans was the mid-fifteenth-century missionary Fra Gryphon of Flanders, who took under his wing a young Maronite by the name of Jibraʾil ibn al-Qilaʿi, and sent him to be educated in Rome in 1470. Ibn al-Qilaʿi would be for Duwayhi what John Eliot was for Mather: an exemplary figure in an idealized story of Maronite history which centered on the notion of "perpetual" fealty to the Roman Catholic Church. Like Eliot as well, Ibn al-Qilaʿi was a missionary. His mission was, significantly, defensive in nature, and was set against an encroaching world rather than being a narrative of Christian conquest of the wilderness.

Utterly remade by his long twenty-three-year sojourn in Italy, where he learned Latin, theology, and science to complement his native knowledge of Arabic and Syriac, Ibn al-Qilaʿi devoted himself to rejuvenating both the image and the condition of the Maronites. He became a missionary to his own people in 1493 but spent only three years in Mount Lebanon before moving to Cyprus, where he became the Maronite bishop of the island in 1507. Nevertheless, between his return to Mount Lebanon and his death on the eve of the Ottoman conquest in 1516, Ibn al-Qilaʿi produced literally hundreds of epistles admonishing his people in Mount Lebanon for lapsing into error, and wrote and translated from Latin many works on church discipline, ritual, science, and dogma. He founded an enduring school of Maronite historiography which profoundly shaped the way the Maronite Church viewed its world. Its principal contention was, and remains, fundamentally simple: the Maronites have always been orthodox, never monothelitic, and have always been obedient to the teachings of the Roman Church.[13]

ᘉ

The importance of the Muslim domination in this Maronite self-representation was crucial, for it provided the foundation on which a narrative of perpetual orthodoxy and the perseverance of Maronites amidst "foreign" nations could be elaborated and plausibly defended.

Ibn al-Qilaʿi did not deny that the Maronites had strayed. He was in fact greatly dismayed following his return from Rome to find many in the Maronite community, including some of its most important secular leaders, in the tight grip of Jacobite heresy. Far too many of them, Ibn al-Qilaʿi lamented, had been seduced by Jacobite missionaries who had taken advantage of the Muslim reconquest of Syria in the aftermath of the Crusades to infiltrate the very heart of Maronite Mount Lebanon. Far too many of his compatriots had not spotted the ravening wolves in sheep's clothing, and had forgotten that thistles produce only thorns and corrupt trees produce only evil fruit. The Maronites had allowed themselves to be led astray by the false teachings of false prophets; they had allowed the introduction of "foreign" customs and rituals, from mixed monasteries (in which monks and nuns shared a courtyard) to coexistence and social intercourse with "unbelievers";[14] they had thus brought God's wrath down upon them. Islam, as Ibn al-Qilaʿi made abundantly clear, was a punishment from God, a warning to the Maronites about the prospect that awaited them should they continue to deviate from their "original" orthodoxy. This was exemplified by the fall of Crusader Tripoli to the Muslims in 1289, and by the burning alive of the Maronite patriarch Jibra'il of Hajula by the Mamluks in 1367. In a manner with which the Mathers of New England could have easily identified, Ibn al-Qila'i fervently believed that the Maronites might be saved if only they returned to their original faith. "Awaken O Maronites," he pleaded in 1496, "and curse Ya'qub al-Baradi'i [Jacob Baradaeus] and his followers because they have corrupted your land which was once blessed."[15]

For Ibn al-Qila'i, the heretic, *al-hartiq,* far more than the unbeliever (the Muslim), *al-ghayr al-mu'min,* represented insidious danger. He infiltrated rather than invaded; he caught men unawares; he seduced rather than dominated overtly. It was not through the sword that he operated but through the book. "Heresy," wrote Ibn al-Qila'i, "starts with the teacher!"[16] The heretic teacher cast doubt on the original orthodoxy of the Maronites; he also ended what had been until very recently a brilliant and unadulterated golden age in a pure Mount Lebanon, which Ibn al-Qila'i described as having "no heretic, no Muslim either, and if there were a Jew, it was only his grave that the crows would reveal."[17] Most ominously, the heretic threatened to destroy what was left of Christianity in its first home. "The wolf," Ibn al-Qila'i exhorted his listeners with an allusion both biblical and familiar to the rural inhabitants of Maronite Mount Lebanon, "is by his nature perpetually ravenous, and is not satiated at all; his mouth remains always open, for if he but once tastes the blood of man, he will not hunt in the wild but rather will invade [the abode of men] and will not fear death."[18] The heretic took advantage of but also made way for the Muslim in every instance. The one summoned the other. The deceptively similar produced the obviously foreign; they had become so tightly intertwined in Ibn al-Qila'i's Lebanon that the Maronites, according to him, had lost all sense of their own identity, their own history, their own Christianity, and thus by definition their own salvation.

&

Ibn al-Qila'i's polemical intensity reflected his Latinized outlook, nourished simultaneously by his profound alienation from his native land and his passion to refute a long-standing Roman Catholic discourse about the original deviation of the Maronites. But it reflected more: the zeal of one who believed himself to be witness to an existential threat to an ancient Christian community. He shared with his Franciscan contemporaries an understanding of the world that saw in the proximity and coexistence between Muslim and Christian a fundamental problem, one that invited and perpetuated, sustained and supported heresy.[19] The salvation of the Maronites, Ibn al-Qila'i believed, would be assured only when they remade their physical and spiritual environment. Ibn al-Qila'i, however, looked not forward but backward. He wanted to restore what he insisted was a historical Maronite world, filled with persons and villages that mirrored an enduring language and landscape, rather than self-consciously (as the Puritans sought to do) recreate an apostolic age of primitive Christianity. He sought to negate the logic of Muslim tolerance that consistently demarcated the subordinate location of *dhimmis* within an idealized Muslim order. He denied, in effect, that there was a place for a Christian community under Islamic rule: in his view, a Christian community could only defy Islamic rule. For Ibn al-Qila'i, the historical moment confronted the Maronites with a seemingly urgent choice: either union with Rome as a Latinized church or evisceration by a more literate and more powerful Jacobite church under Islam.[20] Writing years later, Duwayhi did not see the threat to ecclesiastical order as that pressing or urgent.

෴

By the time Istifan Duwayhi recorded his chronicle, the Jacobite heresy that had consumed Ibn al-Qila'i had long been contained. Relations with Rome were far more regular following the opening of the Maronite College in Rome in 1584, where Duwayhi himself had been sent as an eleven-year-old in 1641, and where he had studied logic, liturgy, Arabic, Syriac, Italian, Greek, and Latin before his return to Mount Lebanon in 1655. Muslim rule, finally, was far more certain after the Ottoman conquests of Cyprus in 1571 and Crete in 1669. What is remarkable about Duwayhi's history is how he managed to reconcile an ecclesiastical subordination to Rome with a political subordination to his Muslim environment, and more important, how he reconciled what for Ibn al-Qila'i were irreconcilable: perpetual orthodoxy and coexistence with a Muslim world.

Drawing on the work of the great tenth-century Arab historian and polymath al-Tabari, the Maronite patriarch evoked tolerance as inextricably tied to the earliest expression of Islam. He described how in his forty-fourth year the Prophet Muhammad issued his call for men to abandon idolatry and worship the one true God, and how he ordered his followers to believe in all the prophets of God including Jesus Christ, for "he believed the Torah and the Bible." Duwayhi insisted that the histories of this era were clear: Muhammad himself had compassion for the Christians, and while he imposed the *jizya* on them, he also protected them and declared that "he who hurts a *dhimmi* has in fact hurt me, and he who oppresses a *dhimmi* will meet his opponent at the Day of Judgment." The Maronite patriarch added that when Christians asked him for security, the Prophet Muhammad told ʿUmar ibn al-Khattab, who would become the second caliph of Islam, "their persons are like ours, their property is like ours, their honor is like ours."[21]

The venerable patriarch did not for a moment deny that Muslims had on many occasions oppressed Christians. *Tarikh al-azmina* repeatedly alludes to moments of persecution, such as when in 1366 the "sultan of the Muslims" imprisoned Christian bishops in Damascus in retaliation for a Latin Christian attack on Alexandria.[22] Yet the cursory nature of such descriptions, their brevity, almost matter-of-factness, their location between other moments of praise for Muslim rulers and their tolerance, especially for the Ottoman sultans Selim the Grim and his son Süleyman the Magnificent, their *historical* context—all of this stood, at first reading, in great contrast to the formulaic *transhistorical* descriptions of the perpetual Maronite struggle against heresy and perpetual Maronite orthodoxy that routinely appear in Maronite supplications to Rome.

In an utterly deferential letter dispatched in August 1671 following his contested election as patriarch, for example, Duwayhi pleaded with Pope Clement X. After relating how Jesus told Simon Peter that he was Peter, the rock upon which the church would be built (Mt 16:18), Duwyahi wrote that "the enemy of our race was embittered and sent forth from the gates of hell the kings of infidels, the followers of the Jews, the soldiers of unbelievers, and the legions of innovators against the Church of Peter." The patriarch set the Maronites at the very heart of the elaboration of Christianity but also indicated a highly exaggerated sense of steadfastness "in the midst of infidels and innovators." The Maronites, in other words, were due compassion and support because they were cast alone in a "sea of hypocrisy" and yet they maintained a pure Christianity.[23] As much as Puritans such as Mather described a sense of Christian solitude in America surrounded by savage Indians, his narrative was expansive and its tempo aggressive. Maronite isolation, by contrast, was defined by an intense sense of siege. Whereas the Puritans chose to settle in a hostile new world, the Maronites stressed their abandonment in the cradle of Christianity.

But for all the difference between the historical and the polemical, between a chronicle intended for edification and letters directed at supplication (as Duwayhi's letters to Rome clearly were), when read together they provide a coherent understanding that the Maronites were not simply in but irrevocably part of a multireligious world. "Our Orient," Duwayhi confessed to the Propaganda Fide in 1671, did not deserve its name, for it was in reality a "chaos of confessions [*caos de confessione*]."[24] From the beginning it had been so, and so it would remain. The trope of Maronite perpetual orthodoxy reflected not, as with Ibn al-Qilaʿi, a repudiation of coexistence but its opposite, a resignation to it.

The intercessions and miracles of God, the saints, and the Virgin Mary protected the Maronites in this enduring predicament of maintaining purity amidst impurity and in championing truth over error. Duwayhi, for instance, recounted that when the Shiʿa emir Musa Harfush attacked Jibbat Bsharri in 1602, one of his men forcibly entered a monastery and struck with his dagger an icon of the Virgin Mary. But when he left the monastery, "his hand shriveled, and in that same night he perished and died." And when the Maronite patriarch Yuhanna Makhluf died in 1633 without having asked the Lord to bless his flock and to protect them as "was the custom," the many Muslims and Christians who had gathered for his funeral were startled to see the dead man raise his right hand and make the sign of the cross.[25] There was, in other words, no fantasy in Duwayhi about eliminating the other, no call to arrest the march of corrupting time, but rather an attempt to effect a reconciliation with its vagaries and oscillations, its constant, indeed its expected, movement between oppression and liberty. This was, at bottom, what defined historical coexistence: a deep awareness of the variability of conditions but also a recognition of the constancy of difference. Duwayhi, in effect, constructed a very powerful historical narrative, disseminated both orally and through manuscripts, which finally grounded the Maronites firmly within their multireligious world under Islamic suzerainty.

※

The heart of this narrative consisted of a victory already won against heresy. Mount Lebanon provided the setting, and Ibn al-Qilaʿi was its principal hagiographic subject. In *Tarikh al-azmina*, therefore, Duwayhi extolled the memory of Ibn al-Qilaʿi and depicted him as the leader of the last epic struggle against heresy in Mount Lebanon. "It is impossible," wrote Duwayhi of the year 1516, in which the famous Maronite bishop of Cyprus died, "to describe his zeal, his knowledge, and his blessedness, for he alone with his two arms propped up his nation when it was surrounded by heresies and on the verge of extinction."[26] Duwayhi added that the many writings of Ibn al-Qilaʿi ensured the survival of the Maronites. It was through these writings that *Tarikh al-azmina* could reconstruct the story of the devil, personified in a Jacobite missionary, and the fifteenth-century Maronite leader he corrupted by the name of ʿAbd al-Munʿim from the village of Bsharri. The devil, Duwayhi declared, took advantage of the "ignorant youth" when he assumed leadership of his village in 1472 to sow tares in the field of the Lord, and to "tear down the edifice that the Fathers had built upon the firm and unshakable rock." Soon, heresy spread across the valley of Qannubin, where Jacobites and ignorant Maronites like "snakes wandered across the garden of our Lord."[27]

While the heretics settled south of Bsharri, it was the seemingly untrammeled movement of their infectious monophysite doctrine, their "grammar of heresy," their conquest of erstwhile orthodox territory, their deceptive missionary character, which was most threatening. They opened schools for boys and girls in which they taught Syriac and Karshuni books and seemed on the verge of overthrowing the Maronite Church. "Evil multiplied," wrote Duwyahi, when the powerful Maronite notable ʿAbd al-Munʿim befriended and protected the Jacobites after they presented him with gifts on his wedding day and a book in Syriac and Karshuni "filled with false evidences and fabricated teachings that alleged that Jesus Christ the Savior was of one nature, not two." The Maronite leader even built them a church and allowed them to settle in Bsharri. The Maronite patriarch at the time, Yaʿqub, was helpless before the Jacobites, and although he was "always at war" with the heretics, his attempt to prohibit all contact with them, and even expel them, failed. The Jacobites were thus lulled into a sense of security, said Duwayhi, and began to preach their seditious doctrines openly and arrogantly, attracting adherents from neighboring villages and from farther east, but the underlying orthodoxy of the Maronites manifested itself. In 1488 the people of Bsharri expelled the Jacobites, who moved to the neighboring land of Batrun.[28]

When Ibn al-Qilaʿi arrived in Mount Lebanon in 1493, Duwayhi continued, he found the fires of heresy once more rampaging through the land, and the heretics, like ravenous wolves, devouring God's children. From Qannubin he wrote, argued, shamed, debated, and persisted after the Maronites who had turned their backs on their fathers' faith, including his first cousin, before tracing the source of the illness to ʿAbd al-Munʿim, who, as a result, desired to kill Ibn al-Qilaʿi. The Franciscan missionary, however, was not deterred. He decided, according to Duwayhi, to prove in writing that the Maronites had been in constant union with the Roman Church. He sent a manuscript to that effect titled "The Blessed Marun" to the Maronite patriarch, who then enjoined all his bishops to read it carefully and to use it to refute the heretics. The tide finally turned, and in 1495 the deceived and ignorant Maronite leader died—"God struck him down before his time," Duwayhi remarked—and was succeeded by his pious Maronite son.[29]

The importance of this narrative, as with Cotton Mather's depiction of John Eliot, lies not at all in its historical accuracy but rather in the broad didactic outline it provides of an idealized Maronite orthodoxy, heresy, tribulation, and redemption, all undergirded by the story of the triumph of knowledge over ignorance, the open against the secret, high against low. God, the Maronite clergy on earth who most elevated his name, and ʿAbd al-Munʿim's son and heir who returned to the "true" faith together defeated the devil—the Jacobites. While there were still occasional moments of heresy in the sixteenth and seventeenth centuries—a Maronite priest in Cyprus, Duwayhi laments in his *Tarikh,* was "deceived" by the Greek Orthodox in 1626, and in 1648 the brother-in-law of the Maronite patriarch abandoned his religion—nothing again approached the scale or seriousness of the Jacobite assault.

This narrative spun so deftly by Duwayhi also provided a template that allowed the Maronites to adapt intellectually as well as religiously in a Muslim Ottoman world. The purification of their community from the disease of heresy facilitated the integration of the Maronites into an Ottoman empire as a cohesive part of a variegated whole. Their perpetual orthodoxy amidst unbelievers, like a rose among thorns, thus became for Duwayhi perfectly compatible with Ottoman rule. Like Muslim jurists but from a very different vantage point, Maronite ecclesiastics proclaimed separation but acknowledged diversity. Neither actively sought to claim the other's flock. Both sought to preserve and celebrate a foundational moment, a notionally pristine condition that was ever under attack by heresy and innovation. The Maronites began to thrive at the very edge of Muslim empire.

இ

The signs of this were everywhere to be seen. No fewer than twenty-seven new Maronite churches were built in Mount Lebanon during Duwayhi's patriarchate, from Mar Yuhanna (Saint John) in the village of Dayr Hrash in 1671 to that of Mar Sarkis and Bakhus in Bsharri in 1701—all, of course, in direct contravention to the stipulations of the Pact of ʿUmar.[30] Duwayhi's *Tarikh al-Azmina,* in fact, anticipated the transformation of the district of Kisrawan, long subjugated to the Shiʿa Hamade lords until their eclipse in the eighteenth century, into an overwhelmingly Maronite region by the nineteenth century.[31] While oppression and injustice could not be discounted in so diverse an empire, the Maronites were able to subjugate themselves to two lords, to speak two languages of deference, and above all, to engage with utter fluency in a third language of coexistence, with its own unwritten grammar of multireligious life, entirely alien to their distant ecclesiastical masters in Rome, and to the nineteenth-century American missionaries who would offer them "true" Christianity.

According to Girolamo Dandini, a Jesuit missionary who toured Mount Lebanon in the late sixteenth century, the Maronites dressed in a fashion similar to that of other "Levantines." They wore turbans and used no tables, but sat "cross-legg'd upon Mats or Carpets spread upon the ground." They ate "just as the *Turks* do, making no use of Napkins, Knives, nor as much as Forks, but have only very pretty wooden Spoons; and when they drink the Glass goes round." They grew beards and shaved their heads as other communities did.[32] This similarity in language, dress, furniture, and food was also reflected in the fact that Maronites studied law under Muslim shaykhs. The most famous of these Christian jurists was the Maronite bishop Abdallah Qaraʿali, who in the early eighteenth century codified Maronite civil law on the basis of the Islamic *sharia* and built such a reputation that even Druzes and Muslims sought his legal opinions.[33]

Duwayhi himself was on excellent terms with the Druze emir Ahmad Maʿn, and it was to the Druze Shuf district that he fled for two years as patriarch in 1683 because of the fighting among Christian notables in the district of Kisrawan.[34] The choice of refuge in Mount Lebanon was not surprising: the famous early-seventeenth-century Druze leader Fakhr al-Din had actively courted Maronite clergy as both scribes and interpreters in his ultimately unsuccessful attempt to consolidate power at the expense of the Ottoman state and rival Shiʿi lords. Duwayhi's *Tarikh al-azmina* recalls that during Fakhr al-Din's reign, "Christians held their heads high, because most of his soldiers were Christian, as were his advisers and servants."[35] Far from being ranged against one another because of their religious differences, Maronite, Shiʿa, and Druze notables in the seventeenth and eighteenth centuries subscribed to the same language of hierarchy, and they viewed their respective communities and the worlds around them from similarly elevated vantage points.[36] They extended similar forms of hospitality (which covered, as the nineteenth-century Scottish traveler David Urquhart would put it so aptly, "a multitude of sins"),[37] noted one another's religious celebrations, took refuge in one another's districts, ate in one another's homes, attended one another's funerals, and mourned their dead in a similar manner. For all the ecclesiastical narratives that accentuated a timeless orthodoxy defined against heretics and Muslims, Duwayhi, like the Druze emirs with whom he took refuge, recognized that the multireligious world necessarily operated outside the realm of formal texts and prescriptions, be they the Pact of ʿUmar or the narratives of perpetual orthodoxy.

This basic reality did not obviate the formal texts, nor did it mean that bloody battles were not fought between different notables of different sects, or that the Ottoman soldiers did not pillage, or that a powerful historical consciousness of the separateness of Maronite religious identity did not continue to develop, especially under the auspices of the Latinized Maronite clergy.[38] It did, however, suggest a far more astute recognition of realities ignored, denied, or covered up by polemical texts. Just as the Ottoman state's tolerance of ostensible heretics and infidels indicated the limits of Muslim polemic, so too did the Maronite existence within a Muslim environment underscore the limits of Christian polemic. Neither Duwayhi or any of his immediate successors nor the Muslim Ottoman state under which they lived could or did push relentlessly for a resolution to the problem of coexistence so much as they continually rehearsed age-old themes of good and evil, heresy and fidelity, justice and injustice. At imperial and ecclesiastical levels respectively, they fought instead to preserve a defining historical orthodoxy that had already been attained. As much as this allowed for a diversity of religions unfathomable to a minister such as Cotton Mather, this reading of the world fundamentally contradicted the idea of a voluntary, conscious embrace of faith at the heart of American Protestantism. It provided, moreover, the antithesis of the millennialist enthusiasm that would animate early-nineteenth-century American missionaries. It was precisely two such men, missionary, Protestant, and American, who would descend uninvited, but not exactly unexpected, upon ancient lands, and who would, as a result, precipitate a collision of two disparate worlds. To this cultural clash, which gave meaning to and took the life of the first Arab convert to American Protestantism, Asʿad Shidyaq, we now turn.

Part II

INTERSECTIONS

Chapter 3

The Flying of Time

American Christians had never combined in any great enterprize or plan for
spreading the knowledge of Christ, or advancing his kingdom; had never sent, from
these shores, a single missionary with the message of heavenly mercy to any portion
of the widely extended pagan word, lying in darkness and in wickedness, without
God, and without hope. Some scattered and transient efforts had indeed been
made, for the benefit of some of the native tribes of the American forests; but without any general union, or any expansive or systematized plan of operation. In these
respects, there was no experience, no example; all was untried, all to be begun.

Letter from Samuel Worcester to Jeremiah Evarts

The fitful Puritan evangelization of Indians had long since run its dismal
course when the American Board of Commissioners for Foreign Missions
was established in 1810.[1] So too, of course, had the covenantal Puritan
theocracy cherished by Cotton Mather. As the largest and most famous
American missionary organization of the nineteenth century, the American
Board represented itself as an expression of a new nation embarking on a
new errand, whose scope and ambition had no parallel in its revered Puritan past.[2] It sought to promulgate "Christianity among the heathen" wher-
ever possible through both the publication of Bibles in different languages
and the support of missionaries to "explain, exemplify, and impress on the
mind, the great truths which the Scriptures contain."[3] The ABCFM was a
product of a New England Congregationalism that had been buoyed by the
success of the American Revolution but alienated by the diversity of its
forms. It recoiled as much from the Deists who wrote a constitution that
strictly separated church and state as from the Methodists and Baptists who
flourished in its aftermath.[4] At the same time, however, the American Board
was borne by the rise of a "missionary spirit" embodied in myriad benevolent associations concerned with elaborating a virtuous evangelicalism at

home and abroad.[5] Though clearly driven by the Second Great Awakening, and propelled forward by the example of British evangelical and Pietist labors across the world, the American Board self-consciously built on what it regarded as the unfulfilled national and missionary promise of Cotton Mather's America.[6]

The ABCFM and its agents were able to propose three things that had never been part of the fabric of American Puritanism while at the same time staying true to one thing that certainly had been. Like their Puritan antecedents, they celebrated an uncompromising orthodoxy, but they moved "the heathen" from the place where the Puritans had located them at the margin of American concern to its center. [7] They departed far from a Calvinism centered primarily on the urgency of one's own salvation in favor of a more universal and therefore more hopeful rhetoric of salvation. Finally, they spoke in national terms, and they emerged on a national stage on which New England was by no means the political or religious center and the Puritans not yet its historiographic center. They had thus to impress themselves competitively upon an expanding nation and a beckoning world.[8] Even as they saw themselves, in other words, as the inheritors of Puritanism, the evangelicals of the American Board totally rethought its implications by assuming, as William Hutchison has written, that Americans were an already blessed people who acted less out of repentance than gratitude, less out of fear than an unshakeable self-righteousness, less for themselves than for others.[9] It was not simply the Old Testament with its theme of exclusive election that they emphasized but the far more expansive New Testament. "The whole New Testament," wrote Jeremiah Evarts, "supports, in regard to all mankind, the great principles of beneficence which the law of Moses had urged upon the Israelites, throughout the code of their national polity."[10] The American Board, then, sought not an escape from the corruption of men, not a means to ward off what Mather had described as the "incroaching and ill-bodied *degeneracies*,"[11] but the precise opposite: it sent forth its missionaries to seek out, to confront, and to overturn ignorance and error across the world and replace it with what it considered to be the singular truth of evangelical Christianity.

✌

For all their recognition of the unprecedented boldness of their enterprise, however, the American Board and its missionaries remained indelibly stamped by the template of the Puritan experience with the Indians. Their relationship with this aspect of the Puritan past was direct yet ambivalent. They muted the triumphalism of Mather but did not disown the conquest of America. They grappled with the same basic paradoxes that had defined and debilitated John Eliot's work. These ranged from the continued primacy of a settler-colonial impulse that produced and undermined missions, to the tension between a context of compulsion and a missionary philosophy that stressed the free and unconstrained choice of Indian heathen, to the cultural imperialism attendant on the spiritual salvation of America and the world's heathen. In a tone far more contrite than the Puritan divine had ever been able to strike, two American Board missionaries at Bombay, Gordon Hall and Samuel Newall, recognized that Christian Americans "who now dwell and plant where their fathers once roved and hunted" still had a duty to bring the Indians to civilization and Christianity. "They have claims indeed upon the American churches which should go home to every bosom," they wrote.[12] Nevertheless, the American Board tempered such oblique criticism of ancestral shortcomings by pointing out that the Puritans had worked "among a people scattered in the wilderness." More positively, it insisted that the "general history of such missions as have at any time been conducted on Christian principles, and with a real regard to the salvation of the heathen, affords abundant encouragement to proceed with vigor, in the same glorious cause."[13]

There had not, after all, been a cessation of missionary efforts in the century that followed King Philip's War, and still less of earnest exhortations for missionary labor. Prominent eighteenth-century theologians like Jonathan Edwards and Samuel Hopkins had strongly advocated missionary work; and men like John Sergeant, David Brainerd, and David Zeisburger had all trod missionary paths.[14] Nevertheless, the American Board's insistence that not enough missionary effort had been made in colonial America now galvanized it to act; the "many discouragements" of prior missions to Indians, while initially propelling it abroad, also inspired it to open up significant new missions in 1816 to the Cherokees, and then to the Chickasaws and the Choctaws—whose first mission station was, significantly, named after Eliot.[15] It sought to make good the "the long and heavy arrears of our country to those poor and diminished tribes of our fellow-beings, whose fathers once called their own the widely-extended territories over which our prosperous dwellings are now spread and continually spreading."[16] The very establishment of these domestic missionary stations seemed to be a gamble—rashly wagered according to some—that somehow a tragic strand of American history could be unspun and rewoven: that Indians could be civ-

ilized and assimilated into a benevolent Christian republic rather than annihilated or expelled from it.[17]

The American Board adopted the same resolute Puritan equation of its
particular Christianity with civilization. Its missionaries exhibited the same
confident, even brazen, mobility that John Eliot had demonstrated nearly
two centuries earlier. Rather than entering unannounced into an Indian encampment at Nonantum, they quite literally traveled the world, from Ceylon to the Sandwich Islands to Palestine, and also to Georgia and Arkansas,
carrying with them the same fundamental missionary belief that the Scriptures themselves contained the power to transform radically the condition
of all men. The seal of the American Board, with the figure of the missionary
handing a Bible to a kneeling heathen, encapsulated the ideal of the missionary searching out foreign climes and distributing the truth of Christianity to as many natives as possible.[18] American missionary labor, then,
provided an opportunity for a glorious global culmination of a supposedly
unfulfilled Puritan beginning.

৯৫

Nothing, however, linked the nineteenth-century missionaries to those of
the Puritan past more than the reverence in which they held the figure of
the mid-eighteenth-century missionary David Brainerd. It was after him
that the first American Board station to the Cherokees had been named in
1817, just as Eliot's name graced its first mission to the Choctaws. Brainerd
was a product, indeed an embodiment, of a colonial revival of religion that
had itself sought to resurrect the apostolic New England piety that Mather
celebrated in his *Magnalia Christi Americana*.[19] His celebrated memoir was
carefully crafted and first published by the great American theologian, minister, and sometime missionary Jonathan Edwards in 1749, and in it the
ABCFM missionaries found an example of self-denying evangelical piety
that was far more intense, immediate, and elaborate than anything John
Eliot had left behind.[20]

Brainerd's memoir began to circulate widely only in the early nineteenth
century. It was strongly recommended by the faculty of Andover Theological Seminary, where most of the early missionaries to the Levant were educated; it was read avidly by Levi Parsons and Pliny Fisk, the first American
missionaries in the Ottoman Empire.[21] That Brainerd was a Presbyterian
mattered little to the Congregationalist missionaries who were inspired by

him. The American Board, although dominated by Congregationalist ministers, encouraged interdenominational cooperation with Presbyterians, with whom the Congregationalists had agreed to a Plan of the Union in 1801 to evangelize the western frontier. While it was Brainerd's piety amidst a "general deadness all over the land" that moved Jonathan Edwards to celebrate the young missionary's most "Christian life," it was Brainerd's selfless evangelism amidst an Indian "wilderness" which ended only with his death at age twenty-nine that impelled later missionaries to identify with Brainerd despite the meager results of his missionary work.[22] Parsons, for example, confessed in his own diary that he wished he had Brainerd's "ardour of piety, that tenderness of soul, that deadness to the world, that concern for sinners."[23] Because Brainerd left such an extraordinarily introspective diary, the missionaries who emulated him could trace across days, weeks, months, and years how a man measured his own sense of inner depravation, of worthlessness, of sin, of shortcoming, of failure in the eyes of God in relation to how he judged the manifest depravation of the "poor" Indian heathen. They could take heart from the fact that his inner struggle for genuine Christian rebirth, with its requisite stages of awakening, doubt, dedication, further doubt, and ultimately a near certainty of salvation, was recorded and resolved through missionary work.[24]

For nineteenth-century missionaries, Brainerd's life lent itself to a reworking of foundational American missionary tropes. His life was a bridge from a Puritan world to theirs, and also from theirs to the outside world. Rather than the debauched English, the emphasis was now on white Americans, the uncouth settlers of the frontier, the wicked unchristian men who harassed poor Indians and frustrated benevolent missionaries, and the pernicious infidel liberal or Deist elites around them who threatened the nation's evangelical calling.

Young missionaries who read Brainerd saw how God's kingdom had slowly enlarged despite the "brutishly stupid" natives, on the one hand, and unscrupulous and "nominal christians" on the other.[25] They found in Brainerd's mission an alternative to a far less edifying secular development over which they had little control. As Boston's population swelled from 24,000 at the turn of the century to nearly 44,000 by 1820, so too did the diversity of its religious institutions, which by 1822 included eleven Congregational, four Episcopal, four Baptist, two Methodist, and three Universalist churches, one Roman Catholic church, and one Quaker meeting house.[26] With this diversity had come the dissolution of any pretense of a uniform

Christian orthodoxy. Thus Parsons repeatedly noted and decried the Sabbath-breaking, ignorance of the Bible, swearing, intoxication, and shameless "infidelity" where "*Reason* is made *omnipotent*" in the United States before he departed for Palestine, even as he took hope in the religious revivals that he himself had read about in Brainerd's memoir, as well as personally experienced, witnessed, and encouraged.[27]

To a man such as Parsons, as for many of his nineteenth-century peers, banished was the notion of the dangerous savage Indians who had stalked Mather's imagination. The totality of Indian defeat in the Northeast was to them plainly apparent. Despite nineteenth-century missionaries' belief that Brainerd, like them, worked simply through the power of scriptural persuasion rather than force, Brainerd's Indians were constantly threatened with the loss of what little land remained to them. They were caught between what Brainerd described, and what the American Board also witnessed, as "the vicious lives and unchristian behaviour of some that are called Christians" and the mercy of true Christians, such as Brainerd himself, who offered the Indians salvation and security, especially if they relocated and settled down under proper Christian instruction and care.[28] More so even than Eliot's evangelism, Brainerd's took on a truly disinterested hue. He acted, in missionary eyes, out of sheer compassion for bedraggled heathen on the verge of spiritual and physical extinction. Brainerd's beauty appeared most radiant because he was serving poor and pitiable Indians in America, which plainly anticipated the missionaries' own outreach to the heathen beyond.

Significantly, the missionary hagiography of Brainerd did not dwell on the historical reasons for the Indians' dislocation, nor did it directly implicate the Puritans in their present plight. Thus even as the members of the American Board, and particularly its corresponding secretary Jeremiah Evarts, implicitly reproached their Puritan ancestors for not doing enough for the salvation of Indians, Brainerd's lonely work among Indians between 1743 and 1747 explicitly vindicated Puritanism. If only the example of Brainerd and Eliot could be revived, there might yet be a missionary nation of whites and Indians, all subordinated to an evangelical culture that disavowed the extreme manifestations of colonial violence but also completely rejected heathen manners and customs. For the early American Board, the fantasy of an evangelical America coexisted with a fantasy of a world devoid of heathen and infidels.

As had been the case with Eliot, there was no question of Brainerd's tolerating Indian culture; indeed, there continued to be an outright refusal to coexist with it, there being no material, fiscal, political, military, or theological reason to do so. Brainerd deplored the Indians' "idolatrous sacrifices," their "heathenish custom of dancing [and], hallowing," the "fabulous notions of their fathers," and the "manner of their living."[29] Reading Brainerd, therefore, bespoke a fundamental tension between what was meant to be a cumulative process of self-doubt on the part of a sincere evangelical Christian, and mission work to heathen that could, for the most part, brook no such doubt. The private, agonizing confessions of unworthiness recorded in his diary constantly competed with strident and unequivocal proclamations that Indians needed and required spiritual and civilizational tutelage, or what Brainerd described as "their utter inability to save themselves either from their sins or from those miseries which are the just punishment of them."[30] As a model Christian, Brainerd demanded self-introspection. As a model for cultural interaction, however, he confirmed a fundamental conceit of mission work: those to be saved were to be the objects of unilateral transformation, their culture disparaged, their history ignored, their equality consistently denied. The missionary ethos of the innate similarity of all people before God was systematically undercut by a far more trenchant ethos of civilizational inequality that separated the generic heathen from the benevolent missionary.

By the same token, foreign missionary activity offered a realm uncluttered by the stubborn realities of American history. It offered a precious opportunity to reformulate the narrative of an American benevolence unsullied by the violence and cruelty that had marked, and continued to mark, white depredations against Indians. Through their own work and their own agency, American churches could be at the forefront of a movement "to evangelize whole nations, and ultimately to renovate a world."[31] Reincarnated abroad, Brainerd's example could explicitly fulfill America's unique promise and providential favor while implicitly expiating its sins. Foreign missionary activity could allow American churches to take their equal place alongside evangelical British churches. It could universalize the American experience by exporting missionaries modeled on the image of Brainerd, but it could also add Americans to a Protestant pantheon in a national way not contemplated by Mather's *Magnalia Christi Americana*. Rather than tell the story of the introduction of Christianity in America in which the heathen, whose annihilation was explicitly justified, remained on the margin, the American Board and its missionaries wanted to be the principal actors in a far more ambitious story. They wanted to introduce true American Christianity to all of humanity, and in the process, to effect the "Conversion of the World."[32]

🌿

To spread American Christianity, however, the missionaries had first to learn it. Andover Theological Seminary was the preeminent missionary recruiting ground of the early nineteenth century. Every missionary who would work in Ottoman Lebanon in the first American Board missions—Levi Parsons, Pliny Fisk, Isaac Bird, Jonas King, Eli Smith, and William Goodell—was educated at Andover. Opened in 1808 "in opposition not only to Atheists and the Infidels, but to Jews, Mahometans, Arians, Pelagians, Antinomians, Arminians, Socinians, Unitarians, and Universalists, and to all other heresies and errors, ancient or modern, which may be opposed to the gospel of Christ, or hazardous to the souls of men," the seminary was designed to impart a rigorous orthodox education to future Congregational ministers.[33] The inroads made by Baptist and Methodist congregations in the early nineteenth century, and the more immediate threat posed in 1805 by the liberal Unitarian triumph at Harvard College, erstwhile bastion of Puritanism, had created a particular sense of urgency over the moral and spiritual decay of America.[34] Leonard Woods, the first professor of Christian theology at Andover and author of its most famous history, recalled that "it was notorious that the minds of many of the youth in our colleges were corrupted by the infidel philosophy which had sprung up and produced such abundant fruit in France, and that Deism and Atheism were more or less openly advocated by multitudes of men, both educated and uneducated, in our community." Far worse, Woods added, many Congregational ministers had been "departing from the faith of our Puritan fathers" and were clearly "infected with the Pelagian and Socinian heresies."[35]

To stamp these out, Andover demanded that its students, who were expected to be proficient in Latin and Greek before they enrolled, be guided through a course of study that would "unlock the treasures of divine knowledge." It had them concentrate on biblical studies in their first year, theology in their second, and homiletics in their third, and throughout their time there to be impressed with the certainty that the Scriptures, not secular reason, formed the basis of sound judgment and interpretation. Between their meals in an unheated common hall, compulsory chapel service, recitation, and prayer, the men who would become missionaries were required to attend lectures in "Natural Theology," "Sacred Literature," "Ecclesiastical History," "Christian Theology," and "Pulpit Eloquence."[36] They were encouraged to pore over the Old and New Testaments, and were taught by Moses Stuart to appreciate the importance of philology in illuminating the meaning the Bible and, more fundamentally, to understand that a single valid meaning of biblical text rested on a proper understanding of the words of the text itself.[37] To the extent that they were meant to receive any education about Islam, it was in the lectures on ecclesiastical history (although the professorship was not established until 1819 and not filled until 1824) which were designed to teach, among other subjects, "the rise and progress of popery and mahometanism" as well as "the state and prevalence of paganism in our world" and the effect "which idolatry, mahometanism, and Christianity have respectively produced on individual and national character."[38] These lectures would have undoubtedly touched on, and at the same time dismissed, the rudimentary elements of Muslim faith and perhaps even sketched the "Imposter's" life. They would have echoed George Sale's "preliminary discourse" which prefaced his hugely influential translation of the Quran, a copy of which Andover's library possessed. They would have also, as the description in the Andover curriculum underscored, related the rise of the "false prophet" to the corruption of Roman Catholicism, and seen in both a common manifestation of a powerful anti-Christian spirit.

※

Andover, however, provided something else besides intellectual training: it provided a bastion from which young men convinced of their spiritual righteousness could march forth. Every one of the students who became a missionary to the Ottoman Empire experienced an intense revival of "living faith" before entering Andover, revivals that were confirmed by their induction into Andover and their subsequent ordination as orthodox ministers and missionaries. There was a certain ritual of being "born again"—Brainerd's shadow here too made its presence felt—that was expected of every repentant Christian of this generation, and it was a ritual whose explicit arduousness the missionaries would, in turn, look to find in the foreign heathen men and women they hoped to convert. Parsons, for example, was overwhelmed by a revival that swept Middlebury College in 1811. His journal recorded the constant introspection, and captured the dramatic fluctuations in his own sense of piety. On the eleventh day of November 1811 he experienced a very powerful and very sudden emotional and wrenching awakening:

> At this moment, I was directed to Jesus, as an all-sufficient Saviour. Then my heart acquiesced in his atonement, and in his dealings with such a vile sinner, as I saw myself to be; and my soul reposed itself on the arm of everlasting love. I felt the chain break; O it was the bondage of sin! I opened the Bible, and read these words, "For this cause, I bow my knees to the God, and Father of our Lord Jesus Christ." It will never be in my power to give an adequate description of my feelings in view of this passage. There was a beauty, majesty, and sweetness in it, which are indescribable. I dwelt upon it until my heart was a flame of love. Jesus revealed himself in his glory. In his countenance shone a divine majesty and benevolence. In a moment, I raised my hands, and exclaimed, "Father, glorify thyself."[39]

So powerful was this experience that the next day Parsons was "insensible till evening," and for two hours he could say only "none but Christ, none but Christ."[40] Fisk, for his part, experienced an awakening on the first day of January 1808 when a friend, who had begun a revival, told him simply: "Remember, you have an immortal soul that must exist beyond the grave either in happiness or woe!"[41] Eli Smith, who was a graduate of Yale, was also inspired by a single question in the course of a sermon he attended on 20 August 1820: "Shall this be your last struggle?"[42] In his turn, Goodell witnessed and participated in what he called a "mighty" revival that occurred in 1815 at Dartmouth College.[43]

The importance of these revivals lay not just in their physicality, for they almost all dwell, as does Parsons's, on the forceful intimacy of the Holy Spirit entering and capturing an individual's heart, or in their exemplification of true virtue as God's unconditional gift of grace, but in their timing. The success of the American Revolution, the disarray of the Catholic Church following the French Revolution, and the extension of British imperial reach in India made the moment seem propitious, even *providential,* for the establishment of an American foreign missionary enterprise. Missionary enlightenment, in this instance, was neither secular nor liberal.[44] That all souls were precious, all were fellow beings, and all should be made objects of universal Christian benevolence in accordance with biblical injunctions to preach the Gospel were certainly crucial factors in justifying missionary work. But these abstractions were rendered suddenly feasible, suddenly realizable, suddenly less visionary by the immediate accessibility of the world.

The benevolent empire of British evangelism beckoned, and to ensure that Americans could see this, the "Society of Inquiry Respecting Missions" at Andover Theological Seminary had Claudius Buchanan's *Memoir of the Expediency of an Ecclesiastical Establishment for British India* reprinted in 1811.[45] Despite the war between the United States and Great Britain, the American Board sent its first missions to India and Ceylon in 1812, and its first station was established at Bombay in 1813.

๛

Crucially, the British imperial context through which idealistic American missionaries experienced the world gave currency to the millennial expectations that had seized America's founding generation.[46] Millennialism made sense to the American missionaries: it reconciled the evident success of British imperialism in Asia with an American Revolution that had broken with the British monarchy; it allowed for a strengthening of ties to British missionary organizations by underscoring a common Anglo-American evangelical quest for an imminent reformation of the world; and it made room for cooperation and, in important ways, identification with British evangelicals without diluting the American consciousness of the American Board. William Carey and Samuel Hopkins, two of the most prominent late-eighteenth-century advocates of missions, had justified overseas missionary work by tying the salvation of heathen to the reformation and reconstitution of the world. The American Board and its missionaries did the same. Above all, millennialism offered a temporal framework within which divinely favored American missionaries could plausibly evangelize the world. "Prophecy, history, and the present state of the world, seem to unite in declaring, that the great pillars of the Papal and Mahommedan impostures are now tottering to their fall," proclaimed the American Board in its first *Address to the Christian Public* in 1811.[47] Timothy Dwight famously delivered a sermon at the fourth annual meeting of the American Board in Boston in September 1813 in which he underscored how the "present is the proper time for this glorious undertaking." He elaborated the broad field of missionary labor and described the "millions of the human race" who awaited their gospel of liberation. "How amazing must be the change," he said, "when the *Romish* cathedral, the mosque, and the pagoda, shall *not have one stone left upon another, which shall not be thrown down:* when the *Popish, Mohammedan, Hindoo, and Chinesian,* worlds shall be created anew."[48]

This sense of a rapidly approaching end of time called for immediate missionary labor, because the Gospel had to be preached to every creature before the advent of the millennium. Even as Dwight indicated the millennium would begin around 2000, others predicted it would arrive even sooner. Jedidiah Morse, building on Samuel Hopkins's 1793 treatise on the millennium and echoing the British millennialist George Stanley Faber, underscored 1866 as the date that would mark the Antichrist's fall.[49] Whatever the year, there still remained battles to be fought, particularly against Islam and Catholicism, and several hundred million heathens to be proselytized, even if many of them would not in the end be saved. In this millennial view of the world, the inevitable collapse of the "two coeval powers of Mahomedanism and Popery," as the English missionary William Jowett styled them, was anticipated by the wondrous increase in missionary societies at the turn of the century in both England and the United States. So ingrained was the conviction that the momentous events that had ushered in the nineteenth century had heralded a new dawn that Morse listed in his *Universal American Geography* as among the great historical epochs (following the entire gamut of recorded history from the Creation, the Fall, and the building of Babel to the establishment of the Assyrian, Egyptian, Babylonian, Greek, and Roman empires, to the revelations of Judaism and the birth and crucifixion of the Redeemer, the birth of Muhammad, and the "irruption" of Islam, and onward through the Reformation, the development of the printing press, and the French and American revolutions) the establishment of the London Missionary Society and the British and Foreign Bible Society in 1795 and 1808, respectively.[50]

American evangelicals knew they could not shorten time as such, but they believed they were divine instruments in the "train of events" that would mark its end.[51] Inspired by readings in the Books of Daniel and Revelation, many among them believed that they were fulfilling prophecy, that despite the magnitude of their task and the formidable obstacles in their path, solace could be found in the certainty of their eventual success. They sensed, as David Brainerd had before them, that "Time appeared but an inch long, and eternity at hand."[52] They believed not only that America was uniquely endowed to play a leading role in the evangelization of the world, but also that the rest of the world awaited its Christianity in this "distinguished epoch in the history of the Church."[53] What appeared at the time to be a spectacularly successful beginning to the American Board mission to Hawaii in 1819, an operation fully independent of the British Empire, further bolstered this millennial enthusiasm. There, even before the arrival of the American Board mission, a Hawaiian king had died and ancient "idols" had been destroyed. When the American Board missionaries arrived in 1820 they were welcomed by the new ruler of Kailua, and were soon able to open several stations and schools across the Sandwich Islands and even eventually send back to Andover the ruined idol of Kekuaokalani, to which human sacrifices had allegedly been offered, but which had now been defiled: the eyes and teeth were torn out and the feathers rubbed from the face.[54]

In this American quest to reclaim the world for Christ, no place figured more profoundly than the Holy Land. Indeed, nowhere across the world was American missionary labor more idealistic, and nowhere were the challenges so stark and the allies so few. If in Bombay British colonialism prepared the way, and among the Cherokees American expansionism opened a path for missionary work, in the Muslim Ottoman Empire the American missionaries labored for the most part alone. The decision to inaugurate a mission to Palestine and soon thereafter to Syria was justified at a meeting of the American Board on 24 September 1818. There, at Andover, nearly five thousand miles away from an empire it sought to proselytize, the board decided to send Pliny Fisk and Levi Parsons "to acquire particular information respecting the state of religion . . . in Asiatic Turkey" and "to ascertain the most promising place for the establishment of christian missions, and the best means of conducting them."[55] By its own admission, the board was to dispatch missionaries to an empire about which it knew virtually nothing. A year later in Boston, as Fisk and Parsons were preparing for their voyage East, the board justified its decision. Tucked between reports of progress in South Asia and among the Cherokees in North America, the few pages devoted to Palestine underscored the expectations that were attached to the mission:

These were the scenes of those great transactions and events, which involved the destinies of mankind of all ages and all nations, for time and eternity; the creation of the progenitors of our race—the beginnings of the sciences and arts, and of civil and political institutions—the fatal transgression, which "brought death into the world and all our woe"—the successive revelations of Heaven, with all their attestations, their light and their blessings—the incarnation, labors, agonies of the Son of God, for the recovery of *that which was lost*—and the first exhibition of that might and gracious power, which is to bow the world to his scepter, and fill the mansions of immortality with his people. They have since been the scenes of dire changes; and the monuments of all their glory have long lain buried in dismal ruins.—But the word of Jehovah abideth forever; and that word gives promise of other changes there—changes to be followed by a radiance of glory, which shall enlighten all lands.[56]

Yet even if Palestine was a "field of no ordinary description," the instructions that were furnished to its first American missionaries referred them to those recently given to fellow missionaries destined for the Sandwich Islands.[57] Thus presented, the overlapping instructions reinforced a "missionary manichee" (to borrow Alan Perry's formulation), the dichotomy between the singular American Christian missionaries and the generic "perishing heathen" they were meant to save.[58] Both sets of instructions counseled patience; both warned against controversy; both reaffirmed the essential sameness of humanity within a hierarchy of civilizations at the peak of which sat the sending American churches. In the face of the unbridled racism prevalent against American Indians, the American Board stood resolutely for benevolent paternalism. As in 1812, when Leonard Woods emphasized to the first missionaries departing for India that the immortal soul of every human was equally precious, "in the savage as well as in the citizen; in the heathen as well as in the Christian; in the Hindoo, the Chinese, and the Hottentot, as well as the polished European or American," so in 1819 the American Board lauded the universal efficacy of missionary labor among all of God's children.[59]

There was, however, a clear difference in the tenor of these instructions, a difference amplified in 1822 when new missionaries were sent at the same time to the Sandwich Islands and to the Ottoman Empire. The instructions for the former dwelled at length on the "untutored," primitive, and barbarous character of the natives but also affirmed the intrinsic equality of all men, in much the same language that Jonathan Edwards had once used before the Mohawks of Stockbridge.[60] For the missionaries Isaac Bird and William Goodell on the eve of their voyage to the East, however, the American Board emphasized the profanity that had been visited upon the ancient birthplace of Christianity "for so many dark and dismal ages" by a multitude of irreligious nations. "The very stones of the pavement," their instructions read, "would seem to cry out against unfaithfulness in this consecrated region."[61] If the board seemed to anticipate upwelling racial superiority in its missionaries to the Indian-like "primitive" heathen of the Sandwich Islands, it alluded to an altogether different danger in Palestine. It feared that the awesome task of trying to revive Christianity in so entrenched and so diverse an empire would overwhelm and dispirit its young missionaries. "You must not despise the day of small things," the Prudential Committee bluntly told Fisk and Parsons at the Old South Church in Boston on the eve of 31 October 1819. It reminded them that they were going "to the Mingled People, now sitting in darkness, in that once favoured Land, where the Light of the world first shone, and thence blessed the Nations with healing radiance."[62] Three years later the committee warned Bird and Goodell of the "strangers and foreigners, men of diverse languages and uncongenial habits" among whom they were to labor.[63]

ℒ

In nineteenth-century evangelical eyes, the profusion of impure religions and nations marked the corruption of pure Christianity in the Holy Land.[64] American missionaries deplored the presence there of what they regarded as idolatrous Christian sects and forsaken Jews. Most blatantly, however, there was the ascendancy of Islam. From the very outset of their mission to the Ottoman lands, the American Board missionaries consistently articulated certain notions about Islam that at once recognized it as a far more difficult and dangerous problem than that presented by the idolatry of the Indians or Hawaiians, but at the same time reduced it to as fragile an edifice as that of any heathen culture. It was considered more dangerous for obvious reasons: it represented, for the missionaries, a recognizably literate monotheistic religion utterly antithetical to Christianity; it was extensive; it reigned supreme in the birthplace of Christianity; and it had produced a series of great imperial dynasties. Pliny Fisk admitted in his farewell sermon of 1819 that the peoples of the Ottoman Empire do not "contemplate the character of Protestant nations with that respect, which is felt for civilized men among more untutored tribes."[65] The missionaries, moreover, subscribed to the long-standing Western polemic, unquestionably reinforced by their education at Andover, against the "artful imposter" and the religion he had spread allegedly through fire and sword.[66] Just as the English missionary William Jowett, whose authority was cited in the original instructions to Parsons and Fisk, declared, for example, in his *Christian Researches in the Mediterranean,* that "Holy War and Consecrated Licentiousness are peculiar to the Mahomedan Creed—foes, implacable to the entrance of our pure and peaceful Religion,"[67] Fisk remarked that Islam "was first propagated, and is still defended by the sword. Cruelty and blood are among its most prominent characteristics."[68]

The American Board and its missionaries subscribed to the notion that the historic triumphs of Islam were predicated on its despotism. The absence of a genuine, loving Oriental family would epitomize this despotism evocatively for the missionaries, several of whom traveled to the East with their wives and children, just as the Barbary Wars did for a more general American public.[69] The harem and polygamy, referred to obliquely in Jowett's description of "Consecrated Liscentiousness," contrasted with their view of a gendered evangelical order at home, where a Christian family was the bedrock of proper moral order. Given this belief in the pervasive tyranny of Islam, American missionaries reckoned that Ottoman defeats in Europe and Napoleon's invasion of Egypt, and the upsurge of nineteenth-century Protestant missionary labor, heralded Islam's much-anticipated end.

For Protestant missionaries in particular, these Muslim reverses indicated the imminent fulfillment of prophecies contained in the Books of Daniel and Revelation.[70] For them, as for a much larger community of biblical scholars in America and Europe, the rise of Islam was foretold in the first twelve verses of the ninth chapter of Revelation, or the fifth trumpet, essentially as the "angel of the bottomless pit" who was to take revenge on a corrupt Christianity. Islam's downfall was also foretold in Revelation. For many millennialist thinkers, and for Parsons, the restoration of the Jews to Palestine and their conversion to Christianity anticipated the end of Islam and the Second Coming of Christ.[71] The pouring out of the sixth vial, the drying up of the Euphrates, would allow Eastern armies to march to Palestine for the final battle of Armageddon, where they would be annihilated by God.[72] In a sermon delivered in Paris on the twenty-ninth of September 1822, just before he embarked for Ottoman Syria, Jonas King drew on Revelation to state: "Though I believe the Millennial day is near, I do not believe it will dawn upon the world without some opposition from the powers of darkness. The Bible and missionaries that are flying through the earth will awaken all the enmity of the natural heart, and Infidelity, and Antichrist, and Superstition, and Paganism will unite their forces, and God and Magog will show themselves on the field of battle."[73] Similarly, Levi Parsons wondered how missionary success would "excite the rage of the enemy, and induce the beast, the false prophet, unconverted Jews, and hardened infidels, to make one fatal struggle for the extermination of true religion?" While not every missionary was as fascinated by the details of scriptural prophecy or as consumed with apocalyptic thinking as were Parsons and King, they did collectively subscribe to its basic outline that Zion "will at length be victorious, and take the undisturbed possession of the world."[74] The disappearance of Islam was to the missionaries as inevitable as the recession of Indian culture.

໒

The early American missionaries to the Ottoman Empire consistently used a plainly militant language to describe their anticipated reconquest of the Holy Land. Fisk, for example, hoped for "spiritual conquests" of Muslims and for the taking of the "strongest fortresses of error and sin."[75] Parsons saw himself embarking on a "spiritual crusade to the land of promise."[76] King admitted that his greatest desire was "to pull down the crescent, and lift up the standard of the cross on the walls of Zion."[77] The Americans, however, were always careful to distinguish between the historical Crusades, whose physical violence they condemned and which, in any case, they associated with Catholicism, and their own self-proclaimed gentle crusade.[78] This point was crucial for the missionaries because it reinforced the association they continually made between Catholicism and Islam. Both, they insisted, were violent, and both intolerant. For Fisk, "Mahommedan piety" manifested itself in the "persecution of infidels and heretics"; for Parsons, the Crusades were "the commencement of a long series of inhuman and savage cruelties; the history of which, is but a detail of persecutions, proscriptions, banishments, and massacres."[79] The Crusaders were, for him, "deluded champions of the cross."[80] The Protestant missionaries, by contrast, were products and proponents of a "holy violence," as Ebenezer Pemberton had described the task of missionaries in his sermon on the ordination of David Brainerd in June 1744.[81] This violence involved, as the missionaries' own intense, dramatic, and above all consistent conversion experiences attested, an involuntary invasion of the mind and the heart by the Holy Spirit. God could erect an empire in the hearts of humans, and could compel an inward sublime surrender to his will, whereas Catholic, like Muslim, persecution ostensibly compelled only outward, essentially empty conformity.

Yet rather than posit "tolerance" as the counterpoint to "intolerance" as we would today, the missionaries presented evangelical "truth" as the counterpoint to Muslim "intolerance." The missionaries were not intolerant in the sense that they did not compel anyone to worship their God. They did not persecute those who opposed them. That their Puritan forebears had made a fundamental choice to vanquish the Indians in Massachusetts rather than to tolerate them was overlooked in the American Board's historical outlook in favor of a narrative that focused on the exceptional nature of John Eliot's and David Brainerd's work.[82] Puritan and more recent American violence to the Indian was construed as incidental, and a betrayal of a glorious heritage and a national calling; Muslim violence, by contrast, was supposedly deliberate, inherent, and typical; it reflected an age-old fanaticism.

Yet the tragedy of American history was also, in the missionary mind, its redeeming quality. The Indians had been persecuted despite the fact that the primitive natives had offered, and still offered, their consensual subordination to the "civilized world." Fisk alluded to this point when he declared in his 1819 sermon that the "savages of the wilderness, and in the islands of the Pacific, have, by intercourse with the civilized world, received the impression, that Christian nations are, in many things at least, their superiors, and qualified to teach them."[83] Although Jedidiah Morse admitted in his 1819 edition of his *American Universal Geography* that Indians would soon "be constrained to migrate to the wildernesses on the W. of the Mississippi,"[84] Levi Parsons remained silent on their bleak fate, as well as on that of the remaining Indians on the eastern seaboard, when he preached in April 1819 to the remnants of the Stockbridge Indians, to whom Jonathan Edwards had once ministered in a failed attempt to promote Indian-white coexistence.[85] Instead, he described how he was shown deep gratitude by the Indian "chief" at Stockbridge, who even contributed money—$5.07—three baskets, a string of wampum, and some gold ornaments for his impending mission to Palestine. Parsons was utterly moved by the evidence of the Christianization of these "once miserable pagans." Listening to the Indian chief, he confided to his father, "I could from my heart call him *brother.*"[86] And when William Goodell visited the Choctaw Indians in 1822, he was welcomed by them and marveled, his biographer said, at the transformation of "savages" into "people of God."[87] Most symbolically, the famous Cherokee Catherine Brown, "the lovely convert from heathenism" celebrated by the American Board because she repudiated her native Indian culture but also because she vindicated missionary labor in the face of white American racism, donated her earrings for the mission to Palestine.[88] Far from reflecting failure or underscoring a history of American intolerance, the domestic errand to the wilderness was made to bless explicitly a much bolder errand to the world.

Pliny Fisk, Levi Parsons, Jonas King, Issac Bird, and William Goodell, the latter two accompanied by their wives, Ann and Abagail, fully expected that the "holy violence" that had motivated Brainerd and themselves would be welcomed by the heathens of the Orient as it had supposedly been welcomed by the heathens of the American wilderness. The missionaries were not just comforted by scriptural prophecy; they were greatly encouraged by the optimistic reports submitted by the British evangelists William Jowett and Henry Martyn, the latter of whom had been heavily influenced by David Brainerd, and who had before his death in 1812 publicly engaged in several controversies with Shi'a Muslims in Persia—stabs aimed "at the vitals of Mahommed," as he vaingloriously put it. Despite Martyn's evident disgust with Muslims, from the "swarthy obesity" of some of their religious leaders to the "Moulwee maggots" who rebutted his missionary polemics, the Englishman had specifically alleged that "Persia is, in many respects, a field ripe for the harvest. Vast numbers secretly hate and despise the superstition imposed on them, and as many of them as have heard the gospel approve it; but they dare not hazard their lives for the name of the Lord Jesus."[89] Citing Martyn's authority, Fisk confidently, if curiously, declared in 1819 that there "are in Persia about 80,000 persons, who, ten or twelve years ago, openly renounced Mahommedanism." He insisted as well, referring to prospects in the Ottoman Empire itself, that "Syrian Christians are nominally under the Pope's jurisdiction; though they are said to pay very little deference to his authority, and are much more inclined than the Catholics, to the true doctrines of Christianity, and to the diffusion of them."[90] The missionaries of the American Board wanted to believe that there were many on the other side of the ocean who, like the Indians of yesteryear, cried out for help and salvation. "We are now to leave our native shores," wrote Parsons in October 1819, "with the joyful expectation of saving some of the heathen. . . . In everything the hand of God has been with us."[91]

❧

So it was that two American missionaries boarded the *Sally Ann* on 3 November 1819 in Boston harbor. They carried with them their formal instructions; their Bibles and the *Life of Brainerd,* among other books; letters of protection from the secretary of state of the United States, the governor of Massachusetts, and the British, French, and Russian consuls; as well as the hopes and blessings of the sending "American churches." Their initial destination was Malta, an important British naval and missionary staging point, and home to a British Bible depository and press. From Malta, Fisk and Parsons were to proceed to Izmir (Smyrna), and from there make their way to Palestine to establish, or at least study the prospect of establishing, a mission station.[92] Upon their arrival at Malta just before Christmas Eve 1819, neither Fisk nor Parsons knew any Arabic or Turkish, nor did either of them have any real sense of the complexity of the "people of all ranks and complexions" they were meant to proselytize.[93] They were often insensitive to local culture. Parsons, for instance, once entered a mosque near Izmir with his boots on because they were "long" and hard to remove.[94] Yet encouraged by a stream of missionary sermons and exhortations, and by the fact that they now trod on the same ground once walked by Saint Paul, they believed that the current missionary age would reproduce the spirit and even exceed the success of the original apostolic age.[95]

Just as the Apostle to the Gentiles had traversed the ancient world to establish Christian churches in the face of determined opposition, so now the American missionaries expected to travel the length and breadth of the western parts of the Ottoman Empire to introduce and revivify faith in ancient lands. Near the spot where it was said Saint Paul landed after his shipwreck, Parsons exclaimed: "On these shores he prayed for a guilty world. Eighteen centuries afterwards, missionaries with the same message endeavor to proclaim the Saviour who came into this world to save sinners."[96] Even as time flew forward to its inevitable end, the missionaries anticipated their fleeting reunion with a supposedly familiar landscape that had lain neglected for centuries. Every observation of local manners and customs, and every visit to such famous places as Smyrna, the Cedars of Lebanon, and Jerusalem, which Parsons reached in the company of pilgrims in February 1820, making him the first American missionary to enter the city, exemplified the Scriptures and reminded the Americans of the role they had assigned themselves in fulfilling its prophecies.

Thus the American battle for the hearts and minds of the peoples of the Middle East was commenced in a land they recognized but did not know. The American Board believed that it was sending messengers of peace to the inhabitants of the Holy Land, or as the instructions to Bird and Goodell affirmed, "embassadors from the churches in this country to their suffering fellow men in the eastern world."[97] But the arrival in the Ottoman Empire of their missionaries constituted the opening act of a dramatic cultural clash. It was dramatic in the sense that this clash brought together two utterly irreconcilable strands of U.S. and Ottoman history, two antithetical temporalities of tolerance and intolerance, two contradictory manners of making facts correspond to ideals. If the missionaries through their voyage east saw themselves fulfilling an evangelical calling at the heart of an idealized Christian America in which Puritan New England occupied pride of place, they also came face to face with a defiant reality of Ottoman coexistence for which they simply could not account. As they contemplated how to win over the stunning variety of the "mingled people," they found themselves locked in a metaphorical war of annihilation with a foreign world infinitely more cohesive and resilient than anything missionaries in America had previously encountered.

Chapter 4

The Artillery of Heaven

"He received us very favorably," wrote Pliny Fisk of the nineteenth-century emir of Mount Lebanon, Bashir Shihab. "He knew something of America, and when we told him we were Americans, he gave us a salutation, and an expressive look, which flattered our national pride."[1] So it was that the lord of the land squeezed between the Mediterranean coast and the Bekaa Valley welcomed the missionaries. He was in all probability as confused about the true nature of their errand as they were about him, for he personified the very coexistence that they sought to overturn. Emir Bashir issued from an ancient Arab tribe that had early converted to Islam and had ridden into Syria in the seventh century as part of the Muslim conquest. Under the watchful eye of the Ottomans, his venerable Sunni family acceded to the rulership of Mount Lebanon when the Druze house of Maʿn died out in 1697, and retained its status despite the discreet conversion of several Shihabs to Christianity in the middle of the eighteenth century. Emir Bashir maintained a studied religious ambiguity. He built both a church and a mosque at his palace at Bayt al-Din in the Shuf district of Mount Lebanon; he was baptized yet observed the fast of Ramadan; his wife converted to Christianity, yet he introduced *sharia* law throughout his domains.[2] He was never referred to as a Christian ruler, or even the ruler of Christians, despite

Figure 3. Map of the Ottoman Empire, ca. 1820. Source: Drawn by J. W. Stoll, Department of Geography, Syracuse University.

the significant Christian population over which he held sway. Rather he was known in early-nineteenth-century literature as the "chief of the Druses," and to the Ottomans as the leader of the "mountain of the Druzes," *cebel-i düruz*.[3]

During his long reign, which began in 1788 and, despite several interruptions, lasted until 1840, Emir Bashir managed to consolidate the various districts of Mount Lebanon into a single administrative unit. He presided over five hundred villages, which included, according to one contemporary source, roughly fifty thousand Christian men (among whom Maronites predominated, but which population also numbered thousands of Greek Catholics and Orthodox Christians but no Protestants), ten thousand Druzes, five thousand Sunni and Shi'a Muslims, and a few hundred Jews.[4] Certain districts of Mount Lebanon were inhabited primarily by one community, such as the Maronite Jibbat Bsharri, wherein lay the village of Ihdin, the Cedars, and the Qadisha Valley, with its famous monasteries of Qannubin and Quzhayya. The Shuf was settled by both Druzes and Christians, and here, wrote a Greek Catholic chronicler in the first decade of the nineteenth century, family alliances cut directly across religious lines, "for there was no difference among them in this between Druze and Christian."[5]

From the northernmost tip of the Lebanon chain above Tripoli to the southern Druze-dominated district of the Shuf which overlooked Beirut, each region of this mountainous land was controlled by and associated with notable families of *aʿyan*, who were themselves divided into various ranks—emirs, *muqaddams*, and shaykhs in that order—but who were collectively distinguished from the commoner *ahali* or *aʿwam*, who made up the bulk of the rural population.

Because rank rather than religion was the defining aspect of local political life under Shihabi hegemony, the leading Maronite families shared an elaborate elite culture with their Druze and Shiʿa counterparts. This dictated even such details as the way they addressed letters to one another, how these were folded and sealed, the manner in which guests were praised and hosted, and the way the paramount Shihab emir greeted those who entered his court.[6] A veritable taboo existed within Mount Lebanon against publicly probing into, let alone denigrating, the faith of others. Ottoman governors readily acknowledged in their own correspondence with Istanbul the suspect, indeed heretical, nature of the Lebanese chiefs, but in their own direct correspondence with these chiefs they invariably avoided broaching the topic.[7] Maronite priests and monks laced their chronicles with references to infidels and schismatics, but in their public dealings and everyday intercourse with those of other faiths they politely avoided giving offense, and in turn expected no less.

For all that these rituals defined a public expression of coexistence, they could not mask the often brutal battles fought by competing elites of various sects throughout the eighteenth and early nineteenth centuries.[8] The eclipse of Shiʿa lordly power in the districts of Tripoli and Kisrawan in the eighteenth century and its replacement by Shihab rule, under which thrived Maronite families allied with Druze chiefs, had sectarian overtones. It was in this period that the district of Kisrawan became overwhelmingly Maronite, and many Maronite monasteries were built there.[9]

The feuds and battles between clans of different sects were not, however, religious in nature. Rather the internecine wars resulted from a struggle for control of certain lucrative tax districts. Hence the *aʿyan*, who were also known by their Ottoman title *mukataaci*—tax farmer or holder of a financial contract—were constantly building, breaking, and resecuring alliances with Ottoman provincial governors in Damascus and Acre, as well as with imperial officials in Istanbul, in whose hands ultimate authority rested. They were expected to uphold law and order, administer basic justice, punish, fine, or beat recalcitrant *ahali,* collect debts, and above all raise the required imperial revenue, of which they kept a percentage. They forwarded the remainder to the ruling Shihab emir, who in turn defrayed his own, often outrageously high costs before passing the rest on to the Ottoman governor of the province of Sidon, ensconced in Acre.[10] To do so more effectively, to assess the population, the fertility of the land, and hence the taxable income of each district more accurately in order to raise as much revenue as possible to satisfy both Ottoman demands and their own, the more powerful *a'yan* surrounded themselves with an army of retainers. These were often drawn from lesser branches of their own families and from village men, but Druze, Maronite, and Shi'a notables recruited scribes almost exclusively from the ranks of educated Christians such as the Shidyaqs.

⠝

The lineage and family history of As'ad Shidyaq thoroughly implicated him within this genealogical geography of Mount Lebanon, in which certain important families dominated the social order and defined the political and religious landscape of the country. Originally from Hasrun in Mount Lebanon, As'ad's family had settled in the village of Hadath, some five easy miles southeast of Beirut. He was related to the illustrious 'Awwad family, from whose ranks had emerged several patriarchs of the Maronite Church, as well as to the eighteenth-century Maronite bishop of Aleppo Jarmanus Farhat and to the famous scholar Josephus Assemani, head of the Vatican library and author of the massive Latin compendium of Syriac history and literature, *Bibliotheca orientalis Clementino-Vaticana.*

Members of his extended family had over the years enrolled in the venerable Maronite College in Rome, while others had become parish priests and still others teachers in Maronite schools in Beirut and Mount Lebanon. Butrus, the brother of As'ad's great-grandfather, was a subdeacon, or *shidyaq,* in the Maronite Church, from which derived the family name. As'ad's grandfather Mansur, also a subdeacon, worked for the Shihab emirs and for the Shi'a Harfush emirs in Baalbek. He made a small fortune at one point, but he was also caught up in several wars fought between rival Shihab emirs and found himself repeatedly exiled, once in Bilad Bishara in northern Palestine, another time in the Hawran region in Syria.

As'ad's father, Yusuf, was known as Abi Husayn, undoubtedly a reference to his own father's connection to Shiʿa emirs. He too worked for several Shihab emirs as secretary, teacher, property agent, and tax collector. He lived a life as unsettled as his father's, and experienced a similar cycle of punishment and pardon, penury and plenty, moving constantly according to the whims of his patrons or the dictates of security. He had five sons, one of whom, Asʿad, he hoped might become a priest.[11]

☙

Asʿad Shidyaq studied at the Maronite seminary of ʿAyn Waraqa, which was located in the heart of the rugged district of Kisrawan. Founded in 1789 by the patriarch Yusuf Istifan on the site of a convent dedicated nearly a century earlier by Istifan Duwayhi, the seminary symbolized Maronite aspirations for reform at the close of a turbulent eighteenth century.[12] Although the establishment of the Maronite College in Rome in 1584 had spurred the creation of several Maronite schools in the seventeenth and eighteenth centuries, most of these were run by separate religious orders and were therefore not directly under the supervision of the patriarch. By contrast, ʿAyn Waraqa not only was modeled on the Maronite College in Rome but also effectively became its replacement under the direct control of the patriarch. Its main function was to educate the Maronite clergy. Two boys from each of the eight Maronite dioceses and two from the Istifan family were selected as its students, but it was also open to other Maronites who paid the necessary fees. The decline in the Maronite College in Rome following the abolition of the Jesuit order in 1773 had underscored the need for an alternative seminary; but more than anything else, the founding of ʿAyn Waraqa reflected the acute need felt by many in the Maronite ecclesiastical community to control more directly the Latinization of the Maronite Church that had been set in motion a century earlier.

The eighteenth century had been a time of immense transformation of the Maronite Church as it came under sustained pressures from the Vatican but also from new Western-inspired Maronite monastic orders to Latinize its ecclesiastical structure, practice, and discipline. These encroached upon the patriarch's authority.[13] Deeply divided Maronite ecclesiastics were thus summoned at the behest of the Vatican to a historic general Lebanese Council in 1736 at the monastery of Luwayze in Mount Lebanon. There a number of resolutions confirming Roman dogma were passed, emphasizing the priest as a dispenser of sacraments, purging all manner of heretical books and ideas, regulating the relationship between the patriarch and his bishops, insulating the ecclesiastical community from that of the secular notables, abolishing Maronite mixed monasteries (in which nuns and monks had traditionally shared a courtyard), and suppressing various "superstitions" considered antithetical to proper Catholic practice.[14] The goal of the Lebanese Council was nothing less than to transform the Maronite Church from an institution rooted in the genealogical geography of Mount Lebanon, and hence inevitably subjected to its vagaries, to an outpost of reformed post–Tridentine Catholicism which visibly separated the sacred from the profane.[15]

The city of Aleppo, meanwhile, had been at the vortex of a major missionary endeavor in Syria throughout the century which had resulted in the conversion of thousands of Greek Orthodox Christians to Roman Catholicism.[16] It was from there that a Jesuit-educated Maronite woman by the name of Hindiyya al-ʿUjaymi moved to Mount Lebanon, where she founded the Order of the Sacred Heart of Jesus at Bkirke in the district of Kisrawan in 1750. Hindiyya embodied and exacerbated the crisis in Maronite identity of her day. The regulations of her order sought to sever the ties that traditionally existed between nuns and their relatives and the lay protectors of their convent. Her embrace of auricular confession, with its obligation to confess frequently and methodically before a priest in a manner that further accentuated the individual over the communal, was, moreover, very much a part of a Latinized sacrament, itself part of a larger attempt to discipline the wayward Eastern Christians and to consolidate Vatican control.[17] Indeed, inspired by Latin Catholic devotional literature introduced to her by her Jesuit tutors and confessors, she claimed to have visions of Christ, to perform miracles, and to speak directly with Jesus through dramatic bouts of mystical union with his body and spirit. She soon found herself the object of veneration as a living saint on the part of many Maronites, including the church's patriarch at the time as well as many members of the influential Khazin family. She also, however, attracted strong suspicion on the part of many other Maronite clergymen and Roman Catholic missionaries. Rumors about her false piety were exacerbated by accusations of torture and murder behind the walls of her convent, sensationalized most famously by the French aristocrat C. F. Volney.[18] Significantly, both her supporters and detractors used torture, and both used inquisitorial procedures introduced by Roman representatives, which relied on written confessions as their main proof, to establish their case.[19]

Hindiyya was subjected to several papal inquisitions; her order was suppressed by the Propaganda Fide in 1779; and Patriarch Yusuf Istifan (who had been elected in 1767 amidst the controversy) was ordered to Rome to answer for—and soon enough recant—his support for the mystic, who was herself confined in various convents, even tortured, until her death in 1798. Her Maronite supporters eventually abandoned her, and the entire affair was blamed on a deluded young woman who seduced an otherwise obedient Maronite nation.[20] The debacle surrounding Hindiyya put in ironic perspective the notion of a monolithic Maronite community for which As'ad Shidyaq soon would be so bitterly persecuted. In the immediate aftermath of the affair, Hindiyya became in European missionary eyes emblematic of Oriental decadence, and embodied the impossibility and inherent irrationality of autonomous Eastern reform as much as she did a contemporary Roman Catholic preoccupation with female mysticism and monastic discipline. In Maronite eyes she became a severe embarrassment, and her case emphasized the need to indoctrinate a more rational, and less superstitious, clergy and community.[21]

ꞵ

The establishment of 'Ayn Waraqa was very much a communal atonement for the Hindiyya affair. At the same time, it was, by its location and history, a deliberate affirmation of Maronite autonomy. It was a result not of Roman urging but of local initiative. A chastened Yusuf Istifan had been rehabilitated by Pope Pius VI in 1784 after spending several years disgraced—in his view unjustly—and in exile in Palestine. Not only had he finally signed a full confession prepared by the Propaganda of his own errors relating to Hindiyya and reaffirmed his utter submission to the Holy See, but also he and his entire community had, declared the pope, utterly rejected "the despicable corruptions of Bkirke and the delusions of the woman Hindiyya and her false visions and teachings."[22] Indeed, the school was chartered in 1789 at Bkirke, the very scene of Hindiyya's alleged crimes. Patriarch Yusuf Istifan, the twelve Maronite bishops (including four from the Khazin family), Ghandur Sa'd al-Khuri (acting as the French consul in Beirut), and twenty-six Khazin and five Hubaysh shaykhs, among others, affixed their seals to the founding charter of 'Ayn Waraqa. The school was placed directly under the sole control of the Maronite patriarch. He was to select its administrators and approve every student who proposed to enroll, and he was to decide where to employ the students upon their graduation.

The school did not welcome its first students until 1797. Pious endowments had first to be converted or established for the benefit of the school.[23]

The Shihab emirs pledged the revenue from land in Damur on the Mediterranean coast south of Beirut, including an orchard with its annual thirty-three loads of mulberry leaves, for the benefit of indigent Maronites; pastoral letters, moreover, made it incumbent on every Maronite family to give to the school—five piasters for the wealthy, three for the middle classes, and one for the poor. When the school did finally open, its curriculum included Arabic and Syriac, logic, philosophy, algebra, geometry, eloquence, and copying. Every one of the eighteen students in each class was to be inculcated with a spirit of orthodoxy that derived from the regulations of the Maronite Council held at Luwayze in 1736. Like their counterparts at Andover Seminary, the students were to be taught how to resist "heretical ideas." Because here the students were boys, not college graduates as was the case at Andover, they were tutored in an obviously more paternalistic manner. They were to lead a regimented life of prayer and study. They were not to leave the school save with permission and under escort, and when on the road they were to keep quiet and not greet anyone, not even a family member. They were under no circumstances to possess any books except those that expressly promoted Catholic piety. And they were to refrain from explaining the moral sciences to the common laity.

Everything about the school, from the strict discipline of dormitory and classroom life, to its isolation from surrounding society, to the pedagogy which explicitly mandated the equality of all students, was designed to produce a literate and articulate clergy rooted in Mount Lebanon and totally loyal to the institution of the Maronite Church personified in its patriarch. This loyalty was to supersede the natural loyalty of students to their families, no matter how illustrious they might be. Every student, including the fourteen-year-old As'ad, who was enrolled by his elder brother Tannus in June 1812, was made to know that he was entering a seminary whose main goal was the production of a devout Maronite clergy. Every student was to pledge obedience to the will of the patriarch, especially in matters concerning Catholic dogma.

Thus at age sixteen As'ad would have sworn on the Bible that he, As'ad, son of Yusuf, from the village of Hadath, did submit himself entirely and of his "own volition" (*bi-tamam ikhtiyari*) to the school's laws and regulations. He would have vowed, furthermore, that both now and later he would always submit to the patriarch's authority and heed his command to engage in benevolent action to save souls.[24]

The establishment of ʿAyn Waraqa confirmed the path Istifan Duwayhi had first cut in reconciling the Maronites with their Muslim Ottoman surroundings. From the outset, the Maronite myth of perpetual fidelity to the Roman Catholic orthodoxy had created an equally tenacious myth of perpetual persecution at the hands of the enemies of the faith, and thus Maronite missives to Rome and Paris throughout the eighteenth century consistently complained of Muslim oppression and Maronite isolation. But as in Duwayhi's time, this was far more a reflection of an astute Maronite reading of Europe than it was a faithful account of the Ottoman Arab world.

In fact, the Maronite community extended its sway across Mount Lebanon. The Qannubin monastery had indeed been abandoned for much of the eighteenth century, but only part of the reason for this lay in the oppression of rulers, which in any event had far less to do with religious persecution than with the insatiable appetite of the secular lords of the land for revenue, which plagued the entire population, Maronite, Shiʿa, and Druze alike. The patriarchs preferred to reside in Kisrawan in newer and more accessible monasteries closer to the coast, and often in properties owned by or connected to their extended families. As the Maronite notable Ghandur Saʿd confessed to Yusuf Istifan in 1788 about the wretched and ignorant state of the Maronite clergy in the aftermath of the Hindiyya affair, "If only there were persecution of the community or some abridgement of your religious liberty or some impediment that prevents your control or administration, an excuse [for their ignorance] might well be found."[25]

The very nature of Ottoman imperial tolerance, which upheld the separateness of religious communities under Islamic hegemony, had allowed the Vatican to embark on its radical transformation of Eastern Christianity in the eighteenth century. The intensity of Vatican involvement in Maronite affairs accentuated the total absence of formal Ottoman concern in the internal divisions of the empire's Christian subjects in Mount Lebanon; by the same token, the bitterness and energy with which many Maronites condemned Roman legates compared starkly with their formulaic pronouncements on infidel oppression. Not only had the Maronites flourished on the margins of Ottoman imperial concern, but they had put down deep roots in the land as well. Their monasteries and those of their Armenian Catholic and Greek Catholic counterparts, almost all built in Ottoman times, covered dozens of hilltops and mountains across Mount Lebanon.[26] Some, like remote Qannubin built into the side of the mountain, bore the hallmarks of an earlier, less secure, less affluent time. Most, however, were built on more exposed tracts that often commanded inviting views of an infinitely more multireligious environment. The spread of monasteries southward into the Shuf was accomplished either by taking over debt-ridden church properties or by purchasing land from non-Muslim *aʿyan*—from Druze notables and Shihab emirs—who actively encouraged the creation of a more organized, more consistent, and more productive tax base under monastic auspices.[27] So much had the Maronite community prospered that by the time the American missionaries arrived in the region, Pliny Fisk could count over a hundred Catholic monasteries in Mount Lebanon and found Qannubin restored as a patriarchal residence.[28]

ᘉ

The hierarchy of the Maronite Church clearly reflected the dominant social order, in which important families defined not only the temporal but also the ecclesiastical landscape of Mount Lebanon. Six of the eight eighteenth-century patriarchs had come from notable Maronite families which had donated much property to the church, but in return had expected, and indeed often demanded, the right to be involved with the selection of certain bishops, and at times even to foist their own kinsmen on the church as patriarchs.[29] Whatever the tensions between the secular and ecclesiastical realms—and there were many in the eighteenth century—the symbiosis between them was manifest.

The American missionaries established their mission station in Beirut just as Yusuf, bishop of Tripoli and son of a shaykh from the prominent Hubaysh family, was elected to the patriarchate. Born 27 April 1787 in the village of Sahil ʿAlma on the bay of Juniya in Kisrawan, he was christened Yaʿqub and baptized at the Franciscan church in Harissa. The Hubayshes epitomized political and social Maronite integration into an Ottoman Arab world: they had initially risen through the ranks of the Turkoman ʿAssaf emirs until their extirpation in 1590, after which they cast their fortunes with the Druze leader Fakhr al-Din and then with the Shihabs. Ghazir in the district of Kisrawan was their main seat, and as with the Khazins, their influence inevitably came to express itself in the Maronite Church. The monastery of Mar Jirjis (Saint George) in Sahil ʿAlma was erected by a bishop from the family in the early part of the eighteenth century. Yaʿqub, like Asʿad Shidyaq, was one of several brothers, and also like Asʿad was sent to the school of ʿAyn Waraqa. He was enrolled in 1809 as its nineteenth student. At twenty-one he was far older than most of the other students, an indication perhaps of a late choice of career for a man who might well have

Figure 4. Maronite patriarch Yusuf Hubaysh. Source: Isaac Bird, *Bible Work in Bible Lands; or, Events in the History of the Syria Mission* (Philadelphia: Presbyterian Board of Publication, 1872), 159.

become a secular lord. Following his graduation, he was ordained a priest in 1814 and given the ecclesiastical name Yusuf, in honor of his ancestor the bishop, in his family monastery at Sahil ʿAlma. He was quickly granted control for life of another family church and its endowed properties and mulberry trees in Ghazir. There he resided until, six years on, when he was just shy of thirty-three, Yusuf was made to travel to Qannubin to accept, very reluctantly, the barren bishopric of Tripoli.

Yusuf plainly did not want to leave Ghazir. He complained bitterly to his friend Butrus Karam, bishop of Beirut, of the arduous travel he had to undertake among so undistinguished a flock. Qannubin was, in fact, only a day's distance, but the Maronites who inhabited its environs were in accent, lineage, and outlook entirely different from those over whom he presided in Ghazir. He dreaded what he described as *wahshat al-ightirab,* the utter forlornness of separation from his native land.[30]

This same Bishop Butrus Karam to whom Yusuf complained had himself been consecrated in 1819, and would help elect Yusuf patriarch of the Maronite Church on 25 May 1823 at Qannubin. He appended his seal to a petition, one of several that followed a long-standing Maronite practice, begging the Roman pontiff to approve a patriarch's election by bestowing upon him a *pallium* of confirmation, carried with the patriarch-elect's personal representative, an Armenian Catholic monk, to Rome. The various Maronite monastic orders seconded these petitions, and the Hubaysh, Khazin, and Dahdah shaykhs also dispatched letters imploring Rome to confirm Hubaysh.

Most important, Yusuf Hubaysh *al-haqir,* the lowly, had signed a vow of total submission to Rome's authority, acknowledging the pope to be the direct successor to Saint Peter, and thus Christ's regent on earth. As an ever vigilant and faithful servant of the Catholic Church, Yusuf formally committed himself to upholding Catholic beliefs and fighting all forms of heresy. Although Yusuf was well under forty, and thus in direct violation of the resolutions of the 1736 Council of Luwayze, Pope Leo XII, on the recommendation of the Propaganda Fide, granted the *pallium* to the kneeling envoy of Yusuf Hubaysh on 3 May 1824.[31] Through its men of the sword and pen the community had apparently spoken in one voice in favor of the student from ʿAyn Waraqa. All the glowing testaments to Hubaysh's Christian character and piety, and all the proclamations of the alleged "joy and happiness"[32] that attended his election, papered over the fact that not every bishop was happy, nor was every Maronite of one opinion or coloring.

As the sixty-third head of the Maronite Church, Yusuf Hubaysh was also the first graduate of ʿAyn Waraqa to take charge of his people. He inherited a divided ecclesiastical community over which the stigma of the Hindiyya affair still hung.[33] Much, then, was riding on the new patriarch's shoulders when he received the papal *pallium* on 7 July 1824. He personified a Maronite Church desperate to turn the page on its recent past at the same time as it clung tenaciously to an ancient, heavily romanticized lineage. Hubaysh decided to celebrate his confirmation at Sahil ʿAlma on 13 March 1825, on the fifth Sunday of the Lenten fast before a huge crowd made up of the heads of all the Catholic churches in Lebanon, the papal legate, the Austrian consul, and the heads of the powerful families, emirs and shaykhs with their retainers and commoners—*fellahin,* or "lowly peasants," is how Hubaysh referred to them—not too far behind, some six thousand souls in all.[34] There was no imperial Ottoman official present, underscoring the degree to which the spectacle inculcated a sense of unshakeable, indeed transhistorical, religious continuity that bound the ever faithful Maronites to Rome. This evocation occurred very much at the margins of, but crucially not beyond, an Ottoman sultanate that barely registered, let alone expressed any concern over, its distant Maronite subjects. A telling imperial absence at one level, however, was more than made up for by its obvious presence at others. Many notables who witnessed the ceremony annually participated in filling the imperial coffers, and all of them, Hubaysh included, were ensconced at the apex of the local social order. For all these notable men, time did not fly forward providentially, as it did for the American missionaries; rather, it moved deliberately and for the most part predictably. The notion of rushing forth to evangelize the world because of the rapid passage of time was alien to an Ottoman Arab culture that prided itself on its stability amidst heresy and infidelity, and its uninterrupted political and religious lineages.

ଯ

It was to this conservative world that the American missionaries announced themselves in the third decade of the nineteenth century. They came not as crude military crusaders but as the redeemed "artillery of heaven," men who were determined to reclaim biblical lands from the god of this world who had long since enslaved the ancient Eastern Christian churches.[35] They wanted to conquer spiritually where others had prevailed through force. More humbly, Parsons and Fisk were simply two idealistic Americans, both just under thirty (the first was born in Goshen, Massachusetts, in 1792 and the second in Shelburne, Massachusetts, in the same year). They were young men of modest means, animated by enormous hopes.

The first two years were difficult ones for the American Board missionaries. Levi Parsons and Pliny Fisk spent much of their first year between British-controlled Malta, where a Bible depot and a printing press were located under English missionary supervision, and Ottoman Chios (Scio) and Izmir (Smyrna) trying to learn Italian and Greek; at the same time, they conducted tours of the Ottoman Levant, literally traveling up and down the Aegean and the Mediterranean from Chios to Cyprus, from Izmir to Alexandria, and from Cairo into Palestine and Syria. Parsons was the first American missionary to visit Jerusalem, which he did in February 1821, but he fell ill and died in Alexandria exactly a year later and was replaced by Williams College and Andover Seminary graduate Jonas King.

The missionaries groped their way across an unknown land, rudely awakened to the enormousness of their self-appointed task. Despite the Greek war of independence, which broke out soon after their arrival in the region, the missionaries were by their own admission not unduly harassed.[36] Single men, they often traveled in the company of pilgrims and were able to traverse great stretches of the empire; they described, as best they could, the variety of the "mingled" people they encountered; they distributed and sold hundreds of Bibles and tracts, but they were not able in three years to produce a single Arab convert. They spoke barely any Arabic, and they were weighed down by the unrealistic American expectations of a speedy yet pacific conquest of the "ancient and mighty kingdom" of Satan in the Ottoman Empire.[37]

It was at this point that Pliny Fisk and Jonas King embarked on their first tour of Mount Lebanon armed with letters of introduction given to them by Emir Bashir Shihab.[38] They were joined by the Reverend Joseph Wolff, a converted Jew and now a zealous missionary for the London Jews Society, and together they researched the "promiscuous jumble of rocky, precipitous hills" and "deep ravines" that constituted Mount Lebanon. The Protestant missionaries became known locally as "al-Inkiliz," or "the English," both because of the association of England with Protestantism and also because the missionaries put themselves under English consular protection. As "English," they benefited from the ascendancy and prestige of England's naval power. Emir Bashir had already established a relationship with the English admiral Sidney Smith during the brief but intense Napoleonic interlude; Lady Hester Stanhope, the niece of William Pitt, resided

Figure 5. Dr. Jonas King, Beirut, 1822–1825. Source: John H. Hewitt, *Williams College and Foreign Missions* (Boston: Pilgrim Press, 1914), 38a (opposite 38)

near Dayr al-Qamar, although she was utterly disdainful of what she described as "the rage of Bibles & misguided zeal."[39] So long as missionaries
were perceived as pilgrims, or as temporary residents tending to their own
affairs, this favorable association clearly outweighed another, narrower, ecclesiastical anti-Protestant view of the English as the champions of the "heretic" Luther, which was an obsession, in particular, of eighteenth-century
Latin missionaries to the East, and which thus clearly found an echo among
the native Catholic clergy.[40]

The missionaries traveled unimpeded. They routinely stopped at Maronite, Greek Catholic, Armenian Catholic, and Syrian Catholic monasteries, and were almost always cordially received. This place is your place—*al
mahal mahalkum*—Yusuf Hubaysh was said to have told Lewis Way in June
1823 when the English missionary rented the former Jesuit college of ʿAyntura.[41] American missionaries soon joined the Englishman, and the Maronite bishop Hanna Marun even provided Jonas King with letters of
introduction for his impending visit to Dayr al-Qamar. Before long the
Americans even visited Qannubin, where they were welcomed by, and
dined with, the patriarch on 6 October 1823.[42] They left their host with a
Syriac New Testament and a printed copy of the Arabic Bible, one of the
many copies of a British and Foreign Bible Society reprint of a Roman edition from 1671, without the Apocrypha, which was regularly forwarded to
them from Malta.[43] They also stopped at Bkirke and asked Maronite priests
there about Hindiyya, whose history Fisk had read about in Volney, but
found them, not surprisingly, unwilling to discuss her case. And finally, in
the middle of October, they visited ʿAyn Waraqa, where Emir Bashir had
recommended they study Arabic, but Fisk found that the "situation of the
place is low, and disagreeable and there is great want of neatness."[44]

Throughout this summer the Protestant missionaries repeatedly challenged, or provoked, the Eastern priests, monks, abbots, bishops, and patriarchs they encountered. They doggedly contested various points of Catholic
dogma, from the veneration of saints and the Virgin Mary to the prohibition on the marriage of bishops and the infallibility of the pope. The local
priests and bishops would often try to change the subject and avoid being
drawn into controversy, but almost always the missionaries would press
home their point that the Scriptures, not the Catholic Church, was the lo-
cus of salvation. King, for instance, exhausted from his travels in August,
sought refuge in a monastery near Sidon. There he found an Arabic Book
of Psalms and a catechism containing the Ten Commandments. As he leafed
through them, and found that they were listed according to the Catholic

tradition, in an outburst of self-described "indignation" he immediately accused the monastery's superior of being impious and a liar for perverting
the commandments of God.

The missionaries spoke loudly but they did not listen; nor did they heed
the many signals, if not outright pleas, from their first native informants,
guides, and teachers to avoid what they believed to be unnecessary controversy. Their attempts to impress upon these men the "plain truths about their
Popish doctrines and practices," as Fisk put it in his journal entry from October 1823, reflected a raw missionary sensibility and a fundamental belief
in the power of biblical criticism to reveal the essential and transhistorical
divine truths contained in the Scriptures.[45] This, after all, is precisely what
Andover Seminary had inculcated in these Americans. But their enthusiasm
also reflected an unwarrantable breach of general propriety whereby these
men enjoyed the hospitality of their hosts only to ignore some of the most
basic stipulations of religious discretion in a historically multireligious land.[46]

Their disputation constituted more than simple eagerness. It was also an
expression of a mission born of a particular moment in American history as
it collided with the realities of an entirely different moment in Ottoman
Arab history. Put more bluntly, it was the translation of a missionary ethos
that arose in a colonialist America in which missionaries were cultural imperialists into a world where they were not. The extraordinary reversal of
position permeates the early missionary correspondence. The privileged men
belonging to established churches preaching in English to broken Indians
in North America had been transformed, indeed had voluntarily transformed themselves, into largely isolated individuals speaking in halting Arabic to firmly entrenched Christian communities living in the shadow of the
Ottoman Empire. The first description sent back from Beirut by William
Goodell in November 1823 captured this precise moment of reversal at the
same time as it heralded another transition: from itinerant and unmarried
men to a more stable, more familial, if still small missionary enterprise that
sought to make Beirut and its hinterland of Mount Lebanon a missionary
field.[47]

ﻻ

"In a short time, boats came, and we found ourselves surrounded by half
naked and barbarous Arabs, of whom we have often heard say, 'Who can
stand before these sons of Anak?'"[48] This Old Testament question that pre-
ceded the conquest of the Promised Land by a people favored by God was

tellingly brought to mind by William Goodell and Isaac Bird as they went ashore in Beirut in the middle of November 1823. If the allusion was to a biblical frontier, the description clearly evoked a more recent American one—the "half naked," "barbarous," and "fierce Arabs [who] leaped out" at the missionaries to carry them ashore recalled the Indians of North America, or at least a certain stock representation of them well established by the early nineteenth century.[49] King thus recounted one harrowing incident in his journal, describing "the Arabs, who poured down upon us like a torrent . . . at the same time setting up a terrible yell, like the war-whoop of the savages of North America."[50] But the language of frontiers, biblical and more recently colonial, also heralded the commencement of a metaphorical war of annihilation in which the Americans' inability to understand, let alone adequately depict, the world they were encountering would lead them to an utterly resounding defeat.

To be sure, the letters and journals sent back to the United States quickly amplified their initially stark description of Beirut's inhabitants. The missionary correspondence would take roughly six months to journey from Beirut to Malta and from thence to Boston aboard American brigs such as the *Sally Ann,* which regularly plied the route between Malta, Boston, and Izmir. As they accumulated, these ethnographic and physical descriptions of the "promising" part of the empire "at the foot of mount Lebanon" first espied by Pliny Fisk on 14 July 1823 provided a detailed portrait of a foreign coastal town and hinterland poised, the missionaries adamantly believed, to receive the spirit of God. Beirut was far smaller than Boston—its population was estimated by Goodell in January 1824 to be not less than five thousand strong—but it had a recorded history that stretched back to Phoenician times and had once boasted a famous Roman law school. In the early nineteenth century it was a walled town with five gates; a few decades back its ramparts had endured a Russian bombardment during one of the many Russo-Ottoman wars; its streets struck the missionaries as "narrow and dirty," its houses, made of "soft, sandy, crumbling stone," appeared to them "dark, damp, and inconvenient." The town also possessed three large mosques and several smaller ones as well as Maronite, Roman Catholic, Greek, and Greek Catholic churches. Ships were forced to anchor about two miles from the city, but the cargoes they loaded there included silks, wines, tobacco, olives, figs, raisins, and other fruits. Those they unloaded contained a variety of colonial commodities such as sugar from the Antilles and Brazilian coffee as well as European manufactures, especially English textiles, much to the satisfaction of the English consul, Peter Abbott, with whom the missionaries established immediate contact, and under whose protection they journeyed up into Mount Lebanon.[51]

The foreignness of Beirut to the Americans was mirrored by the spectacle of unmistakably foreign men wearing English clerical garb accompanied by their unveiled wives and children, with boxes and baggage in tow, arriving in town.[52] There was no question of the missionaries "fitting in": that was neither their objective nor their outlook, and to the extent that Fisk, King, and Bird had made what they described as Oriental outfits, this was never with the aim of passing for natives, as it would be for an intrepid British explorer, Richard Burton. Rather, it constituted a missionary concession to what the Americans took to be local predilection, and to facilitate travel, just as their hosting visiting Roman Catholic and Methodist American preachers in Beirut, improbable if not unthinkable in Boston, constituted another concession quickly made to their new situation.[53] For the most part, then, they openly declared, and in any case could hardy conceal, their foreignness. Their wives sewed their clothing from cloth sent to them by American missionaries in Malta, who also sent shoes and stockings.[54] They ate pork; they sat on chairs and around tables rather than cross-legged on carpets in a house they rented just beyond the walls of the city. Then they set about trying to find Arabic tutors.[55]

Their instinct was to classify what they saw in terms that made sense to them; thus they assumed the diversity of sects they encountered to be a reflection of an indelibly sectarian landscape. Because they privileged religious affiliation over all others, the Protestant missionaries spoke of the "derelict" Jews, the "nominal" or "professing" Christians, and the "Mohammedans" as if they represented segregated communities. In their letters and journals they routinely wrote about "a Catholic" or "a Turk" or "a Greek" or "a Jew" as if such religious identities were static, but also as if they were more "real" markers than those of social discrimination between high and low, notables and commoners, or *aᶜyan* and *aᶜwam*.

A principal, indeed crucial, difference between local chroniclers, or even some Western writers such as Charles Churchill, who had accumulated decades of experience in Mount Lebanon on the one hand, and the American missionaries on the other, was that the latter had little appreciation, and initially precious little interest, in how different communities in Mount Lebanon shared a turbulent history of coexistence, and how this coexistence had elaborated over time a rigid social hierarchy that clearly traversed religious boundaries. While they bemoaned the "chaos of dialects" around them, the Americans could not yet see that a multireligious hierarchy depended on a common language of social order.[56] The missionaries flirted with this language at first in their poorly written Arabic letters, for in a largely illiterate society they used socially laden titles, and of course they received them.[57]

But from the outset they also associated with consuls and met governors; they traveled and had means available to them far beyond what was available to ordinary men. They had servants, they offered their guests coffee and tobacco, and they could hire teachers. They were educated and under English protection. The missionaries, in short, delighted in the expensive fruits of this nonsectarian elitist order without fully appreciating the degree to which the coffee, tobacco, and repasts they enjoyed, for instance, at Emir Bashir's palace or with the Maronite patriarch at Qannubin obligated a reciprocity of treatment between men of culture. They were unable to appreciate the degree to which local society was more than simply the sum of its various parts.

Far more to the point, they also believed that one did not need to learn a culture before trying to convert it. Certainly, they diligently applied themselves to the study of Arabic, and very early on recognized the difficulties of the language. Yet for the American missionaries, the mastery of Arabic was simply the means to a predetermined end. There was nothing, they maintained, that ought prevent them in the meantime from trying to communicate the inherent truths of the Gospels to the people of Syria, Palestine, and Mount Lebanon, just as David Brainerd had once communicated those same truths to the Indians of North America.

Two paths of mission were almost immediately pursued: the first was education. The homes of married missionaries became the setting for informal learning. Bird and Goodell boasted that their wives reflected "the intelligence and influence of the female part of the community in America."[58] They took in a few, apparently indigent boys and girls, and attempted to instill in them a proper Christian and civilized manner. In July 1824 the missionaries established a more formal school for boys, and they hired a native to teach the Bible in Arabic.[59]

The second path was direct proselytization. Of all the missionaries Jonas King was the most competent in Arabic in these first years in Ottoman Syria. More so than Fisk or Parsons, he was able to immerse himself in an Arabic environment. The son of a Franklin County farmer from rural Massachusetts who had taught him to read the entirety of the Bible from Genesis to Revelation by the age of six, King grew into an evangelist determined to instruct the world.[60] Accordingly it was he who pressed the assault in the summer of 1823. Armed with letters of introduction given by both Hanna Marun, the Maronite bishop who lived in Kisrawan, and Lady Hester Stanhope, King stayed in the house of an "Arab"—a Maronite merchant—by the name of Yusuf Dumani of Dayr al-Qamar. King hired his twenty-year-old son to be his full-time Arabic teacher. Despite the welcome provided him by his host family and the courtesy of several visits paid by Maronite priests, King continually cajoled all who would listen about the imminent end of time and the desperate need of all people for regeneration.

For all his stylized self-abnegation—"I am a worm and no man" he told his teacher—King was clearly a confident missionary.[61] Having gone to Andover Seminary and then studied Arabic in Paris under the Orientalist Sylvestre de Sacy, he thought that his intimate knowledge of the Bible and his worldliness gave him an irresistible advantage over the provincial Maronite priests.[62] He repeatedly exhorted his hosts to become born again; he mocked the ubiquitous icons of the Virgin Mary, and always he dueled publicly with clergymen. He attempted nothing less than to shame them into regeneration.

On Thursday 21 August 1823, for example, he was reading the Twenty-second Psalm with his teacher. He had just reached the passage "All the ends of the world shall remember and turn unto the Lord; and all the kindreds of the nations shall worship before thee." A priest entered the room, and King asked him whether that time was past or to come? The priest "hardly knew what to answer me," wrote King triumphantly. Having seized the initiative, the missionary then declaimed before all present—family, guests, and embarrassed priest—that darkness now covered the world. The time was coming when Jesus Christ would reign on the earth and all would know his name. He turned to his Arabic teacher and made him open the Bible and read from Revelation 20:1–3:

> And I saw an angel come down from heaven, having the key of the bottomless pit and a great chain in his hand.
>
> And he laid hold on the dragon, that old serpent, which is the Devil, and Satan, and bound him a thousand years.
>
> And cast him into the bottomless pit, and shut him up, and set a seal upon him, that he should deceive the nations no more, till the thousand years should be fulfilled: and after that he must be loosed a little season.

As he read, all were solemn. His teacher's grandmother wept. King could, by his own account, hardly refrain from weeping. And then he lectured his listeners about how the church of Christ founded by the Apostles had moved away from truth, and how darkness had prevailed, and how every Christian had to read these words to the churches of Asia.[63]

King left Dayr al-Qamar to continue his travels; he went again to Palestine, where he spent the winter, before returning to Dayr al-Qamar in the middle of 1824, where he was once more well received.[64] Now bolder than before because his Arabic was that much better, he disputed again, and now ever more in public. On 24 June he wrote to Isaac Bird in Beirut that "I have been to the Market place, and into families, arguing, disputing, preaching."[65] And in August of that same year he urged his fellow missionaries that "it becomes us surely to study & converse, & preach, as those, who have but little time to labour."[66] The very bluntness of King's style won him admirers, among whom was As'ad Shidyaq, who intensively taught him Syriac in Dayr al-Qamar in the summer of 1825.[67] For all his evocation of the awful scenes of eternity, there was a profound simplicity of manner in a man who presented his fellow men with a Bible they professed to follow and exhorted them to read it for themselves. In 1823 his efforts to declare the essential "truth" of salvation through Jesus Christ alone were dismissed by a Maronite priest because King's disputation suffered from his poor Arabic, but by 1825 this was no longer the case. He could now preach and write fluently in the language, as evinced by an extensive Arabic prayer from Tyre in January 1825 in which the missionary pleaded with God to forgive all and to bestow a "faith that purifies the heart, works through love, and overcomes the world."[68] King was no *jahil,* or "ignorant" commoner; all could see that. "He spoke Arabic well," admitted one resident of Dayr al-Qamar who put to paper the only surviving Arabic remarks describing the American missionary, "but everybody was distressed by him, for, although he was handsome and youthful, they believed he was English and therefore had no religion."[69] There was an undeniable sincerity in the man that moved some to listen to the words of an American whose faith—Protestantism—had no official standing in the empire.

Yet for all his efforts to inspire an American-style revival of faith, King's efforts also recalled the Puritan experience with the Indians. Like the Puritans, he was determined to expose before their flocks the ignorance of his opponents, as well as their impotence in the critical question of salvation. Yet unlike them, he had no General Court behind him to ban supposedly idolatrous worship; he had no militia and no settlers who could subdue the natives directly or indirectly; he had no disease to thin their ranks severely, or any technology that could impress or terrorize them. Yet he desired the same result that John Eliot had vainly sought with many more advantages nearly two centuries before. And unlike Paul on Mars Hill or David Brainerd at Crossweeksung, the American missionaries who operated in the Ottoman Levant worked directly against communities that had a very powerful sense of their own Christianity and were part of an imperial world that was still confident, if no longer certain, of its ability to withstand Western encroachment. If the Spanish conquistador Hernando Cortés appeared, as has often been asserted, as a god to the Aztecs in fulfillment of certain prophecies, and exploited this coincidence to ruthless effect, King and his little band of missionaries appeared decidedly human to the various inhabitants of the Ottoman Empire. For all their contempt for the "ignorance" of the East, the missionaries were themselves largely ignorant of the diverse histories of those they sought to convert. Although they had mastered a certain narrative of American history in which a literal knowledge of the Bible was essential, they now entered into a world that was composed of multiple, often contradictory though coexisting narratives, from the purposefully beleaguered ecclesiastical Maronite to the arrogantly sublime imperial Ottoman.

The Maronite patriarch did not remain idle. Initially thrown off balance by the unannounced appearance of the American Protestants whom he mistook for pilgrims, or for English missionaries concerned only with the salvation of the Jews, he soon surmised that their object was the abolition of his religion and community as he knew it. The American missionaries had commenced what they themselves described as a reconquest of the Holy Land. Patriarch Hubaysh personified the most strident local response. Both sides engaged vigorously in a metaphorical war of mutual annihilation in which no quarter was given. Ostensibly the war was fought in religious terms—true "Christianity" cast against "idolatry" and "perpetual orthodoxy" pitted against "heresy"—but these terms obfuscated the unfolding historical clash. The brittle American narrative about the "mingled people" of the profane East on the eve of the Second Coming of Christ contended with another, equally brittle narrative about a "perpetually orthodox" community that had "never" wavered in its doctrinal purity despite its location among "strangers."

Soon after Joseph Wolff, Jonas King, and Pliny Fisk had dined with Patriarch Hubaysh at Qannubin in October 1823 and left with him a printed Bible without the Apocrypha, word must have reached him of the arrival of Bird and Goodell and their wives at their residence in Beirut, about King's behavior in Dayr al-Qamar, and about the Bibles these missionaries were spreading throughout the land.

๋

"The Apostolic blessing and heavenly grace descend abundantly and rest in layers upon the souls and bodies of our people and our flock, the sons of our Maronite community who inhabit the towns and villages generally, of every rank and measure, the Lord God bless them. Amen." With these words of benediction, the Maronite patriarch announced his first scathing condemnation of the "Libarati," or "Biblemen," on 21 December 1823.[70] His anathema sought not only to regain the initiative from the Americans but also, far more urgently, to define the terms of the missionary encounter irrevocably from a patriarchal Maronite perspective. It located the recent arrival of the American Protestants, described in the *manshur* of 1823 as "some individuals from the sect of the English," within a far older history of perpetual Maronite orthodoxy. Most broadly, the American arrival rekindled a transhistorical struggle between good and evil, between Satan and God, by which the "the artful deceiver and enemy of all good and of the human race" has ever "vigorously attempted to infuse his deadly poison into the members of the mystical body, by which I mean the faithful sons of the Holy Church," and still now seeks "to sow the tares of corrupt teachings in the field of the Lord of Hosts." The patriarch elaborated:

> This [Satan] sometimes does by himself and sometimes by means of his heretical followers, enemies of the Roman Church, mother and teacher of all churches; and thus by deceit of various kinds to mislead Christians and to guide the simple ones [*al-basitin*] toward error and to overstep their bounds, and so, may God shame him, he has in these days instigated some individuals from the sect of the English who are called "Libarati," or the followers of the Book, who have arrived recently into this country and have come to the village of ʿAyntura in the guise of missionaries wearing sheep's clothing but within were ravening wolves. And they began to move among our Maronite nation pretending to be interested in taking in the country but essentially filled with evil and cunning, having brought with them books of the Old and New Testaments printed in several languages including Syriac and Arabic which differ from one another, some replete with errors and others correctly copied regarding what is printed, for they have

deleted from these books seven sacred and divine books which are Tobit, Judith, Wisdom of Solomon, Wisdom of Jesus, son of Sirach, Baruch together with Jeremiah, and Maccabees, although these books are accepted by the Roman Church, and those who do not accept them as sacred and divine are excommunicated according to the hallowed general Council of Trent in its fourth session. Their object is to bring these books suddenly among our Maronite community whose faith is sound, firmly established as it is on the Rock of Peter, and who have never bowed their knee to the idol of Baal.

While the Catholic Counter-Reformation alluded to by the patriarch was certainly familiar to the missionaries, his insistence that these "deceivers [*al-khadiʿun*] did not know that the Roman Catholic faith of the sons of our nation, founded upon the Rock of Saint Peter, cannot be shaken if struck by the winds of these corrupt teachings" evoked a far more intimate legend of Maronite survival in the face of the Jacobite heresy in Mount Lebanon immortalized for the church fathers by Ibn al-Qilaʿi and Duwayhi, but entirely unknown to the Americans (and, to be sure, to the overwhelming majority of the Maronites of the nineteenth century).

Just as Jonas King and Pliny Fisk and the other missionaries had been unable to make sense of the society they sought to conquer on its own terms and instead painted it with the grossest brushstrokes on their sectarian canvas, so the patriarch in turn outlined his utter refusal to understand the "Biblemen" as anything but the ill heralds of a "new blasphemy." Both insisted that they were committed to saving souls, and both claimed biblical knowledge, yet both could articulate their benevolence only through the total repudiation of the other. Hubaysh accused the missionaries of attempting a variety of stratagems to seduce the Maronite faithful. Among them was that they wrote in Arabic; they preached; they journeyed among the people; they pretended to be compassionate and charitable to the poor; they bribed; they bought up authorized Bibles and in their place freely distributed their own copies filled with error. They even tried to seduce Maronites to their own country to teach them there and prepare them as missionaries to return to Mount Lebanon to spread their corrupt doctrines. Plucking a verse from 1 Corinthians 5:13 in which Saint Paul exhorts the faithful to drive out the wicked from among them, citing his patriarchal authority to tend vigilantly over the flock entrusted to him by "our Savior and Lord Jesus Christ," and referring explicitly to the regulations of the "holy Lebanese Council" of 1736, Yusuf Hubaysh decreed:

We therefore prescribe and order . . . all sons of our community, individuals and groups, be they from the clergy or the laity, monks or nuns, regular or secular, of whatever class, or rank or occupation, and we decree irrevocably by the mighty authority of the Word of the Lord that henceforth none should possess their books nor buy, sell, read, or examine them, nor give them as gifts to others, no matter what the excuse may be and even if we determine that in them were contained exact copies of those printed in Rome. Any who have these books, whether from the Old or New Testament, or their books of prayers, or copies of their sermons, or books of their society, or their own works against the Christian religion, we order that all these books be burned or be brought to us at Qannubin because we do not permit or allow that they should remain with those who possess them. . . . We also do not permit anyone at all from our community to join these individuals in all matters pertaining to religion, such as being present at prayer, listening to their sermons, or discussing with them religious affairs. We also do not permit anyone to study in their schools or to read their works.

The punishment for disobeying this anathema was clearly spelled out. Clergymen would be stripped of their authority, and the laity would be excommunicated. The heresies emanating from "strangers" (*al-ghurabaʾ*) who come to divide the flock of God, the patriarch insisted, "must be guarded against totally lest pure minds be corrupted through ruinous intimacy."

Addressed by a Christian patriarch to his flock, proscribing religious contact with the missionaries, invoking church councils and a history of perpetual orthodoxy, this was first and foremost an ecclesiastical document; but it was also laced throughout with a vocabulary that reflected the traditional social order of Ottoman Lebanon. From its opening lines to its depiction of the dynamic of heresy as a process by which simpleminded commoners might be lured to their eternal perdition, the anathema represented a quietist order of things in which all people knew their rank and station under the everlasting solicitude of their secular and ecclesiastical sovereigns. The innate goodness of the common subjects evoked by the term *raʿaya* or *reaya* (the word was the same in the Arabic encyclicals of the Maronite patriarch and in the Ottoman Turkish imperial proclamations) was also their inherent weakness. The danger of the commoner reading an unauthorized Bible supposedly filled with error lay not only in the poison itself infused by the strangers from afar who threatened to overturn a supposedly natural and immutable order of things onto its head, but also in the essential gullibility of the ordinary subject, who had *always* to be herded and disciplined.

The Maronites, in this sense, represented the front line of an incongruous yet coherent Ottoman Arab order of things. This order was religiously and socially fractured in such a manner that the Maronites could thrive in Mount Lebanon, but that also exposed them and other Eastern Christian communities to the brunt of missionary assault. Just as the Catholic push against so-called Oriental error a century earlier had left the Greek Orthodox patriarchate vulnerable, so now the Protestant charge left the Maronite Church in danger. Despite the difference between the American Protestants and European Catholics, Western missionaries exploited the metaphorical as well as the physical distance that separated the *dhimmi* in the provinces from the imperial center in Istanbul. At the same time, both *dhimmi* and Muslim sovereign could and did deploy the conservative language of hierarchy to resist the unsettling intrusion of "foreign" missionaries.

In 1722, for example, long before the arrival of the American missionaries, it took the urgent pleading of the ecumenical Orthodox patriarch in Istanbul to persuade the sultan to revoke an earlier dispensation legitimating Jesuit missionary activity among Orthodox (and other Christian subjects) on the grounds that proper hierarchy and order had been overturned by the missionaries and their converts.[71] The Ottoman rulers' willingness to tolerate missionaries proselytizing among non-Muslims in the periphery of their empire reflected, in part, an Islamic legal ethos in which a particular sect of subordinated Christian subjects was beyond the purview of the state.[72] The literal and legal contemptuousness of the phrase *al-kufr milla wahida*, "all unbelief constitutes one nation," enshrined in a 1750 ruling from the leading Sunni religious authority in the empire reflected not simply Muslim primacy over subordinated Christians but, far more, a concern for Muslim purity amidst plurality.[73]

It was not Western pressure, then, but the manner of the imperial state in its religious and physical margins (especially among the Maronites in Mount Lebanon) that hampered its ability to realize the nature of the American missionary assault. One example of this occurred when Fisk and Bird were arrested in Jerusalem in February 1824. They had worn white turbans, which were reserved for Muslims, and had attracted undue attention to themselves by bringing with them without permission cases of Arabic books, some of which they distributed to Muslims. They were quickly released and allowed to distribute their Bibles in Palestine so long as they confined themselves to non-Muslims.[74] And while the Americans were not able to establish a permanent station in Jerusalem, they were allowed to settle in Beirut and to proselytize among non-Muslims.

It was only when the American missionaries made their obstreperous presence felt in Aleppo in 1824, once more distributing religious tracts, accompanied by the mercurial Joseph Wolff, that the Catholic communities succeeded in prying a *firman,* or imperial proclamation, against the missionaries from their imperial sovereign. The *firman* of June 1824 did not ban the missionaries. It did not even refer to them explicitly. It did, however, condemn books from the "land of the Franks." Because they threatened to upset the religious beliefs of the common people (ʿaqayid al-aʿwam), and thus were bound to create disorder in the public realm, the sultan ordered that these books be returned to Europe. He also prohibited their future importation, sale, and printing in the imperial domains and forbade their possession by Muslims, ordering that any such "false books" (al-kutub al-batila) found among them be confiscated and burned forthwith.[75] The *firman* thus struck a different register of religious purity than the Maronite encyclical. If the latter stressed the perpetual orthodoxy of Maronites beleaguered by a world of heretics and unbelievers, the former emphasized the triumphal sovereignty of Islam.

As different as the Maronite and Ottoman proclamations were—one provincial and the other imperial, one Christian and the other Muslim, one ecclesiastical and the other political—they were not incommensurable. Taken alone and out of context, the *firman* struck the missionaries as a "document most bunglingly patched up, full of absurdities, repetitions, and contradictions."[76] To the extent, however, that the *firman* and the encyclical jointly emphasized the foreignness of the missionary threat at hand, the edicts were emblematic of an Ottoman imperial system that sanctioned the subordination of *dhimmis* to Muslims, and of aʿwam to aʿyan. Taken together, they represented a powerful counternarrative to a missionary view of the possibility and desirability of profound change. Sultan and patriarch each upheld a mythology of conformity and stability supposedly inherent to social order, ecclesiastically Maronite or politically Ottoman. If an entrenched language of legal discrimination between Muslim and non-Muslim opened up the empire to American missionary activity, another equally powerful, far more widespread, and far more widely shared language of hierarchy fettered this activity. Both sultan and patriarch were mutually committed to the quietude of the same subjects whose lives the American missionaries now wanted to transform radically.

৬

"The Firman of the Grand Signor, is, I believe, getting quite cold." With these words penned in Aleppo in 1824, Jonas King indicated his belief that the moment was opportune to sally forth once more. He fully agreed with Isaac Bird that every missionary had to preach like one delivering his last message to dying souls.[77] Convinced that he and his brethren could exploit the tension inherent in a premodern Ottoman world, placating Ottoman rulers by avoiding Muslims yet pressing forth their putative advantage with Christians, the missionaries refused to be deterred by either *firman* or patriarchal command. By the beginning of January 1825 they had already prepared a reply to the patriarch in which they categorically denied all his charges save one: they freely admitted to violating the decrees of the Council of Trent that had denied the laity unmediated access to the vernacular Bible. The words of Jesus Christ were, for them, of far greater authority for searching the Scriptures than the decisions of men. To the patriarch's socially and ecclesiastically laden anathema, the missionaries presented a scripturally laden rebuttal. They also quoted from Jerome, Ambrose, Cyril of Alexandria, the Council of Laodicea, Gregory the Theologian, Amphilosius, and Athanasius, among other church fathers. They called it a reply, or *radd,* and they beseeched the patriarch to give their "suggestions a serious and impartial examination." But in its exegetical nature, its demonstration of missionary erudition, and its appeal to the authority of the fathers of the primitive church, whose direct descendants by way of the Reformation and the Puritans the missionaries considered themselves to be, the reply was less an invitation to dialogue than an unequivocal proclamation. "We wish all men to know," the Americans concluded, "that they are miserable sinners, born in iniquity, by nature children of wrath, and that there is no salvation except through the merits of Jesus Christ."[78]

As the uncompromising lines were being drawn on either side, there were many Maronites who continued to express interest in the missionaries and their message, and Jonas King continued to be hospitably received in Dayr al-Qamar, a town clearly beyond the patriarch's direct reach. Bibles, to be sure, were collected by Maronite priests following the patriarch's command, but the people remained generally, in King's own words, "as friendly as ever, and our discussions are free."[79] His Maronite host, Yusuf Dumani, insisted that his house remained opened to the "Englishmen." Nevertheless, Maronites such as "Saad Ibn Bas," who had read the Bible given to him by King, were obviously far more attentive than the Americans to the local consequences and context within which this missionary drama was being played out. The Maronite Saʿd in particular visited King to find some common ground. He was loath to contradict his patriarch, but King pursued the attack. "Your High Priest," the missionary said, referring to Yusuf Hubaysh, "orders you to destroy the word of God. He is an enemy to God and his

holy word—an enemy to Jesus Christ and his Gospel, and you ought to dis-
obey in the thing, which he has commanded." The Maronite begged King
to "go and talk to the Patriarch." King remained unmoved. "I cannot spend
time to go," he replied, "and see all, who oppose the word of God, nor do
I think it my duty to go and see them."[80] To the extent that both sultan and
patriarch revered, each in his own tradition, a knowledge of how men had
once been won and thus how they must be preserved, the missionaries looked
forward to how men might *yet* be won. For them, men and women had to
be saved, not preserved.

The irony in this soteriological reading of local reality was that of all the
missionaries, King had become the most immersed in local customs and
manners, in dress, and in habit. Of all the founding missionaries—Parsons,
Fisk, Goodell, and Bird—he was the most comfortable in Arabic; by 1825
he could write in the language and expressed himself fluently in it. Like
Paul's famous confession in 1 Corinthians 9:22 that "I am made all things
to all *men,* that I might by all means save some," King readily adapted his
outer habits to gain admirers and converts. And yet for all his immersion in
local culture, King was the most reluctant to compromise with it, and ultimately the least accommodating to its constraints. In effect, he desired and
demanded that natives unmoor themselves from their immediate lives, that
they privilege "Christianity" over culture and text over context. "What is
your Patriarch? What is the Pope himself? a bit of clay!" he told Saʿd the
Maronite. "Your Patriarch may do you harm—perhaps he may be able to
take away your life—but fear not them, said Jesus Christ, who have power
to kill the body only, but fear him who is able to destroy both soul and body
in hell. Whom do [you] chose to obey? God, or man?"[81]

Missionary disdain for local history culminated in a rebuke penned by
King on the eve of his departure from Syria.[82] Crafted as a deliberate Arabic polemic, it was intended to prove to as wide a native Christian audience
as possible why King could not become a Catholic. The so-called *Wadaʿ,* or
"Farewell Letter," explained as well why the Protestantism that he and his
fellow missionaries practiced was the only path of salvation. Completed in
early September 1825 and translated with the help of Asʿad al-Shidyaq, the
"Farewell Letter" was addressed to King's "friends" in Jerusalem, Ramle,
Jaffa, Tyre, Sidon, Beirut, Dayr al-Qamar, Damascus, Aleppo, Tripoli, and
Antioch. Replete with scriptural references, it constituted not just the first
widely circulated missionary statement of a conservative American Congregationalist faith but the first public call for an Arab puritanism: to be
saved, his Eastern Christian "friends" had to become "true Christians" as individuals. Each had to read the word of God and demonstrate faith in Jesus

Christ. Each had to be born again spiritually after being graced by the Holy Spirit, which initial baptism pointed to but did not contain. Those who did not repent would face eternal punishment.

This American eschatological framework was filled in with historical details transposed directly from European history. Not only was the unprecedented attack on Roman Catholic, and with it Maronite, dogma a rehearsal of typical Reformation-era Protestant objections, but also the "Farewell Letter" specifically condemned the Roman Church, and by association the Maronite Church, for the mass persecution of Protestants in early modern Europe. According to King, its garments were indelibly stained by its recourse to "torments too horrible to be named, in her hellish houses of Inquisition, called the 'St. Officio.'"[83] Inquisitions *were* the Roman Church, and the massacre of Saint Bartholomew's Day its essence.[84] The oddness of such a charge was not its historical inaccuracy but its Eurocentrism in the strict sense of the word. Not only did King collapse the vital distinction between Maronite ecclesiology, namely its spurious claim to perpetual Roman Catholic orthodoxy, and a far more complex Maronite history, but also he conflated this history with Latin history. For all his time in Mount Lebanon among Maronites, King did not think it significant to address a solitary word, or add a single fleeting digression in the entire epistle addressed to Arab Christians about their actual world, about Islam or even about the Jacobite heresy, both of which had long been so fundamental to Maronite religious identity.

This was due, perhaps, to ignorance. But although King was shortly to board a Sardinian brig to leave the scene of controversy, his incendiary epistle carried within it an invitation for native, not missionary, martyrdom.[85] Precisely because King believed in the flying of time, the "inestimable treasure of the Word of God" which he had placed in native hands was not lightly to be spurned. He had risked his life and had suffered exile from his land; he firmly believed that his self-appointed task had been completed. In King's view, now it was the natives' turn, even if it meant their embarrassment and shame before their people, indeed, before the world as a whole, and even if it meant the loss of their incomes and jobs and all worldly pleasures, and even if they were to be thrown out of society and considered the filth of the world, and even if they were disinherited by their families and relations, and even if it meant their death. The "Farewell Letter" closed with a fond farewell to his friends: "For I am now going from you to a far distant land, and probably we shall never see each other's faces again in this world. But we shall soon meet in the world of spirits."[86]

Chapter 5

An Arab Puritan

"To my respected brethren and friends: Since many have heard the report that I have become insane, and others say that I have become a heretic, I have wished to write my own brief account so that every discerning man may judge for himself whether I am mad or am oppressed, whether following after heresies or after the truth of orthodox faith."[1] These words, written in Arabic, opened Asʿad Shidyaq's own account of his new faith recorded in the house of the missionary Isaac Bird in Beirut in March 1826. They anticipated the violent passions that would soon end his brief life and reflected the earliest attempt by an Arab Christian subject of the Ottoman Empire to reconcile two antithetical, uncompromising understandings of faith. Asʿad was the missionaries' first Arabic-speaking convert. He became their martyr. He tried, and failed, to persuade the Maronite Church to reconsider its categorical rejection of the Americans, and he himself took seriously their call for Christian renewal amidst a manifestly impure world. His conversion exposed the Maronite myth of conformity and unchanging community, and for this he was persecuted. Yet as much as his life testified to the underlying power of transformation inherent in missionary work, his death also exposed its limitations and costs.

As'ad Shidyaq first came to the notice of the American missionaries in Beirut when he—"a respectable looking Arab," according to the journal of Isaac Bird—came to them offering to teach them Arabic on Monday 28 March 1825.[2] But the Americans already had an Arabic teacher, and As'ad appeared far too eager; he knew, to be sure, about the patriarch's anathema, and asked to read the canons of the Council of Laodicea from which the missionaries had quoted in their response to the patriarch. Moreover, he clumsily inquired whether the patriarch or the ruling emir could injure him should he come to reside in Isaac Bird's house. Because the Maronite carried about him what Bird recalled as an air of "suspicious familiarity," the missionaries rejected As'ad's offer.[3]

The reason for As'ad's overture lay in a tumultuous recent history as teacher, poet, and scribe that the missionaries did not then know about. It was a history, furthermore, that they would never fully understand, for it was inextricably tied to a genealogical geography of Mount Lebanon whose secular contours they would consistently miss. They described As'ad to begin with as an "Arab"—a generic term habitually used by the missionaries in their publications, but in an important respect nonsensical to a Maronite from Hadath whose family had worked across generations for a variety of Druze, Shi'a, and Muslim notables. As'ad himself had graduated from 'Ayn Waraqa in 1818. He spent two years teaching moral sciences at a Maronite monastery near Beirut, and then nearly two more working as the personal secretary for the Maronite bishop of Beirut, Yusuf Karam. As'ad was known for his panegyric poetry, but under Bishop Karam's ecclesiastical patronage he also wrote an important book about the relation between kinship and marriage which was adopted by his church. He soon became restless and moved on to the secular career path chosen by so many in his family before him, and in the process violated the solemn pledge made several years back to labor always for the good of the community under patriarchal authority. As'ad participated in the often lucrative but always turbulent factional politics of the feuding elites of Mount Lebanon. He worked, at first, for a Muslim Shihab emir, but his master quickly fell afoul of the powerful ruling emir, Bashir Shihab. Fearing for his life, As'ad fled to the monastery of Qannubin in 1821, but was eventually expelled from there by the Maronite patriarch. He made his way down to the city of Tripoli, where he took refuge with the Sunni Muslim imam of Emir Salman Shihab. There As'ad engaged in various debates and discussions with Muslim religious scholars, and it was said, or perhaps maliciously rumored, that he came close to converting to Islam.[4] Following a spell in Damascus with exiled Shihab emirs, As'ad joined the service of a Druze notable as his scribe and counselor, returning to his homeland just as the American missionaries were making their first forays into Mount Lebanon. In 1824 Asʿad returned to Hadath to divide up his father's inheritance with his brothers, Mansur, Tannus, Ghalib, and Faris.[5] He went next to the district of Kisrawan to Patriarch Yusuf Hubaysh to plead for employment; the patriarch, however, berated him for abandoning the service of the bishop of Beirut and evidently refused to offer him work. Once more Asʿad returned to Hadath, where he became engaged to the daughter of a Maronite notable from Baʿabda.[6]

Highly educated, engaged to be married, possessed of beautiful penmanship, from a well-regarded family, and very familiar to men in political and ecclesiastical power, yet unemployed, Asʿad was finally introduced to Jonas King in June 1825 by the Greek Catholic Mishaqa family, whose house lay opposite that of Yusuf Dumani.[7] The missionary immediately hired Asʿad, who was six years his junior. He was paid the equivalent of thirteen dollars a month, somewhat over a hundred piasters per month in a year that saw little rain and high prices. He made less, perhaps, than provincial Ottoman treasury scribes in Acre, who were paid two piasters a day in addition to daily allowances of meat, rice, ghee, oil, and a monthly allowance of wheat, as well as very substantial triannual bonuses from the collection of taxes, but far more than manual laborers, who earned less than a piaster a day. The Americans offered him, in short, far more than what the Maronite Church was willing to pay him.[8] Asʿad jumped at the opportunity and remained in the service of King till the latter left Syria in September of that same year, not only teaching him Syriac, the liturgical language of the Maronites, but also correcting, indeed copying, the missionary's Arabic sermons and prayers and engaging in incessant religious discussions and disputations "from morning till night."[9]

Here at last was the kind of man the missionaries had long sought: an individual for whom the Bible could be a transformative text, and for whom the missionaries could be, as they so often proclaimed, an instrument of divine favor. Asʿad could obviously read well, and more important, he *wanted* to read despite the patriarchal anathema against the missionaries and their Bibles. His brother Tannus already worked for the missionaries as a copyist, but Asʿad was bolder and more inquisitive: he did not shy away from religious controversy, and unlike Tannus, he refused to dissociate himself completely from the Americans.[10] Far from it, he engaged them on their own terms, and was "grateful for what Mr. Jonas King had done for him," according to the recollection of Mikhayil Mishaqa.[11]

It was thus As'ad, together with Tannus, who arranged for a visit in late September of the missionaries Fisk, Bird, King, and Goodell to his family in Hadath.[12] As'ad introduced the missionaries to two Shihab emirs, brothers, one Christian and the other Muslim, who lived in the village. They had together lost a desperate struggle for power with their kinsman, the ruling Emir Bashir, who had wasted no time in putting out their eyes and cutting out their tongues to mark them as unfit for lordship. It was As'ad who copied and circulated King's "Farewell Letter," which one of the Shihab emirs had read closely. It was because of all this that King quickly came to value As-'ad as a native informant, and thus encouraged his missionary brethren to hire the man whom they had previously rejected as a grammar teacher for a missionary school located in Bird's house in Beirut. This was done on 23 September 1825.[13]

But what King could appreciate, so too could the Maronite patriarch.

⁂

> The Apostolic blessing encompass our dear son, the beloved and most honorable and revered Shidyaq As'ad, may God bless him with the most abundant of his blessings. After acknowledging the excessive longing to see you in all health and asking after your health, God willing you are in utmost rest. We then say that on this day we have received word that you are residing in Beirut with some English individuals, some Biblemen, having commenced the copying of documents, including our *manshur* issued against them and the document that they call a reply to our *manshur,* and having procured for yourself high income in the process.

A deeply solicitous patriarch sent As'ad Shidyaq a warning in October 1825, as cutting in sharpness as it was obvious in indicating the path toward redemption that it laid out.[14] The preamble was important because it acknowledged As'ad as an educated, knowledgeable member of the Maronite community, and thus defined him both socially, as not one of the ignorant, illiterate commoners, and religiously and locally, as not one of the English. The carefully couched threat of ruination in this world and the next that followed the opening, paternalistic words of the patriarch were but one side of its meaning. The other would have been plainly apparent to any who had witnessed and participated in the cycle of transgression and forgiveness that was such an entrenched part of local culture: As'ad's folly, if indeed the rumors that had reached the patriarch were true, could be overlooked, indeed abolished from memory, were he to play his assigned, subordinate part in the Maronite fiction of perpetual orthodoxy:

> This report [*khabar*] has greatly, greatly astonished us. And had he who informed us of it not insisted utterly on its veracity for he saw you so doing with his own eye, such [a prospect] would never have crossed our mind because this is an outright contradiction: to oppose them by your writing a reply to the *manshur* and by providing them with assistance. This in particular is what makes it impossible to believe this report, for we do not suspect that a man of your intelligence could embark on such actions which would not be expected even from the most ignorant [*aʿzam al-jahala*] sons of our faith. Yes it is indeed possible for Satan, the enemy of good, to lure a human being into error in such trying matters through money as occurred with Judas, for the greed for money leads to such ruinous ends. But in most cases he is not able to entangle men in such a predicament if they are possessed of sharp mind and good discernment, for they would realize that they are bound to lose all that they gain in the ruinous worldly and spiritual ends that surely follow. Because of all this we remain in doubt, and find ourselves most unwilling to believe such a report (unless God has permitted it). Thus it is necessary that we ask you first to tell us the truth lest the reason for the spreading of this rumor be an incident that may or may not have occurred to you (as had occurred previously with you in Acre).[15] We are waiting for your reply day by day, for we do not permit any delay in the matter. May the apostolic blessing encompass you again.
>
> Joseph
> The lowly
> Peter the Patriarch of Antioch
> 16 October 1825

ᘉ

From the journal of Isaac Bird:

> Saturday, Nov. 12—Shidiak received a letter from the Patriarch in which he threatens him, with his brother Tannoos and another Maronite youth, with immediate excommunication unless they ceased from all connexion with the Bible men.

Tuesday 15. After mature deliberation it was thought advisable, for the present, that Asaad should go home to his friends in Hadet, until the fever of alarm and opposition should subside a little. . . .

Mond. Dec. 12: Shidiak returned after nearly a month's absence, to continue with me for a year, risking whatever obloquy and violence might come upon him. He has just been obliged to give up an advantageous contract of marriage, into which he had some months ago entered, because, since suspicions were afloat that he is heretical in his notions, the father of the girl required him to bring a letter from the Patriarch specifying what office he would give him. He now gives up all intentions of marriage. For his greater security, I am to procure for him the usual written protection of the English Consul, which shall ensure to him, while in my immediate employ, all the safety and liberty of an English resident.[16]

※

"Excessive passion"—*al-ʿishq al-mufrit*—for money and missionaries: this is what Asʿad stood accused of by the bishop of Beirut in a letter dated 16 October 1825. His was a far blunter letter than that written by the patriarch on the same day. It was at once filled with the vehement condemnation of Asʿad's putative avarice, and yet at its heart was a desperate plea by a patron to his erstwhile protégé to "return" from the path of perdition on which he had so willfully, so incredibly set himself. The orders of the Lebanese Council against heretics and the patriarch's anathema against the English were unequivocal: excommunication was to be the fate that awaited all those who read, wrote, or possessed the forbidden books of heretics. Repent for what has passed, the bishop admonished, and search for proper work while and until your reputation may be restored. Understand, however, that there shall be no money forthcoming from the church as there has been from the English, for the issue is not money but will. Leave the English and return to your true mother's bosom and your true father's house, for if you do not, then you, *and all those who follow your path,* will most certainly be excommunicated. Enough said. May God grant you the grace to be liberated from this baneful association.[17]

※

When Bishop Karam saw with his own eyes Asʿad's beautiful script rendering Jonas King's "Farewell Letter" into Arabic, he was finally convinced that rumor was fact, and that As'ad had indeed trod far, perhaps even irretrievably, down the path of heresy. The very hand that had once signed a vow of complete submission to the church had now been turned into an instrument that could extract poison from the "pure milk" of faith.[18] The Maronite Church had, after all, at great expense educated As'ad to express what was most enduring about its ancient faith; it now realized that its star pupil, who was meant to confirm perpetual orthodoxy to Rome, was liable to revive accusations of Maronite heresy. Because the scandal involving the disgraced Aleppine nun Hindiyya was still so fresh in the collective memory of its members, the church hierarchy was determined to prevent another Maronite debacle. It not only took the initiative to stop the Protestants but also quickly moved to reassure Rome. Karam, accordingly, boasted to the Propaganda Fide that a sweep for banned books in the diocese of Beirut following the patriarch's anathema turned up not only many of the "corrupt" Bibles distributed by the Protestants but many other books prohibited by Rome as well, including one allegedly written by the Hindiyya al 'Ujaymi.[19]

The bishop of Beirut's condemnations of As'ad's betrayal, and his initial confidence in his ability to crush the Protestants, masked the underlying intellectual anxiety over the sudden missionary challenge, though it could not entirely efface it. He explained in a later missive to the Propaganda that the missionaries had been stymied until "one of them by the name of Jonas King had written on the eve of his departure from these lands a booklet which included some of his corrupt doctrines and slander against the faith and rites of the Holy Roman Church, mother and teacher of all churches, and disseminated it in many of these parts to deceive the simple ones [*al-basitin*]." If it were left unrefuted, King's epistle, he emphasized, would be "very damaging," for it might well cause those "without knowledge" who came across it to doubt their faith.[20]

This Maronite anxiety, which soon developed into fury, was directed against As'ad not simply because he was a principal conduit of foreign heresy but because he, as both informant and disciple, had become its embodiment. As far as the bishop and the patriarch were concerned—and one would venture to add the sultan himself, had he ever heard about the troubles of his *dhimmi* subject on the fringes of his supposedly well-protected domains—there could be no meaningful distinction between high and low, between believer and infidel, between order and chaos in the empire if an individual such as As'ad Shidyaq could sustain an intellectual argument for Protestantism from his position as an obedient Maronite subject. And yet that is precisely what As'ad tried to do, insisting that he was both an evangelical and an obedient Maronite. What his community took on faith, he declared was humanly articulated and thus inherently flawed. Long before the missionaries even recognized Asᶜad as a convert, the Maronite hierarchy identified him as a heretic.

౪

Sabbath Jan. 1 1826 . . . Twelve or fourteen individuals were present at the Arabic service at Mr. Goodell's. After this service we questioned Asaad closely with regard to the state of his heart, and were rather disappointed at the readiness with which he replied that he thought he was born again. For ourselves we choose rather to suspend our opinion. He can hardly be supposed to have acquired as yet, even *speculatively,* very clear notions of what is regeneration, and it would seem quite as consistent with Christian humility and with a true knowledge of his sinfulness if he should speak of himself with more doubt and caution. . . .

A. has often remarked that he is full of anxiety. . . . In many things he sees the Romish Ch[urch] to be wrong and in some things he thinks *we* are so. Our apparent tranquility of mind as to our religious views is a matter of surprise to him. This evening he conversed on the subject with more than usual feeling. "I seem," said he, "to be alone among men. There is nobody like me, and I please nobody. I am not quite in harmony with the English in my views, and therefore do not please *you.* My own countrymen are in so much error I cannot please *them.* God I have no reason to think I please nor do I please myself. What shall I do?"[21]

౪

The main thrust of Asᶜad Shidyaq's protest was remarkably simple, and in this simplicity lay its cardinal transgression, its revolutionary potential: he had not turned "English," or lunatic as many of his detractors claimed, but was a Maronite of ancient stock who had been *convinced,* not corrupted, by the missionaries. Asᶜad wanted to become a puritan in the sense that he wanted to purify his faith of all its temporal encumbrances; he wanted to become a missionary in the sense that he sought to revive what he described as a primitive and genuine Christianity among his people and all others who might listen; and he was an evangelical in the broad sense of putting his faith in the absolute centrality of Jesus Christ, whose imminent return he believed was nigh, for an individual's salvation. The very fact that Asᶜad admitted that he was profoundly influenced by the Americans, and by Jonas King in particular, and yet maintained his own separate identity from the missionaries; the fact that he was entirely open to intellectual engagement; the fact that he demanded to be convinced and not simply commanded; the fact that he *publicly* engaged in controversy; and above all the fact that he was asking questions, protesting, and writing self-consciously as an individual, all these facts accumulated to pose an existential modern challenge not only to the church—for how could one be a Maronite and English at the same time?—but also to the empire in which this church was so comfortably ensconced, for how could one be an obedient subject and yet not part of an established religious community?

As'ad protested not with any intent of revolution; he consistently professed his obedience, and that was precisely the problem. He was not the first Maronite to protest, or the first to be persecuted; and he was certainly not the first to be receptive to new ideas about faith. Long before him there were many sustained contacts between East and West. The problem was that he was the first to embrace the message of the American missionaries so seriously; he was the first to try and reconcile hitherto irreconcilable constructions of faith, the first to try to disassociate American ideas from American culture rather than, as the missionaries had habitually done in the United States among Indians and did again in the East, subsume Christianity within American culture.

🌿

As'ad was urgently summoned by his patriarch to the monastery of Mar Jirjis 'Alma in January 1826. He immediately obeyed the summons, and together with the patriarch's brother, the priest Niqula, he made the day's journey from Beirut to Kisrawan. He remained at the monastery, save for a single trip undertaken with the patriarch's permission to the nearby Armenian Catholic patriarchate in Bzummar, until midnight on the second of March, when he fled the place, seeking refuge again in Isaac Bird's house in Beirut. Almost immediately Bird asked As'ad to write an account of his experience, which As'ad did. In dense but clear handwriting across thirty-four small pages, he recounted in Arabic both the nature of his association with the missionaries and the history of his recent confinement. The tale As'ad told was defiant yet hopeful. "I reside here," he said, referring to Bird's house, "not because I hold the opinions of the English or the Biblemen, nor because I learn my religion from them. Not at all! I am committed to the infallible word of God; I believe in it, and it is according to this word that I want [to live] my life and [to set] my heart."[22]

As'ad did not deny his obvious debt to Jonas King. The missionary was central to Shidyaq's own transformation—he never used the word "conversion"—for it was through discussion, dialogue, and debate with the American that he had come to what he considered to be a proper understanding of faith. Indeed, while preparing a reply to King's "Farewell Letter," and specifically after reading the twenty-ninth chapter of Isaiah, As'ad claimed to have been overcome with dread. He stopped his work on the reply, and instead began rereading the Bible, partially because he was searching for evidence to refute King, but also because he wanted to find in the prophetic books incontestable proof that Jesus was the long-awaited Messiah in order to debate Muslims and Jews. Only upon reading from verse 14 of chapter 52 of Isaiah to the end of chapter 53—verses about the suffering servant, interpreted by missionaries as a prophecy about the vicarious suffering of Jesus Christ—did "my heart rejoice greatly by my finding this testimony, for it tore away the darkness of doubts from me." This was a defining moment for As'ad. By his own admission, henceforth "my desire to read the New Testament increased, and I sought to know the best way to act in accordance with the teaching of Jesus, and desired to free myself from every selfish desire."[23]

The letters of Jonas King and As'ad Shidyaq were evangelical in nature. Both men were steeped in readings of the Book of Revelation, which As'ad cited repeatedly in his statement; both men demanded immediate public preaching of the "pure" Gospel before an anticipated end of the world; both decried certain Catholic and Maronite rites and practices, ranging from the veneration of saints, to an alleged violent Roman injunction against heresy, to the denial to ordinary believers of the ability to read and contemplate the Scriptures independently, and thus the opportunity for Jesus Christ to seize and transform their sinful hearts, and, most scandalously, to the interposition of the church between humanity and its only means of salvation, the unadulterated Word of God. Both thus appealed to the authority of the Scriptures and the early church. The two men ended their letters with almost identical challenges to doubters that they must be proved wrong with evidence if they were to abandon their faith. This similarity underscored the degree to which As'ad emulated King. "I plead with all my compatriots of the Maronite community, and anyone else from the other communities who loves truth," wrote As'ad, "who see me in error to prove it to me so that I might leave error and adhere to truth." He emphatically denied seeking money or office, for what was at stake, he was convinced, was not worldly pleasure or suffering but salvation and the glory of God. Therefore he insisted that he was prepared to suffer disgrace and banishment, opprobrium and defamation, even death for the sake of Jesus Christ, "the sole mediator between God and man," always living and interceding on our behalf with the Lord, the atonement of our sins:

> If someone were found who could prove that I am in error and that there is no salvation for me save through following the pope, or at least to demonstrate to me that it is lawful to do so, I am prepared to abandon all my subjective views and submit to anyone in the Lord. But without evidence that they are in error, I cannot forsake them and submit to the obedience of the blind, unless it is not only said about me that I am mad, but that I do indeed truly go mad, and reason is indeed stripped from me, and unless they burn not only the Bibles printed by the English but every Bible in the world. But I beseech God to preserve these two things for me and for all Christians and to preserve you all, my masters and friends in the Lord.[24]

So rhetorically close was Asʿad's statement to King's "Farewell Letter" that it constituted an ideal response to American missionary exhortation. What King had called for was introspection of the Bible by those who professed to know it; Asʿad had risen to the challenge, only to admit his own intellectual defeat. This free admission helped bring about what he considered his own intense spiritual regeneration of heart and mind. The missionary crusade had won a signal victory.

Yet as much as Shidyaq's conversion vindicated an uncompromising assault on what the Americans saw as the corrupted churches of the East, his public statement was hardly commensurable with the missionary self-congratulation and cultural myopia so apparent in King's "Farewell Letter." There was, to be sure, an obvious difference between missionary and convert: for King, spiritual knowledge was always imparted *to* the East, never received *from* it, whereas Asʿad sought both to acquire and to dispense knowledge. Indeed, the emphasis Asʿad placed on his own evangelical rebirth as an evolving process of meeting, dialogue, and debate with American missionaries and Maronite ecclesiastics, a rebirth that compelled him to seek the salvation of others, underscored the degree to which Jonas King and his compatriots had departed in the Orient from their own initial understanding of Christian conversion. What had been construed in America as an ongoing process of cumulative transformation of self and other, exemplified by David Brainerd's obsession with self-mortification and the salvation of Indians, had been quietly, perhaps even inevitably, abandoned by the missionaries. They spoke less and less of their own spiritual state with each passing month, only of the dismal situation of the natives. In the missionaries' thinking, a conversion experience begun in America was completed there and then exported, just as printed and leather-bound Arabic Bibles were shipped in crates, presumably to be adopted *in toto* in the heathen parts of the world. The very title of King's "Farewell Letter" captured the one-way flow of missionary movement from American center to less blessed peripheries. King's sojourn in Syria and Palestine was over; now he was moving on to save other perishing souls as the end of time drew near.

Yet Asʿad could not, like King, simply get up and leave after delivering an unprecedented public attack on local beliefs. There was no Sardinian brig waiting to take him to safer shores as there was for King. There was no "Western" garb for him to assume, as King, Isaac Bird, and Pliny Fisk had adopted "Oriental" garb. For him, any movement, whether to the Armenian Catholic patriarch in Bzummar, to a former teacher of his at ʿAyn Waraqa, to Bishop Karam or Isaac Bird in Beirut, or to the Maronite patriarch at ʿAlma, exposed his difficult, intermediary, exilic location between mutually exclusive "English" and "Maronite" worlds. Asʿad clearly now privileged scriptural truths over what he called al-ʿada wa al-marba, custom and upbringing, but he never expressed his rejuvenated Christianity as a repudiation of the culture in which he was so thoroughly rooted. He wanted to be convinced by his former Maronite tutors and patrons, not simply to engage them in controversy. Therefore even as he gradually rejected the spiritual primacy of the patriarch and steadily alienated himself from the Maronite Church, he constantly attended to the decorum of social rank. He eventually stopped attending church services, and later refused to confess, but he meticulously kissed the hands of his superiors, addressed them by their proper titles, and otherwise fully engaged in the customary practices of everyday life.

❧

Asʿad Shidyaq expressed a desire for what he called *tagharrub,* the separating from his native land, at first to find Catholic theologians in some distant realm who might convince him with evidence about church teachings, later to find a corner in an American house in Beirut where he might contemplate, unmolested, the word of God. His dissenting impulse represented the antithesis of Patriarch Yusuf Hubaysh's *wahshat al-ightirab,* the loneliness of an enforced bishopric in Tripoli but a day's distance from his privileged landowning family and property in Kisrawan. The disagreement between the two men epitomized the clash between a radical intellectual position and a deeply conservative one in an early-nineteenth-century Ottoman context, between an individual and a community, between missionary and institutional Christianity, and most basically between a millennialist and an amillenial interpretation of the world.

ℛ

As῾ad wrote about his stay at ῾Alma to demonstrate how greatly his own evangelical consistency diverged from the "laughable" contradictions that ensnared the Maronite ecclesiastics. He illustrated this by recounting numerous instances in which his superior knowledge of scriptural "truths" had baffled his intellectually and spiritually "weak" opponents, who, defeated, more often than not abandoned a heated discussion or impugned his character. "I do wonder as well," wrote As῾ad, "at how they mocked me and said of me that I was mad, yet would then be afraid that a madman could best them in a debate, or corrupt the minds of people, or turn them from truth to error." He also meticulously recorded the variety of accusations leveled against him. He noted that the Maronite clergy not only whispered that he was mad but also continually insinuated or openly accused him of being corrupt, rehearsing an ancient accusation against converts while anticipating what was to become the standard Ottoman interpretation of Protestantism in the nineteenth century.[25]

To be corrupt was one thing, to be insane another. That his accusers leapt back and forth between the two was proof, in As῾ad's mind, of the basic injustice that he faced, and also of the hopeless confusion that confronted the Maronite Church and community. Most telling and damning in his eyes were the several attempts by Maronite clergymen to pressure him into stating publicly what they knew he did not believe, and thus to privilege false public profession over true inner faith. During the first month of his confinement, As῾ad recalled, the patriarch, in the presence of a bishop and another priest, urged him "to declare that my faith was in accordance with the Roman Church." Both the bishop and the priest pressed Shidyaq to do so. "I said that I was afraid to lie for I was not thus convinced in my mind. They both told me that *sayyidna* [lit. "our lord"] the patriarch would absolve me of such a lie." As῾ad turned to the patriarch and asked him if he would indeed absolve him. "He answered in the affirmative, that he would absolve me so as to lie."[26]

But what As῾ad regarded as unacceptable hypocrisy, his patriarch and those who surrounded him saw as clemency toward an errant man. For the nearly three months that he remained at the monastery of ʿAlma, the Protestant objections made by Asʿad alternatively astonished, flummoxed, and angered the Maronite patriarch. Although he eventually become so enraged with Asʿad that he threatened him in a "most unusual manner," never once did he physically harm the dissenter. Asʿad himself portrayed Yusuf Hubaysh as a tragic figure: a sincere man who represented a corrupt church, an individual who wanted to help Asʿad but knew not how. Time and again Patriarch Hubaysh asked Asʿad to state and write that he believed as did the Roman Church. Time and again Asʿad refused. Patriarch Hubaysh at first allowed and then prohibited religious discussions with Asʿad. He sanctioned and then confiscated Asʿad's books. He engaged and then retreated from trying to persuade Shidyaq to desist from the path of heresy. He threatened Asʿad with excommunication but allowed him to visit the Armenian Catholic patriarch in Bzummar, hoping that a different authority might be able to impress Asʿad where his own had evidently failed.

The patriarch was indeed taken aback by the extent of Asʿad's heresy, and to a large extent the inconsistencies that Asʿad noted reflected his genuine indecision and doubt as to Asʿad's motives. The imputation of madness to Asʿad during his three-month stay at Asʿad Alma was, however, almost certainly rhetorical at first, and clearly secondary to the charge of bribery, that is, the accusation that the Americans had bought Asʿad's loyalty with employment. It was, if anything, more akin to the way the word "crazy" is used today than any sustained identification of an unusual malady or *junun*. Asʿad was not physically confined as was often the case with madmen in Islamic history, or sent, like some of his compatriots, to the rich monastery of Quzhayya near Qannubin to be treated by the monks of the order of Saint Anthony; he was not bound by chains or beaten at ʿAlma. And he was not initially considered demonically possessed, although the bishop of Beirut did on at least one occasion tell him that "there is a devil in you."[27]

The patriarch considered Asʿad's "English" turn very dangerous. But because he believed Asʿad to be rational, he consistently urged Asʿad to confess his Catholic creed. So long as Asʿad formally obeyed the church, his manifest errors, his heretical ideas, his association with the Americans could all be deemed transient. Money may have seduced Shidyaq; benevolent admonition might yet bring him back. Youth may have confused him (as his confessor suggested); wisdom might yet enlighten him. The Americans in Beirut may have beguiled him; removing him from their midst might yet save him. It was only when Asʿad obstinately refused to return to the fold, only when he deliberately spurned abundant opportunities to repent, that the depiction of As'ad as mad became a dominant trope. With each passing day at the monastery, As'ad grew more defiant, even as he grew more impatient with his seemingly indefinite detention. By the same token, with each passing day his evangelical demeanor was considered by the Maronite clergymen increasingly symptomatic of a hopeless derangement.

More than anything else, the Maronite patriarch could not and would not understand As'ad's insistent desire to go out and plainly preach the Gospel in colloquial Arabic. To tolerate heresy, let alone actively support it, was to destroy the church; to ask him to accede to such a missionary desire constituted an impossible, even absurd, expectation. Patriarch and common priest, therefore, considered As'ad's repeated requests to proselytize publicly as if they were uttered from the mouth "of a madman [*min rajul majnun*]." The ultimate logic of As'ad's evangelism, and his invocation of imminent judgment, constituted a direct challenge to the conservative language of quietism, separateness, and past achievement that allowed different religious communities to coexist under Ottoman rule. Moreover, it violated the widely held taboo among all communities in heterodox Mount Lebanon not to engage openly in religious controversy.

The very intellectual nature of As'ad's evangelism—his constant recourse to books and to arguments, his refusal to accept shades of meaning— made him impossibly different in a largely rural society where religion in and of itself was manifestly not a matter of public debate and where Protestantism was not legally recognized. His evangelism was premised on a conviction that centuries of Maronite struggle against heresy, or at least the representation of Maronite history as the perseverance of faith in hostile surroundings, was devoid of any enduring significance. To base evangelism on Revelation, to connect primitive Christianity with future salvation exclusively by way of universal missionary action, was to deny the importance of locality and history that defined Maronite church and community. Thus when the patriarch despairingly asked As'ad "What is the church?" he answered defiantly that it was the community of believers in Jesus Christ and his law. And *where* is this church? the patriarch continued. The world, said As'ad, for it is a community made up of all nations and sects. Including the English? Indeed, replied As'ad.[28]

🙚

"And I heard another voice from heaven, saying, Come out of her, my people, that ye be not partakers of her sins, and that ye receive not of her plagues." Moved by this verse from Revelation, which he copied and left on his bed, As'ad made good his escape from 'Alma just before midnight on the first day of March 1826.[29] He reached the protected "English" house of Isaac Bird in Beirut by dawn the next day, exhausted but relieved to be back in the company of the missionaries, while the patriarch's men searched in vain for the pitiable *majnun*. His troubles, however, were only beginning, for within days of his flight from the monastery, As'ad became notorious in his community. His precipitous actions had now forced into the open the scandal that the patriarch had tried first to avert and then to contain.

By sheer coincidence, the ongoing Greek revolt against the Ottomans, which had begun several years earlier, spilled into Beirut at this very time, causing widespread panic. Twelve Greek vessels landed hundreds of marines in the middle of March in an attempt to scale the city walls; upon its failure, they unleashed a heavy bombardment. The Muslims of the city, who lost nine men repelling the invaders, turned in revenge on the native Christians. Many fled to Mount Lebanon; others took refuge with the missionaries whose "English" houses, though beyond the city walls, were considered far safer than those of ordinary Christian subjects. The Ottomans mobilized all available troops and rushed them to Beirut. Suspecting treason on the part of their *dhimmi* subjects, they also harassed the Greek Orthodox, Catholics, and Maronites of the city and ordered all their properties confiscated. Looting was rampant. William Goodell's house was plundered. The missionary schools shut down; soldiers and mercenaries wandered the streets. Only a month later, with order fully restored, were the Ottoman authorities satisfied that the local Christians, contemptible, weak, and silly as they allegedly were, had not in fact collaborated with the "rebellious infidels." They therefore remained subjects worthy of mercy and protection.[30] The pendulum of imperial toleration had swung once more.

Under these circumstances, which enlivened the fears and prejudices of all concerned, the Maronites and missionaries continued their bitter struggle for the body and soul of As'ad Shidyaq. His fate, both sides passionately reasoned, augured ill or well for the future of Christian community in the East. If his conversion was allowed to stand, and even more, if he were allowed to publicize his convictions and explain how he freely arrived at them, and how religion had to be accepted and not simply inherited, a brittle Maronite identity would be thrown into crisis, and with it an entire conservative social order thrown into doubt. If his conversion and his arguments were not allowed to stand, the American project to reclaim biblical lands would lie stillborn.

Brothers, relatives, messengers, and even As'ad's mother made their way from Hadath to Beirut throughout the first half of March. Their object: to cajole As'ad into leaving the protected house of the missionary; as long as he remained there, he "brought an insupportable shame upon the family."[31] The patriarch once more urged As'ad to quit the missionaries immediately ("in very plausible terms," confessed Bird).[32] As'ad would have none of these efforts to change his mind. As much as he maintained the required social obeisance and declared his willingness to "repeatedly kiss the earth" upon which the patriarch's feet had trod, the convert adamantly refused to submit ecclesiastically to the Maronite Church. He again denied "taking" his religion from the Biblemen, and denied seeking any material gain. "All I want is simply that you not compel me into believing certain teachings by power of threat alone," wrote As'ad, "but by the strength of correct evidence [*al-burhan al-sadid*], without which I cannot believe." He once more explained his basic evangelical principles: the necessity for immediate missionary labor among "the people" to awaken the fundamental need for the spiritual rebirth of all believers through the spirit of Jesus Christ. If the Maronite Church could not allow that, then quoting from Revelation, As'ad desired, precisely as Puritans once had, "to remove myself from its midst, not out of hatred for the character of its adherents, but out of fear of joining in their practices, for the church which does not love Jesus I am commanded by the Word of God to leave."[33]

His family, at least those who spoke on its behalf, namely As'ad's uncle, with three daughters to marry, and his older brothers Mansur and Tannus, as well as his mother, could not understand why he was so determined to evangelize. To a great extent they did not care what As'ad personally believed: for them that was hardly the point. No argument, recalled Bird, "could convince the disconsolate mother. Asaad had repeated the name of Christ, and the word of God so often, that she, at last, in a fit of impatience exclaimed, 'Away with Christ, and the word of God; what have we to do with them!'"[34] As'ad's disgrace was potentially his family's as well; the mother clearly did not want to lose her son; and with their father dead, his brothers could not afford the stigma of heresy. They could not and would not so easily abandon the crucial patronage of the church, the employment opportunities it offered, the marital alliances it sanctioned, the dowries it blessed, and the social standing it legitimated.[35] In his journal Bird recorded them telling As'ad that to be secure in the community, "you must hold your tongue, and not broach your new opinions among the people." When As'ad objected to such a stipulation, pointing out how it would contradict the free exercise of his conscience, his brothers and uncle tellingly rebuked him for such absurdly selfish considerations. "Why do you not go," said they, "to the Druses, and the Moslems, and preach the Gospel to them? You answer, because there is danger. So there is danger in the present case; this is not the land of liberty, therefore be silent."[36]

A principal danger thus lay not in Asʿad's personal convictions as much as in the missionary nature of these convictions, not what he believed per se but the manner in which he expressed his belief. For Asʿad and the missionaries, of course, such a distinction was untenable, for evangelical expression was a fundamental tenet of their regenerated faith and a fundamental means to reach out to others. Yet the bluntness and directness of the *kiraza,* or preaching of the Gospel directly to common people which Asʿad consistently enjoined, was impossible to reconcile with the fiction of stable and obedient communities so fundamental to Maronite, and indeed all established, religious identity in heterodox Mount Lebanon. Moreover, the public demonstration and testament of a rigorous new faith was utterly contradictory to the discretion that had typically accompanied *individual* conversions to Christianity in Mount Lebanon. Conversion to Islam was, for obvious reasons, an entirely different matter. The few individuals in Mount Lebanon who publicly professed their Islam before a Muslim judge in one of the coastal cities rarely if ever sought to convert their own people. Many of the formerly Sunni Shihabs and the Druze Abilamʿs converted to Maronite or Greek Catholic belief from Islam in the eighteenth century, and theoretically from an Islamic point of view, had become apostates. But they never dwelt on their conversion publicly, let alone tried to foist their views on others; nor did the churches that won them publicly celebrate their gains, and thus rarely suffered any imperial or local retribution from Muslims.[37] Bashir Shihab, the ruler of Mount Lebanon at this time, was perhaps the most famous example of this ambivalence.

※

From the journal of Isaac Bird, 17 March 1826:

> Four of the relatives of Asaad came down, and succeeded with persuading him to accompany them home. He said he could not believe, after all that has been said, that they would do him violence, and he strongly expected that his visit to Hadet would do good. A majority of us opposed his going, with all we could say; but he thinks he knows the people here better than we do. He left us toward evening, expecting to be absent only a few days.[38]

From the journal of William Goodell, 10 April 1826:

> Asaad has again fallen into the hands of the enemies of the Gospel, who threaten his life. We have some fears that he will suffer martyrdom, and have a daily prayer meeting on his account. His youngest brother will probably be obliged to leave his father's house, in consequence of adopting the same views of divine truth. He has already been beaten, and threatened with every thing terrible. But though his understanding is convinced, he does not appear to have felt, like his brother Asaad, the power of the religion in his own soul. Never has this mission called more loudly for the prayers of God's people.[39]

From the journal of As'ad Shidyaq, 6 April 1826, at the monastery of 'Alma:

> [The patriarch] then asked me, are you following the sect of this person or that, but I said to him my name is Christian, my church Catholic, and I am a Maronite of ancient stock, but in matters of belief it is inevitable that people will differ . . . and when we reached the sea he began to ask me whether I wanted to be bled; with him was Yusuf, deacon of Batrun, who said that there was a doctor at hand who had seen me and had immediately recognized my condition from my appearance and had said that I needed to be bled. The patriarch declared that only God governed the lives of men and that I could not say no and the priest added that if I were not now bled my condition would only grow worse. Thus I was put upon by both of them and I told them that I did not want [to be bled] and that I knew my body was healthy and that I knew that it was said of all those who first became Christians that they were *majanin* and then they were expelled. The reason I said this is because I understood their intent that even if I objected they were determined to have me bled because the *majnun* does not know his own condition, for if he knew he would not be the way he is. . . . I said to the patriarch that the Kingdom of Heaven is like an expensive pearl and it is not much to lose everything for it. He replied, for heresy, it is.[40]

As'ad Shidyaq's prayer of Monday, 10 April 1826:

> O divine God my exile in this world has long endured and it is on me a crushing burden. O you who said, "Come unto me, all ye that labour and are heavy laden, and I will give you rest" [Matthew 11:28], here I am O

Lord, desiring to come to you but my sins prevent me, and so you who came to call the sinners to repentance accept me as one of your servants and let me know what I should do in this period of exile. I would dare say to you that I am ready to leave all things for you but I am afraid to be arrogant and a liar because I know my weakness and I am not capable of anything without you.[41]

As'ad Shidyaq left the house of Isaac Bird on 17 March never to return. He sensed the danger of his new situation, especially after his younger brother Faris impetuously fled the oppressive atmosphere of the family home in Hadath, seeking the protection of the very same missionary from whom As'ad had so reluctantly removed himself. As'ad's room was ransacked, and eleven of his books, including Bibles, were burned by his older brother Mansur. Rumors flew that the missionaries had been killed and that Yusuf Hubaysh and Emir Bashir wanted As'ad dead. "I am like a prisoner here, resistance from without, fear within," wrote As'ad.[42] By the beginning of April he was once more in the company of the patriarch at 'Alma, and he sent his missionary patron a short note begging him to arrange an escape to Malta. Fragments of his journal from this, his second spell at the patriarchal residence, reveal a fascinating, if ambiguous, scene: the clergymen around him were now quite convinced that he labored under the weight of *al-sawda'*, or a degenerative melancholia, because of the moroseness of his demeanor and his apparent loneliness and anxiety. Influenced by still prevailing medieval Muslim notions about mental illness, they considered As'ad overwhelmed by black bile. The patriarch thus encouraged him to be bled, and on the evening of 9 April an attempt was made to that effect.[43] Yet As'ad was also provided with a certain measure of liberty so long as he vowed not to speak against the church; his journal placed him variously in 'Alma, Batrun, Tripoli, al-Burj, and Kfar Zayna. No matter how often he described As'ad as mad and heretical and no matter how often he threatened him with excommunication, the patriarch shied away from more forceful measures. Priests, moreover, conversed with As'ad, as did the Syrian Catholic patriarch, despite Yusuf Hubaysh's repeated prohibitions of any engagement with As'ad in matters of religion; they all recognized that he was extremely well versed in the Scriptures, and one priest even provided him with a New Testament and asked him to vocalize it.

What his antagonists described as a malady As'ad regarded as sincere piety. His missionary-inspired puritanism, even disinterested benevolence, had become ever more apparent. He refused to be idle, and he abandoned poetry, especially the panegyrics for which he was well known and which were so often composed for the local secular and ecclesiastical elites. He recorded fourteen signs of true faith which he showed the clergymen who surrounded him. The most important of these, he stressed, was a love of Jesus Christ as intense as the passion a lover feels for his beloved. This love had to be felt and not simply thought, or else faith remained illusory; it had to encompass one's relatives, overlook disagreement, and triumph over malice. It had to strive to bring others closer to God, to remove from the heart all worldly desires, and not make its object the praise of men. Rather, it had to take the most complete joy in rebirth through the work of the Holy Spirit and know that no matter what good an individual did, he was always deficient; no matter how hard he worked, he was wretched for not doing more. Living faith was to acknowledge the truth even if it brought distress; to renounce error even when this error had provided comfort; to admit a mistake even if such an admission brought shame from people. Faith meant always to pray to God that all things be done according to his will, and to be happy in the recognition of God's will being done even if this caused pain. And in the face of severe trials, it was to submit to God as a child submits to his father to beg succor, and if deliverance were not forthcoming, it was not simply to resign oneself to the will of God but to plead actively for its fulfillment.

As'ad's decision to keep a journal was highly unusual for people in the region at this time.[44] He emulated the Protestant missionaries whose company he so intimately kept, but his emphasis was far less ethnographic and far more a record of his own evangelical tribulations amidst a "sea of unbelief" (*bahr al-kufr*); it was far less obviously polished and premeditated, far more sincere and haphazard. It depicted a man genuinely moved by his faith, torn and tempted in a manner the protected American missionaries in Beirut could only imagine, beset by a patriarch who was desperate to regain him but also determined to ward off so clear a threat to his inherited sovereignty. As'ad literally begged his interlocutors to understand that he simply followed in the footsteps of the ancient church fathers and apostles, and to understand that the real church "is the community of believers, not stones," within which empty rituals were enacted and ineffective icons hung.

He reserved his most scathing condemnation for what he described as the "great ignorance" that resulted from a church utterly entangled with worldly power. He specifically denounced the practice of confession and absolution which, in the individual form in which As'ad knew it, had only been introduced among Eastern Christians by Catholic missionaries and Latinized Maronites in the late sixteenth century.[45] As'ad insisted that the ritual of confession sanctioned in people a wanton disregard for their own salvation, because they believed that they could sin with impunity now, and hoard the transient treasures of this world in the false hope that they could always repent later. But this, he said, was a dangerous delusion, for human beings did not move perpetually between sin and grace, nor did they know the time or place of their final earthly hour. There were only two states for all, he asserted. The first was a corrupt physical birth from a mother's womb, and the second a spiritual rebirth (*tajdid al-wilada*) accomplished only through the grace of God.

In a similar vein, As'ad rejected the prevailing belief that theft was the greatest of sins, the rest of which could be forgiven after repentance and confession. The truth, he said, was that no sin could be forgiven through confession, only through the genuine transformation and renewal of the heart. Icons, he said, could not intercede on behalf of the faithful; only reading the word of God, prayer to God, and the continual contemplation of God and his religion could do so. "Search the Scriptures," Jesus commanded, he reminded his audiences. Therefore to forbid the preaching of the Gospel and to prevent people from delving into religion, as was the custom of the land, constituted a "shocking ignorance" (*jahl fazi'*).

Such was the tenor of defiance that As'ad *al-Inkilizi,* "the English one," exhibited for a month in conversations, in writings, and in an unauthorized sermon he preached in Tripoli on 13 April. In the face of such reckless determination to interpret the Gospel independently, to turn the world upside down, to deny authority and religion, to act the part of the ravening wolf in sheep's clothing, the patriarch despaired. "We keep putting up with you, keep putting up with you," he finally snapped, "but nothing comes of it." It was whispered to As'ad that the patriarch would soon send him to the secluded monastery of Qannubin and there "imprison me and put a chain around my neck." As'ad immediately implored the patriarch to release him, and contemplated Malta once more. Yusuf Hubaysh refused and instead ordered As'ad to follow him to Qannubin. Left alone for a few hours one day in mid-April, As'ad was at a loss. He was as terrified at the prospect of obeying the patriarch as he was afraid of fleeing. Mocked by those who made him out to be insane, abandoned and betrayed, he thought, by family and friends, As'ad turned to God: "I cry out to you but you do not answer me, or look toward me; you have become hard on me, and with the sternness of your hand, you oppose me and to death deliver me; but do not extend your hand to annihilate them [who oppress me] and even if they fall save them in the name of our lord Jesus Christ. Amen." One of the patriarch's men suddenly appeared and told him that the time for delay was over. He was to take As̄ad at once to Qannubin.[46]

※

Letter from the Propaganda Fide to Patriarch Yusuf Hubaysh, dated 7 October 1826:

> Most illustrious and respected Eminence:
> Tearful news has reached this Holy Congregation about a ruinous development among the students of the college of ʿAyn Waraqa. It is said that the student Asʿad Shidyaq [Felice Scidiac] has become Protestant and that he is in full collaboration with the chiefs of the English Protestants resident in Beirut, and that not only is he implicated in his own heresy but also that he is determined to deceive others, teaching and debating against the Catholics to the grave scandal of pious people. In addition to these anxieties caused by the aforementioned student, it has been reported that other teachers in this school have exhibited suspicious and ruinous behavior. Your Eminence knows how critically important it is for you to build a fence without delay to prevent so great an evil if indeed it is present. You must urgently investigate to find out the truth of these allegations, and then to take whatever remedies your wisdom and piety see fit to stop the development of this encroaching evil. Inform this Holy Congregation in full detail about this, and about the nature of the advisers and teachers of the college so that this Holy Congregation might devote itself to another course that will result in the spiritual welfare of this nation that has always been characterized by its attachment to our holy religion. With great desire we anxiously await your reply.[47]

※

The persecution of Asʿad Shidyaq began in earnest after his arrival at Qannubin. Evidence from his journal and letters indicates that he maintained his strident evangelism throughout the month of May. He was increasingly haunted, however, by the prospects of his own religious failure in the face of relentless pressure to conform to the Maronite myth of perpetual ortho-

Figure 6. View of the Monasteries of Diman and Qannubin in Mount Lebanon. Source: Blatchford Collection, Archives and Special Collections Department, Jafet Library, American University of Beirut, Ph 1/231.

doxy. He reminded himself and others that this was a treacherous and deceitful world, for it promised to bestow all manner of power and glory on those who would forsake their spiritual salvation. He wrote that those who were tempted were indeed granted what they thought were beautiful horses and mighty swords to fight the army of true believers, but as soon as the battle was engaged, their bearers found themselves forsaken to the cruelest fate, utterly hopeless and abandoned, neither borne by steed nor protected by steel. Had not some of the great lords of this land recently suffered precisely this fate—probably a reference to Bashir Janbulat, the preeminent Druze leader, ally of the emir Bashir Shihab, esteemed vassal of the sublime state, and great landowner, who amassed enormous wealth only to be betrayed by the emir, cursed as a heretic, and delivered up to an Ottoman gibbet in 1825.[48] He tried to remain steadfast in his evangelism, to bear in mind the transience of this life and the permanence of the next; but Maronite impatience with his dissidence was inexorable, especially after the Propaganda Fide bluntly expressed its concern with the patriarch's reported inability to stem the tide of heresy.

Several times over the course of the next few months As'ad unsuccessfully sought to escape. The various narratives of his last confinement are confused. Some say that he escaped from Quzhayya, where he had been sent to be cured of his supposed possession. Others claim that he had escaped from Diman, a patriarchal summer residence an hour's distance from Qannubin, where As'ad was kept for a short period, or from Qannubin itself, where he was first sent in late April and where he eventually died.[49] All the narratives do agree on one point: that As'ad's physical punishment escalated dramatically after each of his attempted escapes. This cycle reached its peak following his final attempt to flee, when he was subjected to what the patriarch referred to as a "torture commensurate with the totality of his ruinous evil." As'ad was beaten mercilessly on the soles of his feet with green branches, more flexible and thus more whiplike, for eight consecutive days.[50]

Amidst these scenes, interrogations continued but in far more attenuated form. Between the bouts of punishment, As'ad apparently broke down and repented several times, only to reverse himself later, restating his Protestant objections and his determination to preach the Gospel.[51] Along with the beatings, therefore, the patriarch confiscated As'ad's pipe and Bible, and then ordered a heavy chain to be placed around his neck and secured to a wall. At last, after As'ad's final attempt at escape sometime in November and his refusal to recant, the patriarch ordered that As'ad be forced indefinitely into a cramped cell and had it blocked up with earth and stone. The only opening was a tiny window through which his meager rations were passed. He was to be kept there until he might finally come to his senses or else perish without spreading his "poison" to others. The patriarch reassured the Propaganda Fide on 5 January 1827 that he "remains till this date under torture and painful imprisonment."[52]

The pain inflicted upon As'ad reflected, in part, a typical course of medieval exorcism undertaken across the land, in Christian monasteries such as Quzhayya as well as in the Muslim *bimaristan* or mental asylum. Beating was supposed to drive out the evil that inhabited the body and poisoned the mind, and solitary imprisonment in a cave with a heavy chain was a course prescribed by the monks of Quzhayya and elsewhere.[53] The patriarch acknowledged as much in a letter of 23 June to a Shihab emir in which he explained that he was treating As'ad for his *junun,* but admitted that As'ad remained utterly unpredictable, submitting one moment, rebelling the next.[54] Yet the fact that Asʿad was also apparently encouraged to repudiate in writing his association with the Protestants in this period indicates that his torture went beyond traditional remedies for madness. It recalls what was novel about the Hindiyya affair—the adoption by Maronites of Roman Catholic inquisitorial procedures to extract a written, that is to say, definitive, confession from a heretic.[55]

The torture was also, almost certainly, impulsive and vindictive, more an expression of sheer frustration and outrage over the tenacity of Asʿad's heresy—his faith—than any systematic or thought-out course of treatment for one possessed. This was not the first time a Maronite patriarch had physically oppressed one of his own community: the monk Arsanyus Dyab, who leveled some of the first charges against Hindiyya, was defrocked by Patriarch Yusuf Istifan in 1769, thrown into a cell for several days, and allegedly severely beaten on the soles of his feet; a few years later the disgraced Hindiyya herself was imprisoned in a filthy cell at ʿAyntura for months by Deputy Patriarch Mikhaʾil al-Khazin; she was beaten, denied food or water, and threatened with being burned and flayed if she did not implicate Khazin's rival, the deposed patriarch Yusuf Istifan, in her activities at Bkrike.[56]

The persecution of Asʿad was a blunt lesson in terror, intended not simply to punish Asʿad but to deter others from adopting his ways. The severity of Asʿad's punishment, the patriarch freely confessed to Rome, "has become a warning to all who see him or hear his story."[57] The patriarch's treatment of Asʿad was generally condoned by the elites of Mount Lebanon. The bastinado, or the beating of the soles of the feet, was a standard corporal punishment in the empire, and its use in remote Qannubin against Asʿad the *majnun* would not likely have raised any undue concern as a miscarriage of justice. The Shihab emirs refused to intervene actively on behalf of a man who so defiantly and hopelessly challenged the existing order of things. Bashir Shihab flatly rejected the abject plea of his "slave" Ghalib Shidyaq to intervene on his brother's behalf, and blamed Asʿad for his dangerous association with the missionaries. Milhim Shihab, in turn, declined to help.[58] The men of Abdullah Hasan Shihab, who governed Kisrawan on behalf of the ruling emir, captured and returned a bedraggled Asʿad to Qannubin after his final bid for freedom. The British consul himself admitted that there was little that could be done for him because Asʿad was considered to be intimately connected to the Maronite Church, and because his was an affair of religion and hence was under the church's jurisdiction.[59] Because of this perception, the missionaries never directly or indirectly pursued his case with the Ottoman government.

Although Christians in the cities of the Ottoman Empire resorted to Muslim courts when they felt that their own leaders had failed them, and in cases of conversion sought Ottoman protection to escape persecution from their former communities, in Mount Lebanon, Asʿad's family remained within the Maronite fold. They initially acknowledged that his behavior was not simply scandalous but unsettled, and thus forcibly delivered him to the patriarch at the end of March; as much as Asʿad considered himself *mazlum*, or unjustly oppressed, justice in Mount Lebanon, theoretically based on Islamic law, was actually inseparable from the will of the powerful lords and patriarchs who considered Asʿad insane and thus in need of ecclesiastical care.[60] The patriarch enjoyed a free hand to deal with Asʿad as he saw fit, and as this changed from patient counsel to violent punishment, there was no recourse for Asʿad other than supplication to God—or, of course, conformity and submission. Much as the saga of Hindiyya had unfolded across several major Vatican investigations in stunning obliviousness to the Ottoman context in which it was set, so now Asʿad suffered his fate, ironically a casualty of Ottoman tolerance if ever there was one. He may have lived in the Ottoman Empire, but he died beyond the purview of the imperial state.

Asʿad belonged to a prominent but not a powerful family. His station was not one that could command the deference or respect enjoyed, for instance, by the Druze lords of the Abilamʿ family who converted to the Maronite faith in the eighteenth century.[61] Nor could he take refuge in a mass conversion as did many of the Greek Catholics in Syria in the eighteenth century.[62] Nevertheless, the brothers of Asʿad had great misgivings when they realized how severely he was being treated by the patriarch. Tannus and his mother visited Qannubin in late July and were shocked to see Asʿad in his chains. They beseeched the patriarch to release him to their care, or at least to let him out of his miserable cell. In response, the patriarch allowed him to walk freely on the monastery's grounds, but warned Tannus that Asʿad had many times previously appeared better only to revert to his heretical ways. Tannus therefore begged Asʿad to be discreet, and he apparently agreed. No sooner had Tannus crossed the valley to Diman, however, than Asʿad sent him word—though how he did so is not clear—that he could not desist from preaching the Gospel. The patriarch immediately returned him to his prison.[63]

۞

With the coming of winter, and with snow covering the terraced mountainside of Qannubin, Yusuf Hubaysh relented as a priest begged for one last opportunity to bring As'ad back into the church. He granted the priest, who knew As'ad well, permission to enter As'ad's freezing prison, to loosen some of his chains, and even to return some of his clothes. But he was not to return his Bible. For weeks, perhaps longer, the priest urged As'ad to grasp this last line to salvation, to beg the Virgin Mary to intercede on his behalf, and to understand that icons were venerated because they recalled the Savior, just as the cross was kissed in memory of the man who was crucified on it.[64] It is almost certainly because of this priest that As'ad Shidyaq managed to record on a few scraps of paper a sense of his own faltering faith and impending doom. He confessed that he was tormented by apparitions of a false Christ, by Orthodox saints, and by many idols, all of whom presented themselves for worship. He described as well how he was overwhelmed by the "true Virgin Mary," who offered to intercede with her Son on his behalf. He admitted to embracing her fervently, and as a result experiencing great comfort in his heart. The night he did so, he wrote, two angels descended upon him in his prison cell and guided him, amidst the brilliant lightning and deafening thunder, amidst howling winds and terrifying sights, once more to worship God alone. He confessed that he could no longer tell what was true and what was imaginary. The only thing he knew to be certain was that to venerate icons was false superstition, to devote oneself to the word of God true faith. He thus begged his interrogators to provide him with a Bible and to understand that as unjustly tried as he was, and as close to an undeserved death as they had brought him, he could not prostrate himself religiously to any but God, or in good conscience state what the church demanded. He could only say what he believed to be true.

In the face of these expiring notes of defiance from this "miserable wretch, deceived by the Devil and dragged by him to the lowest levels of hell," the patriarch himself entered As'ad's cell, and seeing As'ad spurn his solicitude, cursed him for being a fool and beat him. He declared to all present that he was innocent of As'ad's sins and washed his hands of his fate.[65]

By the time Yusuf Hubaysh recorded his missive to the Propaganda Fide in early January 1827, the patriarch no longer referred to him as As'ad al-Shidyaq but simply as *al-ta'is,* the wretch, and as Rab Shayul, Syriac for Lord of Hell. He defended the students of 'Ayn Waraqa, who he claimed so desired the "extirpation of this wretch, it is as if they want to dismember him limb by limb." He insisted that their hatred of As'ad was so great that *they* labeled him "Rab Shayul, or the Lord of Hell, because by the grace of God

Almighty and the goodness of your blessings they cannot bear those who want to forsake the obedience of their Mother, the Holy Roman Church. We and they are continuing the struggle [*jihad*] with all our power against those Biblemen."[66]

For the myth of perpetual orthodoxy to stand, much had to be suppressed: the patriarch's initial welcome of the missionaries; the extensive and unimpeded tour they had made in Maronite-dominated regions; the genuine interest among many Maronites, including Asʿad's brother Faris, who by now had been spirited away to Alexandria by the Americans, in the message if not the manner of the missionaries; and of course the very complex history of the Maronites themselves. Asʿad's name, and thus his location and identity and place in society, was obliterated, and with it, the patriarch fervently hoped, the memory of his unforgivable, and in an important sense impossible, transgression. Asʿad Shidyaq could never have been.

🙚

When in August 1827 Isaac Bird sought the village of Ihdin to escape the oppressive heat of Beirut, he was chased out forthwith. The American missionary knew full well, of course, that he could not have chosen a more provocative place to visit, for Ihdin was a Maronite village that overlooked the Qadisha Valley and the monasteries of Qannubin, where Asʿad Shidyaq languished, and Diman, where the Maronite patriarch resided in summer. The country was already on edge because of the Greek war, and the patriarch had issued in December a second, even stricter anathema against the missionaries, prohibiting all manner of contact with the "Biblemen."[67] Goodell even admitted that what happened "is nothing more, than was reasonably to be expected."[68] Yet armed with a letter of protection from Emir Bashir (secured by the British consul) and the personal invitation of a Maronite shaykh associated with the British consulate, Bird, family in tow, sauntered into the heart of Maronite Mount Lebanon. The patriarch immediately excommunicated his hosts; villagers then beat them severely. Bird and his family were quickly forced into a humiliating flight from the village. They took refuge with a Muslim notable farther down the mountain before making their way despondently back to Beirut. Bashir Shihab subsequently castigated Bird, noting that "all people cherish their own religion." He added that foreigners had long traveled in his domains and had never once been hurt, and "nobody would have interfered with this Signor Bird if only he refrained from defamation in matters of faith."[69]

Bird pleaded innocence and was outraged at the treatment he had received. He insisted to the British consul that he had done nothing wrong and broken no law.[70] Perhaps, but that was hardly the point. By walking into Ihdin, Bird had openly defied local sensibilities and again violated the taboo that forbade public religious controversy in an unequal but religiously pluralistic empire. An old Maronite priest tellingly rebuked the American for seeking to undermine what he described as the obvious order of nature. "Look at the trees," Bird quoted him saying. "Each one bears its own fruit: the vine, the mulberry, the oak, each has its fruits peculiar to itself, and you cannot alter this course of nature. It would be foolish to attempt to make the vine bear mulberries, or the mulberry acorns, or the oak figs."[71] For all his deliberate defiance of the will of the patriarch, Bird unwittingly played the part of the once dreaded Jacobite missionaries who had long ago plagued the Maronites in these same regions. He provided a church desperate to highlight its Catholic credentials with the perfect opportunity to rehearse a familiar drama.

According to church legend, the medieval Syrian Orthodox heretics who arrived in the Maronite heartland carrying false books were defeated by the innate goodness of a Maronite people under ecclesiastical supervision. The patriarch was able to boast on 9 August to Maronite notables that "our Christian people favored by God rose upon them at once, and with perfect zeal, drove out from among them those ravening wolves."[72] He elaborated this theme in a report to Rome on 4 October 1827. Contrasting the wealth and means of the American missionaries with the dire poverty of the Maronites, he reassured Rome that he had once again prevented the Biblemen from seducing the "simple ones" (*al-basitin*) of his community. Bird, he wrote, had tried to settle in Ihdin with the pretense of "changing air" but was in reality "filled with evil." Although the patriarch had commanded a boycott of the missionary, a call that was so thoroughly heeded by the Maronite "shaykhs and peasants" that Bird was "himself forced to fill his jug of water from the spring," it was "the people of Ihdin" who evicted Bird from their midst of their own accord.[73] What the American missionary presented as the unwarranted fanaticism of nominal Christians, the Maronite patriarch easily transformed into an existential question of the survival of Christianity in the East. The Americans were, for the time being, bested at their own game.

꽃

In the beginning of May the following year, 1828, with prices high and the plague and famine stalking the land, As̄ʿad Shidyaq still lay imprisoned when his American champions boarded a chartered Austrian vessel to depart Ottoman shores. The Greek war had once more taken its now customary toll over the past year. The battle of Navarino, a rumor of the sultan's death, and another about the imminent massacre of Christians had rattled the small European community in Beirut.

But as the missionaries, two Armenian converts, and several Franks boarded the Austrian vessel, some twenty-one souls in all, on that first Friday of May, they left behind them more than the man they would soon herald as a martyr. In effect, they conceded the battle they had themselves initiated, and admitted that for now at least, facts had trumped their ideals. They proffered, once more, rationalizations: the prospect of war, the want of an asylum in case of war, the want of consular protection, their solitary situation and pecuniary embarrassment, the plague which had just appeared in Beirut, the scarcity of vessels, and the call for some missionaries at Malta.[74]

Months before at a similar moment of uncertainty and fear, having removed his own wife and valuables to safety, William Goodell had tried, though without avail, to reassure his native neighbors that the missionaries had not forsaken their friends. "They would have it," he confessed, "that our actions spoke louder than our words."[75] And now, despite their many words about their determined spiritual militancy, and despite all their idealism, the missionaries were simply not prepared to endure the consequences of their self-proclaimed mission to revive faith in the Ottoman Empire.

᭐

A set of astonishing epistles by the missionary Joseph Wolff to the Maronite patriarch and nation concluded the first, and for As'ad Shidyaq disastrous, round of evangelical mission.[76] To the great embarrassment of his American peers, the English Jewish convert to Protestantism peremptorily demanded the immediate and unconditional release of As'ad Shidyaq. The problem was not merely in the haughty tone of the letters but in their manic style, their outrageous content, and their atrociously poor Arabic. More than any other document, they marked the missionaries as foreigners out of place in the Orient. The shorter of the two letters began with a formulaic address to "our dear" patriarch, and bestowed "apostolic blessings upon you and your chin from my hand and inform you that we are now present in Alexandria preaching the gospel to Jews, Muslims, and Catholics." Clearly Wolff was reversing roles and mocking the language of Eastern ecclesiastical authority. Just as clearly he was crossing the line into absurdity. "I have been informed," he continued, that As'ad Shidyaq remains in prison upon your orders. Therefore I command you to release him at once, and if you do not release him upon receipt of this letter, and kneel before him . . . and kiss his hand and beg his forgiveness, I will excommunicate you, and all the Maronites, and the pope who is the Deceiver in Rome, and you [will] go to hell because I know that our Lord Jesus Christ who died for us looks upon the saints such as As'ad Shidyaq and has mercy upon him. But you will die from a stomach ache and you will eat your own shit. Therefore repent and believe in Christ.

The letter was signed "Yusuf Wolff al-Inkilizi," the Englishman, "apostle of Jesus Christ."[77] In his longer letter which he addressed to the Maronite community generally, Wolff declared that "Druses are better than the pope, and better than your patriarch, and better than the nation of the Maronites. The Jews who killed 'Isa [Jesus] are better than you, and Pontius Pilate is better than the pope in Rome, and Herod and Judas Iscariot are better than your patriarch." The letter, furthermore, described the eponymous patron saint of the Maronite Church, Mar Marun, as *majnun,* or insane.[78]

"We are all more or less made answerable by the people for his wild and unevangelical extravagancies," confessed Isaac Bird.[79] The American missionaries pitied but were also exasperated by Wolff, whose outbursts they made sure to conceal from the evangelical public at home. Bird wished that Wolff would "find his way back to England . . . where every madman may find his bedlam."[80] Yet Wolff's letters testified, in an unmistakable sense, to a passing stage of mission, and to the failure of the zealous frontal assault that had animated much of its initial course. Just as Wolff had become a caricature of an "English" missionary, his letters were a parody of Jonas King's "Farewell Letter." Tellingly, Wolff accused his colleagues, among many other things, of having betrayed Luther and of having become far too "prudent" and calculating in their approach to mission. His frantic calculations that the Second Coming was bound to occur in 1847 underscored the degree to which the raw belligerence and millennial urgency that had been so clearly a part of the initial American mission had dissipated by 1830. However absurd his demand that As'ad be released forthwith, it did recall the inability of the Americans to save their prized convert.

William Goodell had moved on to Istanbul, but Isaac Bird had returned to Beirut in mid-May 1830. He was still committed to the self-proclaimed revival of religion in a "dark" region of the world. Although he had acquired a measure of Jonas King's fluency, Bird himself possessed none of his charisma.

Soon enough, on 12 November 1830 word reached Bird that As'ad Shidyaq had died at last. A chapter in the history of American missions had finally closed.

۞

A letter from Asʿad Shidyaq to Yusuf Hubaysh, which the patriarch showed to Asʿad's brother Tannus Shidyaq at Diman in 1829 to prove Asʿad's insanity:

> I ask you, if you will, to liberate me to witness for my beloved Jesus that he is the son of the living God and to preach his Gospel because he revealed himself to me and told me that he wants me to evangelize and to state that he is the true Messiah. And if you need a miracle to believe here are Mikhayil and Sirhan who are dead. If you want me to appeal to my lord Jesus Christ to raise one of them from the dead so that you may leave me to preach, then write me a note and let me understand if you want me to do so, that if I raise the one I want, you will set me free to serve the Gospel of my lord. Tell me what it is you want. There was Shaykh Khalid who had died but I raised him in the name of Jesus Christ on one condition that he accepted in spirit after his death that he come to me but that his left hand across his chest be not shriveled until he comes. This is another miracle in case you need it. Say what it is that you want and I beg you to let me know what will reassure you enough to believe . . . to allow you to free me. Command me if you want this or not. And may the name of God the most holy father who raises the dead and gives them life be blessed.[81]

An undated scrawl, probably from 1829:

> I Asʿad Shidyaq when I was imprisoned at the monastery of Qannubin because of my embrace of the heresy of the Biblemen and my belief in their false teachings, evil spirits, fiends appeared before me and told me to follow them so that the could make me a false Messiah. They informed me that Sirhan and Mikhayil and Shaykh Khalid died and I was deceived by them and thought them to be godly spirits. They told me that we want Shaykh Khalid to be resurrected by your hand so that the name of Jesus can be embodied. I agreed that Shaykh Khalid be resurrected and that his left hand remain shriveled across his chest. And then spirits appeared to me [and told me] that fire was going to descend from heaven and burn me because of my sin and this occurred. Thereafter they told me that the Day of Judgment would happen in a day, or two days, or even today, but then I re-

alized their deceit and their malice and understood that the society of Biblemen were deceived by the fiends and because of that I cursed their corrupt
teachings and believed in the Apostolic and Holy Roman Church.[82]

⊯

In clearer handwriting, also undated:

I Asʿad the fool [*al-bahlul*] believe that the Devil told me that he would
make me the false Messiah but I did not accept because I mocked him and
he was not able to kill me. Therefore I believe according to the faith of the
Apostolic, Holy, Universal Roman Church. I bless all that she blesses and
curse all that she curses.[83]

⊯

In a long report from December 1831 dutifully prepared for the Propaganda
Fide, Patriarch Yusuf Hubaysh recounted his victory over the Americans.
Predictably, he drew an utterly simple portrait of the Maronite faithful surrounded by a sea of unbelievers and schismatics in which the missionary
threat was simply the latest in a long line of heresies to confront a beleaguered but resilient nation. Maronites, he wrote, had from their earliest history been prepared to shed blood and to be martyred to please God and the
Holy Roman Church, and in this spirit they had fought and won the war
over the body and soul of Asʿad Shidyaq. "All submitted immediately to my
shepherd's voice," he asserted—all except Asʿad Shidyaq. The Protestant
convert was reduced to a solitary, and ultimately insignificant, exception that
proved the rule of Maronite perpetual orthodoxy: his voluminous writings,
protests, and pleadings summarily dismissed as the ravings of a deranged and
dangerous man. Although he retreated from his earlier, enthusiastic description of Asʿad's torture, the patriarch was unrepentant. Asʿad Shidyaq, he
confessed, "died in prison in his state of obstinacy and heresy."[84]

The paradigm of steadfast resistance sketched out by the patriarch captured the full ambivalence of Christian subjecthood under Islamic imperial
sovereignty. On the one hand, the Ottoman rulers were the most powerful
of "strange nations" who besieged the Maronites; on the other hand, the
patriarch freely acknowledged that the Muslims—"al-Islam" is how he referred to them—perceived and reacted to a common danger represented by
the missionaries, who respected no limits, were subject to no local author-

ity, and sought to seduce subjects from all communities. He admitted, therefore, that Maronite subjects and Muslim rulers had acted in common if uncoordinated cause to repel the missionary onslaught.

Wrapped up in his evocation of Maronite perpetual orthodoxy were basic assumptions about quietism shared with Muslim rulers which gave meaning to a deeply conservative, pluralistic, and extremely hierarchal social order. The commoners, Muslim and Christian, were at once inherently faithful and yet also fundamentally ignorant; they could thus be seduced by the wiles and stratagems of foreign manipulators, but also defended by the paternal solicitude of their rulers, both secular and ecclesiastical. The insidious danger came not from the masses below but from the men of knowledge, those willful rebels against God's authority embodied in the American missionaries in the first instance and in the "erudite and eloquent and very much attached to English sentiments," Asʿad Shidyaq, in the second.[85] So it had always been, and so it should always remain.

So long as no one other than Asʿad Shidyaq publicly repudiated church hegemony, so long as local notables and Ottoman authorities tacitly endorsed his persecution, and so long as a rigid social order stood unchallenged and Protestant converts had no officially recognized community within which to take refuge, this patriarchal depiction of social and communal integrity would stand. That this notion of unyielding and unchanging identity bore little resemblance to the far richer and varied history of Mount Lebanon; that the Maronites were hardly as isolated as their patriarch made them out to be; that their church had been riven by the Hindiyya controversy; that the Propaganda itself notoriously took a dim view of Maronite claims to perpetual orthodoxy; that the patriarch had initially welcomed the missionaries; and that Asʿad Shidyaq was more than simply a crazed individual—all this was ignored by the patriarch. Asʿad's determination to be convinced and not commanded into obedience, his plea for a new kind of freedom of conscience, his desire to remain a Maronite but liberated from traditional Maronite religious authority, to dissent publicly, to privilege individual experience over community or rank: all this anticipated a more modern Ottoman age that had not yet dawned.

Part III

REORIENTATIONS

Chapter 6

The Apotheosis of
American Exceptionalism

Henry Harris Jessup, the eminent late-nineteenth-century American Protestant missionary to Syria, was not entirely wrong when he believed that
the remarkable story of Asʿad Shidyaq was a "simple narrative."[1] The conversion, persecution, and subsequent death of Asʿad Shidyaq was a tale in
need of almost no embellishment. Yet for all the elements of truth in it, the
story of Asʿad Shidyaq's martyrdom was, and has largely remained, an American missionary tale. The men who told it clearly did not invent his persecution, but they did seize upon it to regain a lost initiative and to turn
outright defeat on the field of missionary battle into evangelical triumph.

Whereas the Maronite community—and with it the representatives of
an Ottoman Arab order of things—had overseen, or at least acquiesced in,
the methodical destruction of an individual whose ideas were deemed
heretical, the Americans deliberately crafted a narrative of his martyrdom
that bore little resemblance to the history and context within which Asʿad
had met his wretched fate. Over the course of the century, they narrated his
story in at least two different ways, reflecting a change in the priority and
scope of the mission itself. From an exemplar of evangelism removed from
all worldly attachments, it was eventually scripted into a parable of mod-

ernization. His drama was stripped of its context in a particular time and place in order to apotheosize the American nation.

A single encounter became a keystone for an entire nineteenth-century edifice of American missionary interpretation that simultaneously idealized the United States and orientalized the East. This interpretation built, of course, on earlier understandings and histories of mission but increasingly infused into them a far more explicitly racial dimension in an era of manifest Anglo-American empire. In Beirut, heart of the Syria mission, millennialism was superseded by a far more comfortable missionary establishment, which was as mute on the racialist nature of domestic American politics as it was strident about the religious fanaticism of Eastern society. This fanaticism was exemplified for the missionaries by As'ad Shidyaq's persecution by the Maronite Church within a larger Muslim world, and was confirmed, in their eyes, by unprecedented sectarian violence between Maronite and Druze inhabitants of Mount Lebanon which erupted in the mid-nineteenth century. Time no longer providentially flew to its much-anticipated end; it worked far more gradually. What had begun in the early nineteenth century as a project to redeem America through missionary work in the world had been transformed by century's end into a project that assumed America's redemption. From the summit of American progress, missionaries looked down at, and no longer simply across to, distant native worlds.

Such a shift was not entirely smooth, nor was it without dissent or contradictions, but it was palpable. A mission that had once urgently framed missionaries and heathen at home and abroad in a single view now ever more segregated America from the world upon which it acted, and posited the missionaries as modern, objective translators of foreign regions and races for a white, Anglo-Saxon, evangelical American public. There were two main events that bounded this transformation and modernization of mission. The first was the failure of the American Board to prevent the passage and implementation of the Indian Removal Act of 1830, which sanctioned the deportation of Cherokees and Choctaws, among other Indian tribes, across the Mississippi. Although American Board missionaries were at the forefront of opposition to Indian removal, and although they won a Supreme Court decision in 1832 which ruled that the state of Georgia had no authority over the Cherokees, President Andrew Jackson pushed ahead with the ethnic cleansing of the Indians. The American Board was dealt a signal defeat. In the name of kindness to Indian tribes who he said were doomed to extinction among superior whites, he ordered federal troops to enforce a cruel and methodical mass deportation of tens of thousands of Indians throughout the 1830s.[2]

The second event was the sectarian warfare between Maronites and Druzes that devastated much of Mount Lebanon in 1860. The reasons for this war were complex, and were rooted in a series of tumultuous political events between 1840 and 1860 that undermined the traditional elitist Lebanese social order, including the collapse of Bashir Shihab's emirate in 1840, a European-instigated partition of Mount Lebanon along religious lines in the name of bringing order to it in 1842, and the initiation in this same period of Ottoman imperial reform which was predicated on the equal treatment of all subjects regardless of religious affiliation. Suffice it to say that the Druzes and Maronites, the two major communities of Mount Lebanon, struggled for two decades to take advantage of their location at the heart of what the Europeans called their "Eastern Question," and entered into a contest to consolidate sectarian control over a land that had never been ruled on the basis of sect. Repeated bouts of violence were interspersed with spells of calm. In 1860, however, Druzes and Maronites engaged in total war in the southern, Druze-dominated part of Mount Lebanon. Entire Christian communities were either massacred or forced to flee their homes.

"Massacre Summer" is how the missionaries would later recall the unprecedented scenes of outrage. Whereas Indian removal in the United States chastened the American Board and underscored the vital importance of the foreign arena for an idealization of America, the war of 1860 horrified its missionaries stationed in Syria, drawing a clear line for them between the backward and savage Orient and the advanced, scientific, and civilized United States.

The irony of this interpretation lay in its silencing of the Arab evangelical voice of As'ad Shidyaq which the early missionaries had worked so hard to cultivate. It also lay in its refusal to listen to, or at any rate take seriously, other natives who were inspired by him, and who were products of the intersection of cultures in which American missionaries played so prominent a part.

℩⅊

Five years into the mission to reclaim the lands of the Bible, with nearly twenty thousand tracts and four thousand Bibles or portions thereof distributed, there was still not a single Arab Christian convert.[3] A scattering of Armenians had indeed broken with their apostolic church, but by and large the mission had precious little to show for itself. As early as 1823 Pliny Fisk had sought to dampen hopes by declaring that the "man who goes into the wilderness to cultivate it does not expect to see flourishing cities at once."[4] Jonas King echoed this prognosis when he wrote: "Let not missionaries, or missionary societies, be discouraged because they see no present fruit of their labors. Seed time and harvest seldom meet together. They shall reap in due time, if they faint not."[5] From Malta in mid-1826 Daniel Temple sounded an even more somber note of caution: "Our hopes concerning most of those who show themselves favorable to the Protestant religion are now dashed to the ground. Most of them turn out to be villains; two of them are now in prison, and many more of them I believe ought to be there. The God of this world triumphs."[6]

№

From Boston increasingly pointed inquiries were made by anxious American Board officials who pointed out the great successes and "wonderful changes" that were being garnered in the Sandwich Islands and among the native Americans. Rufus Anderson, the assistant corresponding secretary of the American Board, forwarded Isaac Bird copies of his own memoir of the Cherokee Catherine Brown and hoped to send another of the Hawaiian queen Keopuolani. In turn he asked the missionary: "Can you not make a tract respecting Palestine, which will be popular? Some of you surely can. Send it home to be printed, as the production of one of you, or as your joint production, or in anyway that suits you."[7] No matter how great the difficulties in the Ottoman Empire, Jeremiah Evarts, the American Board's influential corresponding secretary, reminded Jonas King, men "are apt to grow cold in the best of causes, and great and constant exertion is necessary to keep them from fainting."[8]

There was good reason for Evarts's concern. The proliferation of national benevolent voluntary associations in the northeastern United States such as the American Home Missionary Society, the American Tract Society, the American Sunday School Union, and myriad other, smaller missionary organizations, most of which were similarly committed to purging the national frontiers of Methodist and Baptist revivalists and to transforming a disparate population into evangelical American Christians, competed with the American Board for the attention and purse strings of an American evangelical public.[9] At the same time, the message of organizations with a foreign emphasis, such as the American Colonization Society, which focused on restoring "degraded people of colour to their own native land," resonated with a white evangelical public that held free blacks at a distance.[10] The ABCFM, by contrast, from its inception had to contend with critics who accused it of involving itself in exotic overseas ventures. Far more problematically, it also had to respond to, and eventually succumbed before, severe criticisms of its efforts to assimilate Indians into the United States.[11]

All these pressures demanded tangible success in biblical lands, whose mission had been accompanied with great expectations. The *Missionary Herald,* the official and most important journal that covered the American Board missions, inadvertently added even more pressure. Its emphasis on the putative success with the "heathen" of the Sandwich Islands and among the Cherokees inevitably underscored failure in Palestine and Syria. The gross generalization encapsulated in the word "heathen" that was at the heart of an evangelical fantasy to convert the world now seemed to work against the missionaries in the Levant.

There was also trouble on the horizon, as Evarts knew full well. The American Board's multiracial Foreign Mission School in Cornwall, Connecticut, had to be abandoned in 1826 because of the uproar sparked by the marriages of two Cherokee students to local white women. The racist implications of this decision were not lost on Jeremiah Evarts. "Can it be pretended at this age of the world," he wrote, "that a small variance of complexion is to present an insuperable barrier to matrimonial connexions, or that the different tribes of men are to be kept forever and entirely distinct?"[12] This local fiasco was an omen of national things to come. Andrew Jackson's campaigns against the Creeks and Seminoles, and the agitation by Georgia for the dispossession of Indians, clearly anticipated the callous systematic expulsions of eastern Indians formalized by the Indian Removal Act, and with it the evisceration of an original American Board ideal to redeem America through its evangelization of the Indians.[13]

※

In the face of this relentless pressure to demonstrate the efficacy of evangelism in the Orient in terms intelligible to the domestic patrons of missions, that is, in terms of conversions made, idols smashed, and Mohammedanism vanquished, the missionaries could only temporize and offer increasingly hollow promises of the anticipated harvest to come.[14]

But however the problem at hand was analyzed and reasons for it assigned, from the depravity of the human condition to the overarching despotism of Islam, the fundamental conceit of the missionary project—that there should be a universal errand to the world and that the Americans were uniquely blessed to undertake it—was never seriously questioned. Instead, the natives were blamed. "It would be really gratifying," wrote William Goodell in June 1824, "to find one man of common honesty in these parts."[15] Temple echoed these sentiments when he affirmed that the "unthinking multitude lies buried, as ever, in idolatry."[16] And Eli Smith a few years later admitted that "experience has proved, that so thoroughly is deceit bound up in their hearts, that even when divine grace takes possession, a clear discrimination and just estimate of truth is one of the latest of its fruits to ripen."[17]

The Eastern Christians were especially condemned not only because they were "bad specimens of Christianity," as Smith put it so dismissively, but also because, more obviously than any Muslim or Jew possibly could, they disputed the exclusivity of American missionary Christianity.[18] There was little to indicate this degree of hostility to Eastern Christians at the outset of the mission. Yet within a few years those natives with whom the missionaries had had the most intimate and intense contact, with whom they had the most in common, whose clerics put up the most vehement resistance, and those, in the Maronite case at least, who combined, in missionary eyes, the abominations of the papacy with the degradation of the Orient, created in them an almost visceral reaction. As much as they were objects of pity because they were at the mercy of the "*arrogance and cruelty* of Mohammedans," native Christians were considered by the missionaries to be fundamentally more debased and dishonest than Muslims.[19] "The universal testimony of Frank merchants in the Levant is there is more honesty . . . among the Turks," declared Goodell in the beginning of 1826, "than among the Christian sects."[20] Eli Smith, in turn, agreed. "Europeans in Turkey," he said, "almost uniformly declare that the native Christians are worse than the Turks."[21] Although the term "nominal" Christian was borrowed from an American frontier context where it was usually applied to unprincipled whites, and where it evoked a sense of *disappointment* with the sins of drunkenness, profanity, and duplicitous treatment of Indians, when applied in the Orient it betrayed a feeling of unmistakable *superiority* over natives.

Even the American Board, despite its private criticisms of the missionaries, publicly apologized for them in the *Missionary Herald*. Juxtaposing missionary work in the Ottoman domains to the situation of a "riper age" in the "favored" United States, where ministers who worked with "far more highly gifted communities" often had to wait decades before a revival of religion manifested itself, it urged patience and "reasonable expectations":

> To that portion of the earth the god of this world seems to have directed much of his attention. There he has seized upon the artillery of heaven, and turned it to the defence of his own kingdom. There he fights under advantages, which, in lands purely heathen, he does not possess. In those portions of the Christian church, therefore, which he has bound in chains of darkness, and plunged into corruption, we may expect him to make his firmest, most deadly stand, and there doubtless, will be the most painful struggles and the fiercest conflict.[22]

۞

The echo of a Puritan discourse of Indian America as the stronghold of the devil providentially conquered was meant to inspire an evangelical public to keep faith in the mission to biblical lands. It also, of course, underscored the present predicament of missionaries. The absence of colonial advantage in the Ottoman Empire was clear as the missionaries were unable to save Asʿad Shidyaq. To a far greater extent than John Eliot, the American Board missionaries were forced to rely on the power of persuasion alone in their efforts at conversion. In the process, without the constant threat of militias or disease to herd the remnants of a politically broken native population into praying towns or to plead for Puritan benevolence, the nineteenth-century missionaries were confronted with the limits of the Word to transform ancient worlds. An exasperated Isaac Bird wished for an increase in "English or American influence" in the empire.[23] William Goodell was far more explicit when he lamented:

> It is a great grief to us that we can do nothing, directly, to diminish the political evils of this country; nothing to insure protection for the innocent, or to bring the guilty to justice, nothing to abate national guilt, by being instrumental in promoting a national reform. In this respect our circumstances are widely different from those of our brethren at the Sandwich Islands, or among the Indian tribes of the west, whose labors have a direct and efficient bearing on the body politic, and an influence more or less

powerful on the minds of those, who enact laws, and who control the opinion and practices of others.[24]

☙

So pervasive was missionary distrust of Ottoman subjects that As'ad's initial
approach to Isaac Bird was rebuffed. His first declarations of his own sense
of salvation were dismissed out of hand not simply because evangelical conversion in America mandated a process of self-conscious spiritual struggle
preceding a final triumph of spirit, but also because of an ingrained distrust
of the "corrupted Christianity" of the East. In January 1826 Bird tellingly
informed Evarts only of the promising developments regarding a "young
native" who had defied his church but who was in no sense yet a "a humble, penitent believer in Christ."[25] By March 1826 Bird had to confess that
the "Arab youth" he had first mentioned to Evarts now seemed to have endured the first "trial of his faith." And so he wrote: "We tremble for him, lest
he should be deceived in his *hopes,* and *we* in *him,* but at present we may almost say he bids fair to be a Syrian Luther. Do not forget him in the hour
of secret retirement, when you pray 'thy kingdom come.'"[26] In May, now
convinced that As'ad was sincere, Bird first mentioned "Asaad Esh Shidiak"
by name. In September, William Goodell referred to As'ad as a "suffering
brother" in Christ.[27] And in October of the same year Temple wrote to
both Bird and Goodell, admitting:

> The account you gave us of Shidiak was truly affecting to us and at the same
> time encouraging. We hope the Lord *has* delivered him, and will deliver
> him, out of the mouth of the lion and preserve him unto his heavenly king-
> dom. Such fiery trials are likely to do much good. They will do good to
> the natives and will save you probably from the inconvenience of being
> hounded and teased by false friends pretending to be of your opinions in
> religion.[28]

Indeed as fragments of As'ad's story began to appear in the *Missionary
Herald* in 1826, American readers were given their first details of success in
the lands of the Bible. The 1827 publication of the "Public Statement of
Asaad Shidiak," translated by Bird, who deleted all references to As'ad's physical obeisance to the Maronite patriarch, gave crucial witness to Shidyaq's
"profound regard for the Scriptures."[29] Here was an entirely voluntary native admission about the importance, and hence the viability, of mission. As

much as the mission board and the missionaries had been acutely aware of their failures, now they clutched at a tangible success.

News from the Palestine mission, and about Shidyaq, was emblazoned on the front page of the *Missionary Herald* from February through October 1827. The fortuitous arrival of the last of Jonas King's Syrian journals from 1825 corroborated Asʿad's declaration of faith and significantly provided a *beginning* to the narrative of his martyrdom. King described a moment when, after long discussions with Asʿad in the summer of 1825, the latter took up the New Testament and said to him that the first passage his eye fell on would be "for the English." And so his eye settled on the "word" at the beginning of the Gospel of Luke. He then closed the book and again declared that he would open it and that the first passage his eye would fall on would be "for the Pope." And so his eye fixed on the word "unclean."[30] What would undoubtedly have been read as a mere vignette of a hopeful convert was now taken as a sign of effusing grace, a prelude to an expected conversion experience, which took hold of Asʿad Shidyaq.

With each issue of the *Missionary Herald* more news was published on the fate of Asʿad drawn mostly from Bird's journals and letters. Finally in June 1827, just over fourteen months after Asʿad's initial confinement, the journal announced to its readers:

> That he will escape from the hands of his enemies except by death, is possible, but, we fear, not very probable; that, overcome by pain, and broken down by oppression, he should, like Cranmer, recant, though it would grieve, it should not greatly surprise us; but, that he will, through the divine assistance, persevere to the end, and be a distinguished monument of evangelical piety rekindled upon the ancient altars of Christianity, is what we are entitled of hope, and what all should make an object of their continued and fervent prayers.[31]

The foreshadowing of martyrdom even as Asʿad still languished in prison, alive but out of the reach of the missionaries, was an integral, and even inevitable, component of this narrative. His torture at the hands of "papists," his refusal to recant, and his oppression in a gloomy "dungeon" in the lands of Islam fed American Protestant prejudice. Rufus Anderson had complained bitterly to Bird about the Catholic invasion of America in October 1825. "Already they form a powerful hierarchy in this land of light and freedom," he warned, "and yet carry on their operations so quietly and slyly and civilly that our churches all feel secure and some of them, that is the *liberal,*

seem heartily to bid them God speed. Continue therefore to expose the policy and wickedness of that ch[urch] as you see in Palestine."[32] The missionaries, in short, certainly did not want Asʿad to die; Bird desperately
sought ways to liberate him and continued to forward whatever scraps of
news about Shidyaq's fate he could find. At its annual meeting in 1828 the
American Board reported hopefully that Asʿad's persecution had relented
somewhat, although it also admitted that its missionaries had hastily and
reluctantly departed Beirut for Malta.[33] Ultimately, Bird and his fellow laborers did not shrink from the idea of a native death that so clearly confirmed their preconceived notions. The blood of martyrs "would be like
good seed sown in a prolific soil," noted the *Missionary Herald* in April 1827,
and Anderson urged Bird in June 1828—the latter having already abandoned a still living Asʿad in Mount Lebanon—to prepare speedily "a brief
memoir of Asaad Shidiak" for Sunday school that would constitute "a narrative more continuous and more popular in its form."[34]

⁂

Asʿad Shidyaq was martyred *before* he died. The Maronite patriarch sent
word to the Shidyaq family in late October 1830 that Asʿad had finally succumbed to a fever. His family observed the customary mourning period.
The emirs of Hadath offered their condolences, though Isaac Bird point-
edly did not.[35] In the time-honored tradition of Mount Lebanon, secular
and ecclesiastical notables came together to lay the tragedy of Asʿad Shidyaq
to rest. The Americans, however, refused to give up so easily, and encouraged by rumors that Asʿad was still alive, clung to their hope that he was enduring terrible persecution with "Christian meekness and patience."[36]

⁂

It would take an upheaval in the affairs of the Ottoman Empire to provide
the missionaries with conclusive news of Shidyaq's fate. The Greek revolt,
which had began the year Fisk and Parsons arrived in the Levant, and which
had served as the backdrop to the Asʿad Shidyaq affair, led to the independence of Greece in 1830, the same year that the U.S. government voted to
deport eastern Indians to the western banks of the Mississippi. Indeed the
embers of the Greek revolt, during which the Ottoman fleet had been destroyed at Navarino in 1827 by European navies, were still smoldering when

the ambitious Ottoman governor of Egypt, Mehmed Ali, openly rebelled against imperial authority and sent his son Ibrahim Pasha to invade Syria in 1831. The Ottoman Empire appeared to be on the brink of collapse. The missionaries, as usual, saw providential design unfolding, and a zealous Scottish merchant by the name of Robert Tod, who had followed the missionary accounts of As'ad Shidyaq, sought out the victorious Ibrahim Pasha.

From him he obtained approval to force the Maronite patriarch to reveal what he had done to the Protestant convert, the "persecuted brother" of the American missionary men.[37] At Acre, Ibrahim Pasha ordered Emir Bashir to provide Tod with an escort of troops, and with them the Scot marched to the distant monastery where As'ad had been imprisoned. But he was disappointed, for he found no trace of As'ad Shidyaq. Tod described how a frightened and now obsequious Maronite patriarch, in a "profuse and vapid manner," tried to deflect attention away from the question at hand. But at length Tod commanded the patriarch, "By authority from the Emeer Besheer I require at your hands Asaad Esh Shidiak."[38]

The patriarch insisted, under Tod's imperious interrogation, that As'ad had long since died of a fever. Tod refused this explanation, and in a letter, written in Arabic, to Faris Shidyaq asserted that "there is no doubt that the patriarch is his murderer."[39] Tod's account of his visit, which was published in the *Missionary Herald* in 1833, transformed a resounding defeat, the imprisonment of As'ad and the failure to persuade other Maronites thereafter to risk conversion, into a highly symbolic victory. That troops could be led by an evangelical Protestant into the heart of the Maronite patriarchate, that they could force the patriarch and his obsequious clergy to submit to a humiliating search, that they could brandish the authority of secular powers against the Maronites—all this momentarily turned on its head the balance of power that had thus far defined the tragedy of As'ad Shidyaq and set the stage for a foundational missionary story about the transformation of the East.

೮

Although As'ad was not publicly executed, although his suffering was not openly witnessed, despite the patriarch's avowal that Shidyaq died of a fever, and despite the fact that Qannubin was searched in vain by Tod, the missionaries and their sympathizers continued to insist that As'ad had met a martyr's fate. "The spirit he manifested," declared the *Missionary Herald* in

1833, "was that of a martyr."[40] Joseph Tracy, author of the first general history of the American Board, insisted that under torture, As'ad had died "a constant witness to the truth."[41] Jonas King claimed:"If he died because of the horrible sufferings in a dungeon, without door or window, or in a five by four cell with a small hole for a window, or if he was massacred by his inexorable persecutors—enemies of the truth of the Bible which they profess to believe in, we do not know. However it may have been, he was a veritable martyr, and rested firm in his faith till the very end."[42] And Rufus Anderson stated that "he must ever have an honorable place among the Christian martyrs of modern times."[43] Such professions of an exemplary martyrdom were most fully elaborated in several missionary hagiographies of As'ad, beginning with *A Memoir of Asaad esh Shidiak; An Arab young man of the Maronite Roman Catholic Church, in Syria* which went through several editions, but continuing with Tracy's and Anderson's mid-nineteenth-century testimonies, and culminating with the fullest versions in the late nineteenth century by Isaac Bird and Henry Harris Jessup.[44]

In both its early and later versions, the missionary commemoration of As'ad Shidyaq reflected, in part, the impulse evident at the founding of the American Board which treated the differences among human beings as ephemeral and upheld a notion of the underlying unity of all peoples. The remarkable elevation of As'ad from lowly native to suffering brother in Christ was a vindication of Leonard Woods's memorable exhortation to the very first missionaries of the American Board. "Learned and ignorant, refined and rude, honorable and base," the Andover professor had insisted in 1812, "are all on a level in point of accountableness to God and immortality of soul. Rise then above all the distinctions which misguide our judgments and our hearts, and seek the salvation of this *great family of immortals.*"[45] To describe him variously as a "Syrian Luther," "the first Protestant martyr," and the "Martyr of Lebanon," and to say of him that he was more "steadfast" than Thomas Cranmer, was also to confer on As'ad a signal honor of inclusion in a Protestant pantheon of saints that stretched back to Foxe's *Book of Martyrs.*[46] In this sense, although As'ad's story was reproduced within an established hagiographic tradition that dictated formulaic roles for Catholic persecutor and Protestant martyr, As'ad was unique among all natives who came into contact with the American Board missionaries. Never again would one be so generously referred to, so championed, and so sincerely respected.

Therein lay the problem, for undercutting this elevation was a simultaneous, and ultimately more powerful, reduction of As'ad Shidyaq to the role of native exemplar, "great for his age and his nation," as the *Missionary Herald* put it in May 1827.[47] For all their evangelical pieties about the oneness of man, the missionaries would not abandon their sense of cultural and religious superiority. The sanctuary of Bird's house, its evangelical order, its civilized and Christian habits, its location as an abode of missionary instruction, patience, and truth accentuated for the missionaries the absence of such values at the Maronite monastery of Qannubin. As'ad's betrayal by his family, the wailing of his mother, the violence of his elder brothers and his uncles, their deliberate handing over of As'ad to a persecuting church, as well as his own gentle demeanor in the face of all this, indicated for the missionaries the depraved Oriental setting as much as it evoked a more general and ancient Christian story of betrayal and persecution. The missionaries could not discard their practice of missionary work as transmission, not elaboration, of faith and as hierarchy, not fellowship.

As'ad Shidyaq's proper place was most obviously fixed among other famous native converts already familiar to the American missionary community, including the Hawaiian Henry Obookiah and the Cherokee Catherine Brown.[48] Whereas the memoirs of missionaries exemplified the fundamental significance of American Christianity, those written about the natives, whether Catherine Brown, Henry Obookiah, or As'ad Shidyaq— it mattered little who was the actual native—illustrated only the fundamental irrelevance of foreign culture. Whereas missionary memoirs written in the formulaic style of Jonathan Edwards's famous biography of David Brainerd exhorted Americans to live a more Christian life, those of natives assumed that that life was already being lived in America. Whereas memoirs of missionaries might have functioned as exercises in self-reflection and criticism, the memoirs of natives authored by missionaries encouraged an emergent sense of American destiny and confirmed a sense of tutelage over those the missionaries routinely called "hopeful converts" who were "but mere babes, who can digest nothing but milk, which must also be given in small quantities."[49] The sentimental death of the missionary underlined the vitality of evangelical American culture; the death of a convert, or in the case of Shidyaq his embellished martyrdom, underscored only the barrenness, not to say barbarity, of local culture. As'ad's own words, and the myriad documents in the possession of Isaac Bird and the American Board which painted an altogether different picture of the failed American missionary assault, were eclipsed by a representation of his tragedy that not only distorted the reality of the Ottoman Empire but also obscured that of the United States.

The martyrdom of As'ad Shidyaq was quickly added to the totality of American missionary interpretation that understood mission lands alone to be the objects of change. The structure, as well as the narrative, of the epic triumphalist histories of the American Board reflected this. Chapters progressed year by year and station by station, gradually covering huge swaths of the globe, from British India, to Hawaii, to the Ottoman Empire, to the American West following the forced removal of the Indian tribes from the southeastern states. The movement charted was always unidirectional, moving from center to periphery, from light to darkness, from civilized to savage, from white to nonwhite, in a word, from a Christian America to the unchristianized world.

Although this perspective on missionary expansion was evident from the first proclamation by the American Board of its intent to spread the Gospel to the world's heathen, the later-nineteenth-century histories of foreign missionary work were a great deal less antagonistic to the virulent racialist currents that dominated American politics, and ever more careful to segregate the tumult of American history from that of the heathen world. The profound changes in New England, the bitter struggle with the Unitarians, the disestablishment of the Congregational Church in Massachusetts in 1833, the anti-abolition and anti-Catholic riots that swept New York, Philadelphia, and Charlestown, including the burning of the Catholic Ursuline convent in 1834, were passed over in silence. Mission histories euphemistically explained away the precipitous closure in 1826 of the Foreign Mission School at Cornwall after the racist riot there in the aftermath of white-Indian marriages as simply a discontinued "experiment" that "had fully shown the importance of educating native assistants for the missions, in the countries where they are to labor."[50]

The utopian reworking of American society that found expression in the earliest American Board endeavors with foreign peoples, the notion of a redemptive mission to the world that would cleanse America of its notorious treatment of Indians and would justify the providential favor that graced the United States, was visibly muted as the century progressed. "May a gracious Providence," Evarts pleaded in 1829, "avert from this country the awful calamity of exposing ourselves to the wrath of heaven, as a consequence of disregarding the cries of the poor and defenceless, and perverting to purposes of cruelty and oppression, that power which was given to us to promote the happiness of our fellow-men."[51] The desperate battle waged by

American Board missionaries and Evarts to fight the expulsion of Indians from Georgia was in a sense the climax of this effort to reconcile the realities of American history with the ideals that inspired foreign missions.[52] So invested was Evarts in this conviction that American exceptionalism was a work in progress rather than an accomplished fact that he supported American Board missionaries in Georgia as they fought Indian removal all the way to the Supreme Court. The subsequent failure to prevent the mass deportations of Indians marked the end of an era, and with it the inevitable dwindling of interest in what was seen as a lost cause.[53]

The collapse of American Board work with Indians east of the Mississippi was reminiscent of the failure of John Eliot's Puritan mission. The effort of the American Board to position itself as the benevolent and evangelical intermediary between powerful, white civilization and "poor" Indians failed as decisively, and significantly, as had Eliot's attempt to position himself between English Puritans and the native objects of his mission, save now the scale was larger, the violence more official, and the perpetrators American rather than English. Even beyond the Mississippi, the missions to the surviving Cherokees and Choctaws were abandoned in 1859 amidst intense controversy about the relationship of the American Board to slavery.[54]

                                                        ⓡ

Rufus Anderson steered the American Board in the aftermath of the Indian Removal Act of 1830, and he became the chief advocate of an entirely evangelical, not civilizational, approach to mission work.[55] "There is light hanging over the future," he said in 1840. "There is light, too, abroad—in Syria, in Ceylon, in India, in the Sandwich Islands, and the other side of the Rocky Mountains. But here, in what we have fondly regarded as the Goshen of the world, the shadows thicken around us, and portend evil to all our institutions which depend on mere benevolence."[56] An apparent decline in revivalist religion in Boston, and a temporary mid-century diminishment of contributions to the American Board, emphasized the crucial and privileged ideological space won by overseas work.

Although Anderson, like many of his fellow American Board members, equivocated under severe abolitionist criticism for his refusal to take a firm public stance against slavery within the United States, he also oversaw the American Board's mid-century expansion across the globe.[57] Its missionaries were sent abroad to more stations than ever before in the 1830s, operating in West Africa, South Africa, Greece, Persia, India, Siam, China,

Singapore, Java, the Sandwich Islands, and the Ottoman Empire. The mission to Palestine that had been launched with two unmarried male missionaries in 1819 had by 1842 expanded into Syria and counted nine male missionaries, two physicians, a printer, nine female assistant missionaries, and six native helpers located in three stations.[58]

With this expansion came a more overt American, as opposed to English, stamp on the mission. A commercial treaty signed between the United States and the Ottomans in 1830 paved the way for a U.S. ambassadorial presence in Istanbul. The nearly decade-long Egyptian occupation of Syria between 1831 and 1840 had done little to hamper mission work; far from it, the first consul for the United States in Beirut was appointed in 1836, which coincided with, and furthered, a growing sense of entitlement on the part of missionaries to be protected directly by their own government.[59] American warships routinely called at Beirut, and American flags fluttered over missionary homes.

As the American Board became wealthier, more established, and more powerful, it also became more conservative politically and intellectually— as its mission numbers increased from a handful to over three hundred by mid-century, and notwithstanding intermittent financial crises, its revenues increased dramatically from less than $1,000 in 1811 to over $200,000 in 1841. In this surge the mission to "Palestine" had been renamed as one to "Western Asia," and included under its heading several autonomous missions, including one to "Syria" based in Beriut, and one to "Constantinople" in the imperial capital. By 1860 the Syria mission alone boasted nine stations, nine out-stations, eleven missionaries, a physician, a printer, fourteen female assistant missionaries, five native preachers, and thirty-six teachers and other native helpers.[60] Although the assimilationist fiction of a benevolent "Christian America" had been exposed at home, it was maintained abroad.

≈

Joseph Tracy's officially sanctioned *History of the American Board of Commissioners for Foreign Missions,* first published in 1840, was emblematic of this shift in the meaning and location of America's exceptional role in the world. From an emanation of a blessed, but imperfect, America whose fate was bound up with the conversion of the wider world, the mission became defined by an exaltation of national purity.[61] The ongoing debacle of the Indian deportations tempered but did not contradict the mission narrative

Figure 7. Early Missionaries 1. Rev. and Mrs. J. Edwards Ford; 2. Mrs. George E. Post; 3. Rev. and Mrs. William Bird; 4. Rev. and Mrs. Eli Smith; 5. Rev. and Mrs. J. L. Lyons; 6. Rev. and Mrs. D. Bliss; 7. Dr. and Mrs. H. A. De Forest. Source: Henry H. Jessup, *Fifty-Three Years in Syria*, vol. 1 (New York: Fleming H. Revell Company, 1910), 51a (opposite 51).

Tracy chronicled. The first sentence of the first chapter set the tone of a glorious unbroken missionary history and laid the foundation for an enduring narrative of disinterested missionary benevolence that at once legitimated settler colonialism and at the same time disavowed its most obvious aspect: to dispossess the natives. "The first settlement of New England was a missionary enterprise," Tracy declared, adding that the "Pilgrims were the pioneers of the Protestant World, in their attempts to convert the heathen of foreign lands."[62] As had Mather, Tracy declared that King Philip's War was not provoked "by any injustice or injury received from the colonists." But while he did concede that Philip of Pokanoket had "resolved to exterminate the Europeans," he pointed out that it was a natural for the Indian chief to resist Puritan encroachment.[63]

Tracy was clearly cognizant of the still ongoing cruelty toward the Cherokees, and he openly indicted "the unprincipled white men" who relentlessly sabotaged the underlying promise of missionary America.[64] "The doctrine that Indians cannot be civilized," Tracy wrote, "is the mistake of men who are ignorant of history, or the slander of those who covet their lands."[65] His condemnation of the "people of Georgia" highlighted more than a regional tension between a glorified New England and aggressive southern states: it compared what was a foundational, necessary, divinely inspired, and inevitable dispossession of native Americans in the Puritan period with a nineteenth-century despoliation that seemed naked in its materialism and unjustifiable in its opportunism.[66] As spurious as this contrast may have been from a native perspective, it was utterly important for Tracy, as for Evarts before him, to distinguish between the two bouts of settler colonialism, for the former supposedly embodied the essence of Christian America, the latter its betrayal.

Yet whereas Jeremiah Evarts had died disillusioned at the treatment of the native Americans, and had grappled with the implications of white avarice for the meaning of America, Tracy's history would brook no such despair. No sooner was the cruel treatment of the Indians noted than it was superseded by tales of valiance and the ongoing perseverance of white American missionaries both at home and even more so abroad. They and they alone remained at the center of a redemptive history that with each passing year pushed the Indians ever more to the margins. Some missionaries moved west with the remnants of the Indians, restarting the work of civilization and Christianization as if the uprooting of natives had never taken place; others expanded the frontiers of American Christianity in Africa, Asia, and the Pacific islands. For Tracy, the modest beginnings of the American

Board, when Samuel J. Mills, reared on the stories of Eliot and Brainerd "and of other missionaries to the heathen,"[67] was inspired in the fall of 1807 to pray with fellow students Gordon Hall and James Richards beside a haystack in the middle of an open field at Williams College, presaged an epic story of American progress.

ھ

It was fitting, then, that the second edition of Tracy's *History* would conclude in the year 1841 by recounting overseas events in the Sandwich Islands and Syria, especially the outbreak of sectarian violence in Mount Lebanon in 1841 between Maronites and Druzes. The disturbances occurred in the immediate aftermath of a British-led campaign to evict the Egyptian occupiers of Syria and to restore the "legitimate" authority of the sultan. Ottoman rule was reestablished, but it was subject to the incessant interference of European powers and to an internally driven Ottoman reformation. If the problem in America was how to integrate disparate people and denominations into a single expanding republic, in the Ottoman Empire a similar problem arose from a different angle: how to prevent an imperial system, with its enormous geographic, cultural, and religious diversity, from fragmenting. The imperial state, in other words, wanted to promote a unifying identity that could transcend previously privileged local, religious, and ethnic affiliations. This reordering of the empire, or the *Tanzimat* as it became known, constituted an ideological revolution that in its broadest sense spanned the entire century.

The problem that plagued the Ottoman Empire was that European powers, particularly Britain but also France and Russia, constantly intervened in its internal affairs, each power claiming to defend one or another oppressed community in the empire, each suspicious of the motives of the other. The Ottomans may have been sovereign, but they ruled in the shadow of Western hegemony. It was the English navy, after all, that ended the Egyptian occupation of, and restored the Ottomans to, Syria in 1840. It was this same navy that had transported Bashir Shihab, who had turned a blind eye to the persecution of As'ad Shidyaq and who had collaborated with the Egyptian occupation, into exile.

In the resultant power vacuum in Mount Lebanon, a new culture of sectarianism took shape, further eating away at the social order of the old regime. Christian villagers demanded freedom from their Druze lords, insisting that they had the right to be ruled only by Christian lords. The

Druzes demanded what they insisted were their ancient privileges of land and the subordination of commoners. Both sides believed that Ottoman reform and European powers legitimated their position, and both were encouraged by contradictory promises and pledges given to them by English agents and Ottoman officials. In such unsettled circumstances, a fracas between Maronites and Druzes turned deadly and led in 1841 to the first sectarian clashes between and among Maronite and Druze communities. The Maronite patriarch was still Yusuf Hubaysh, and as sympathetic as he may have been with the Maronite villagers in the southern districts, he urged an end to the fighting on the basis that "the position of each be respected according to his rank."[68]

Because of the As'ad Shidyaq affair, and because of the ongoing hostility of the Maronite Church to the American mission, the American missionary stations in Mount Lebanon were located in the southern, Druze-controlled districts; the missionaries were consequently on far more familiar terms with Druze notables than with Maronites, and it is among the former throughout the 1830s that they had hoped to win mass conversions. Tracy, working with documents evidently supplied by American missionaries on the ground such as Eli Smith and William Thomson (Isaac and Ann Bird having returned to America in 1836), construed the complex events in far simpler terms. He took his readers right back to the familiar moral terrain surrounding the martyrdom of As'ad Shidyaq.

With obvious relish, Tracy related the demise of the same Maronite patriarch who had so bitterly persecuted the famous Maronite convert. Having already reproduced the basic missionary account of Shidyaq's tribulations, Tracy insisted that when British-backed Ottoman rule was restored to Syria and Mount Lebanon in 1840, Patriarch Hubaysh, whom he portrayed as bigoted and venal, had attempted once more "to expel the American mission, and to crush the Druzes, who were disposed to receive their instruction." He had instigated a "crusade" against the Druzes, who had reacted, "rather desperately," with a furious defense.[69] "How signally has the blood of the martyred Asaad," Eli Smith himself said at the time, "been avenged upon him even in this life."[70]

Tracy's description reflected a fleeting mid-century sympathy for the Druzes of southern Mount Lebanon, the heterodox community which the missionaries embraced in the wake of the Shidyaq affair, and which they curiously identified as an "excrescence of Mohammedanism" with "a free and independent spirit in the midst of despotism."[71] Although within two decades this overt sympathy with the Druzes would be entirely reversed, for now it conformed perfectly to the perennial American missionary trope of the eager heathen, the noble savage who awaited, indeed called out for, salvation at the hands of the missionaries. "If the 'Macedonian cry' is ever uttered by those who have no knowledge of the gospel," said Anderson of the Druzes in 1840, for example, "it was by that people."[72] As Tracy would have it, the year closed with the patriarch's power "broken." Amidst a ravaged landscape of destroyed Maronite villages and ransacked churches, thousands of Maronites turned for help to the Americans and now "cursed him [the patriarch] for bringing ruin upon themselves and their families."[73]

৺

The arrival of the missionary William Benton, a graduate of the Theological Institute of Connecticut, and his wife, Loanza, to reinforce the Syria mission in 1847 reflected on the ground what Tracy described from a vast distance: a vindication abroad of an American missionary purity greatly challenged at home. "The whole world," Loanza confided in her remarkably intimate diary on 4 July 1848, "has reason to rejoice in the independence of America. How much light and truth have been sent from there to all the dark corners of the earth. . . . O that our free country were free from the stain of slavery and war."[74] The heady era of evangelism, when the redemption of Indians was an integral aspect of the American Board's vision to redeem America and the world, was coming to a close and being replaced by a harder, more nationalist evangelical racialism that would define American mission work in the post-1860 era. The Bentons, more than any other missionaries in Syria, captured this moment of transformation—and ultimately fell afoul of it. William, like members of the first generation of missionaries, had read the life of David Brainerd. At Williams College he had been inspired by hearing of Jonas King, then a missionary in Greece, and listening to a lecture by Henry Bingham of Sandwich Islands fame. Both he and Loanza loved the idea of America but also drew back from a reckless embrace of it.

Loanza's grandfather had been taken captive by Indians in western Massachusetts in 1746; she herself had initially wanted to work in the "western wilds to labor for dark savages" in emulation of her sister, who evangelized among relocated Choctaws.[75] That she recognized the paradox of a "free country" that condoned slavery and colonial expansion, and that she often juxtaposed references to the "poor Choctaws" and the "poor Arabs," the "poor mountaineers," or most routinely the "females of Syria," whom she described as a "poor ignorant and oppressed race of beings," recalled the sensibility of the original American missionaries, for whom the Indians were the archetypal heathen, but also alluded to the unhappy fate that so many of them had suffered since the turn of the century. It recalled, too, the work of the first wife of Eli Smith, Sarah Smith, who had died in 1836. She was famous among missionaries for her dedication to the education of Syrian women; she was also horrified at, and vigorously protested, Indian removal in the United States, and often compared her work with the Syrians with missionary work to the Indians, both of whom, she said, "have long dwelt in ignorance and insensibility."[76]

The Bentons were significantly less seized with millennial urgency than was the first generation of missionaries to the Levant but were as steeped in its paternalistic language. Despite their initial lack of Arabic, like Pliny Fisk and Levi Parsons three decades earlier, they did not hesitate to condemn the culture and morals of the natives among whom they worked. It came as effortlessly to them as did their easy denunciations of Muslims— followers of the "notorious imposter," said Loanza—or Eastern Christians, whose religion William Benton described as "encased in superstitious customs, and fatigued by the traditions of ages."[77] Just as their brethren in China were unable to compromise with their Chinese environment, but in a setting markedly less coercive, these missionaries dressed as if still in New England, wore no jewelry, and furnished their homes with rocking chairs, white curtains, and iron bedsteads, or what Loanza referred to as "tokens of civilization."[78]

But in other respects, the Bentons were different from most other missionaries. Unlike many of their peers who lived in Beirut or in larger cities, the Bentons, after a sojourn in Aleppo, settled in a small village called Bhamdun in Mount Lebanon. There they were protected by the local Druze leaders and elders. Loanza in particular gained local repute for her confidence in prescribing medications. In Bhamdun they both learned Arabic, and raised their children to become fluent in it as well.

胤

A picture of mid-century American benevolence overseas, the Bentons became fully committed to ministering to a tiny community of converted Christians and evangelizing the Druzes, in whom Rufus Anderson had put so much hope. From their outpost five hours' distance from Beirut, they could take solace from the fact that the mission had firmly established itself

Figure 8. Burj Bird, the Old Mission House built in 1833 by Rev. Isaac Bird. Photo taken in 1863. Source: Henry H. Jessup, *Fifty-three Years in Syria,* vol. 1 (New York: Fleming H. Revell Company, 1910), 42a (opposite 42).

in that city. An American missionary press, which had been established in Beirut in 1834, became active in the 1840s; a native church was founded there in 1848, followed by Ottoman legal recognition in 1850 of Protestantism in the empire. Tensions remained, of course. The eastern churches, and a revived Jesuit mission thoroughly alarmed by the spread of Protestant influence, continued to fret about the presence of so many American missionaries. By and large, however, the intercourse between the Americans and their immediate environment was far more regular, and far less confrontational, than when Pliny Fisk and Levi Parsons had first entered these lands.

The Bentons wanted to believe that on As'ad Shidyaq's martyrdom a pure evangelical church might yet be built. So adamant were they that their small outpost offered excellent prospects for proselytizing, they defied their missionary peers in Beirut who believed that the station was too small, and that American families should not live alone. William and Loanza were at length instructed to close their station and consolidate with other missionaries. They rejected the views of their missionary brethren, and so in 1859 they were ordered by the American Board to return to the United States. The Bentons refused. "I am inclined," wrote William defiantly to his brother, "to jeopardize my connection with the Board rather than my obligations to preach Christ and him crucified upon this mountain."[79]

≈

As this missionary scandal was unfolding, unknown to the small native Protestant community, the traditional social order of Mount Lebanon was unraveling. The collapse of the Shihabite emirate in 1840 had been followed by a European-inspired partition of Mount Lebanon and by Ottoman reform in 1856 which declared the equality of Muslims and non-Muslims in the "civilized" eyes of the Ottoman sultan. Some Maronite villagers yearned to be free of what they now called "Druze" rule, and in turn, Druze lords resented what they considered the uppity behavior on the part of their erstwhile subordinates. A revolt by Christian peasants in the northern part of Mount Lebanon against their own Christian lords in 1859 stoked sectarian tensions in the southern part, where the majority of landowners were Druze and many, if not the majority, of the villagers were Christian. The missionaries could certainly sense the unsettled situation, for all their stations in Mount Lebanon were located in the Druze districts. In late May 1860 an incident set off general fighting between Maronites and Druzes, which the American missionary William Thomson perceptively described as "simply a rising of the *people* against the wishes of the ruling classes on all sides."[80]

The Druzes carried the day, routing the disorganized Maronites. They pillaged entire villages in Mount Lebanon and ransacked many homes, including that of Asʿad Shidyaq's brother Tannus. By the end of June the Druzes had committed several unprecedented massacres of Christian villagers and townsfolk in Dayr al-Qamar and Hasbayya. The confusion and panic of the war forced most American missionaries and their families to abandon Mount Lebanon and seek the safety of Beirut and the European gunboats lying just offshore.

The Bentons stayed put in Bhamdun and relied on the protection of neighboring Druze shaykhs; most other missionaries assembled in Beirut, rattled by rumors of an impending massacre of Christians in the city. They abandoned their earlier view that the war was the result of a local, if destructive, contest for supremacy between Druzes and Maronites. Instead they now perceived the events as signaling a broader "natural" Muslim hatred of all things Christian which imperiled the entirety of civilization in the East. One missionary wrote that "as in the wars of savages, as when wild beasts have been let loose upon lambs, so have the Druzes and Mohammedans joined in mercilessly slaking their thirst in the blood of Christians."[81] Henry Harris Jessup warned that the massacre of Christians was of horrific proportions, "in the same character with Cawnpore and Delhi."[82] So terrified were the missionaries by the "moral perverseness, heartlessness and cruelty which have characterized the Moslems" that Jessup wished for any other government "rather than endure this imbecile and wicked Turkish rule any longer."[83] A separate massacre of Christian subjects in Damascus at the hands of a Muslim mob occurred in July and seemed to confirm American fears.[84]

From objects of solicitude and great hope between the 1830s and 1850s, the Druzes had in an instant become for most missionaries the incarnation of satanic Muslim fury. The Bentons, however, having remained in Bhamdun, and having refused to leave their native converts, would not scapegoat the Druzes. They tried in vain to correct the impression that the war being fought was a "religious war," and instead, sympathetic to the Druze shaykhs with whom they coexisted, pointed out that it was the Druzes who fought to defend themselves in what amounted to a vicious struggle over land.

※

Europe was appalled by the outrages committed against Christians. So too was a deeply embarrassed Ottoman sultan. Both the French and the Ottomans rushed separate armies to pacify Mount Lebanon and Damascus. A

European-dominated ("international") commission of inquiry was established, the first of its kind, to investigate the massacres. In Mount Lebanon, Ottoman authorities sentenced practically the entire Druze leadership to death (though, in the end, these sentences were not carried out) despite the fact that they, and many of the international commissioners, agreed that the Maronites were also to blame. In Damascus, the Ottoman military rounded up scores of alleged rioters, summarily tried them, and had them shot or hanged. Jessup was thrilled when he heard that Beirut had been occupied by six thousand French troops. "The Moslems are humbled to the dust," he exclaimed in reporting the executions of Muslims in Damascus.[85] William Benton, however, recoiled at what he regarded as a cynical Ottoman appeasement of "the wrath of Christendom." He asked his American peers a frank question: "The Lord gave them [the Druzes] a fearful victory and now we welcome the armies of Europe to ask and demand the rights of the conquered Christians; But suppose the scene exchanged; had the Christians accomplished their most unchristian design 'Not to leave a Druse alive on Lebanon,—who would have asked after the rights of the poor heathen Druses? Who?"[86]

The entire mission project lay exposed by the question of one isolated missionary; therefore his letters remained confidential and his view ignored. He and his wife believed sincerely that they belonged in Mount Lebanon, and that for all their sins, the Druzes could yet be saved. As long as the board was willing to let things be, he and his wife were willing to continue with their labor, for as Loanza wrote to the board, "We beg you, urge us no more to return to the U[nited] States—we have put our hand to the plough and with us there is no turning back, while we have life and health to labor for the poor Arabs of Lebanon."[87]

వ౩

Henry Harris Jessup was by far the mission's most preeminent American chronicler. For him there was no question of the enormous changes that had been wrought over nearly a hundred years of missionary work. Just as the United States had been transformed beyond recognition following the abolition of slavery and the transportation revolution, so too had the Ottoman Empire, and specifically Ottoman Beirut, drastically changed as a result of the *Tanzimat,* notwithstanding the massacres of 1860.

The center of the Syria mission went from being a small town of roughly five thousand at the turn of the nineteenth century to a modern capital of

Figure 9. Henry H. Jessup, 1855. Source: Henry H. Jessup, *Fifty-three Years in Syria*, vol. 1 (New York: Fleming H. Revell Company, 1910), 30a (opposite 30).

a newly created imperial province in 1888 with a population closer to a hundred thousand; it was linked not only by a modern carriage road to Damascus and by telegraph to Istanbul but also by steamships to Europe. A new municipality, new building codes, new neighborhoods, and an urban layout with widened and more "regular" streets, conspicuous mansions, kerosene lighting, a quarantine and harbor, and above all a vibrant mix of peoples and nationalities, came to define a city that was home to the most important American missionary institution in the Ottoman Empire, the Syrian Protestant College, which had been founded in 1866. The college was independent of the American Board, which four years later transferred its Syrian mission to the Presbyterian Board of Foreign Missions.[88]

Dress, food, furniture, architecture: everything that defined the city and its inhabitants was obviously changed. The 1860 crisis, if nothing else, had galvanized Ottoman and Western interest in Beirut and Mount Lebanon and prompted an outpouring of Western Christian sympathy for the Christian victims of the massacres. New missionary societies and charitable agencies from Germany and Great Britain arrived to assist refugees and orphans, marking a new, expanded phase of Protestant missionary work in the region.[89] A new Arabic press, urban literary circles, anarchist movements, Western tourists, Ottoman governors, prying European consuls, French Jesuits, and reformist Muslim intellectuals defined the contours of a vibrant American Protestant missionary world. In 1865 American missionaries and their Arab assistants completed a new Arabic translation of the Bible. In 1897 there were, according to Jessup, seventeen thousand children (of whom eight thousand were girls) in Protestant schools in Syria and Palestine, five orphanages, and thirty-six hospitals and dispensaries. In Syria alone there were 150 American schools.[90]

The explicitly illiberal first flush of American evangelism, utterly out of place in the Ottoman Empire, had metamorphosed into a far more *outwardly* accommodating sense of mission very much in keeping with the late empire. As much as both Americans and their Maronite opponents still distrusted each other, the metaphorical war of annihilation that had marked the outset of the encounter had long since been overtaken by an intense competition among Americans, European Protestants, Jesuits, Arabs, and Ottomans to dominate, or at least profit from, a distinctive, multinational and multireligious Ottoman modernity.

It was this progress, and an interpretation of its monocultural Western, and specifically Anglo-American, origin, that Jessup unabashedly celebrated in his history of the American Board presence in Ottoman Syria. Published in 1910 in two volumes, the 795 pages of *Fifty-Three Years in Syria* moved chronologically and thematically across the nineteenth century; from Beirut as a small, insignificant walled provincial town to a major city that boasted an enormously successful mission; from the "utter stagnation" of Syria intellectually to an educational renaissance embodied by the missionaries; from the oppression of women to their gradual emancipation; and above all, from obdurate native fanaticism to the undisputed triumph of American benevolence.

Like the enormously popular account *The Land and the Book* by his fellow missionary William Thomson, Jessup's work was in equal parts ethnography and history, detailing the customs and manners of the natives. But far more deliberately than Thomson's account, *Fifty-Three Years in Syria* also chronicled the great strides made by missionaries in the East to uplift, educate, and civilize the myriad men and women who inhabited the ancient lands of the Bible. In other words, Jessup made missionary work synonymous with enlightenment, science, and an American modernity which, he believed, had made great inroads into, and would inevitably triumph over, the supposedly stagnant, sectarian, and segregated landscape of antagonistic religious communities in the Ottoman Empire.

＊

As part of this broader civilizational narrative, Jessup modernized the story of As'ad Shidyaq. For him, As'ad's fate represented much more than the difficulties faced by mission or the sufferings of a native martyr. It constituted a vindication of a modern Protestant civilization in confrontation with an antiquated Orient, which could have been anticipated from the outset of American missionary work in a hopelessly stagnant land. The basic outline of the drama was culled from earlier iterations. Jessup's *Fifty-Three Years* referred readers for details to Isaac Bird's *Martyr of Lebanon,* published nearly a half-century earlier in 1864 by the American Tract Society, which itself essentially reproduced and elaborated the same stereotypes, the same edited snippets of dialogue that originally appeared in the *Missionary Herald.*[91] The patriarch remains a caricature of himself; As'ad retains his evangelical purity, and the Americans their disinterested benevolence.

A graduate of Union Theological Seminary, Jessup and his wife arrived in Beirut in 1856, together with the future founder of the Syrian Protestant College, Daniel Bliss, and his wife, Abby. In Jessup's interpretation of their work, his generation of missionaries (with the exception of William and

Loanza Benton, who are scarcely mentioned in his history) provided a seamless continuity with the venerated first generation of "pioneer" missionaries—Levi Parsons, Pliny Fisk, Isaac Bird, William Goodell, and Jonas King—with whom the name of Asʿad Shidyaq was indelibly linked. Thus the death of the first Arab convert to American Protestantism, whom Jessup referred to as the "proto-martyr of modern Syria," exemplified in his account the unreformed moral condition of the peoples of the East, their bigotry and superstition, and also their premodern stasis. The avatars of modernity clashed with those who recalled the "Spanish Inquisition."[92] It was not simply that Asʿad Shidyaq died "from disease induced by the dreadful filth of his narrow cell, and the torments of those who visited the convent," or that he was killed for his beliefs. His fate epitomized the stakes of this encounter: a clash between the Muslim-dominated East and a now global Protestant civilization, but also between entirely different moments of time on a continuum of human progress. The East, as fellow missionary Cyrus Hamlin declared, was "centuries in the rear."[93]

This temporal disjuncture between Protestantism and Islam was confirmed in the eyes of nineteenth-century missionaries by the outbreak of the infamous 1860 war. The cruelty of Yusuf Hubaysh of the 1820s was cut from the same cloth as that of the Druzes in 1860, which in turn was understood to be part of the broader fanaticism of the Eastern world, where, said missionary James L. Barton, "all religion is racial."[94]

Jessup drew on his own vivid recollections as well as on the polemical work of a British resident, former officer, and self-declared expert on local manners and customs, Charles Churchill, to recount a gripping and even poignant history of how missionaries and their native helpers survived the ferocious sectarian violence that he alleged was stoked by Ottoman Turkish malice and innate Muslim bigotry. To William Benton's question about who would have cared for the Druzes had they been victims, he had no answer, and more to the point, he had no need to give one, for Benton had been dismissed by the American Board in 1861 for his allegedly disordered mind. The true significance of "Massacre Summer" was, for Jessup, less in its details than in the manner in which the carnage, and the era that followed it, were related as thesis and antithesis.

The thesis was basic: these massacres were symptomatic of a "native" Oriental world inherently segregated by religion and race, and unable to modernize of its own accord. The violence the Druzes and Muslims enacted was, for Jessup, utterly incomprehensible in modern terms. It was certainly, for him, incomparable to anything that had occurred in America, which was itself in 1860, of course, on the brink of civil war, and which had by then a well-documented history of religious and race riots, to say nothing of slavery and the massacres of Indians. Rather, the sectarian horrors that transpired in Mount Lebanon and Damascus illustrated for the missionaries how a premodern native world prodded down the path of enlightenment would lash out, much as the Indian sepoys allegedly had in 1857, or the Jamaicans would in Morant Bay in 1865, in an enraged but ultimately futile burst of atavistic *native* fury—"heathen rage," as Jessup put it in 1884.[95]

The antithesis was equally basic: this primitive native violence constituted a turning point in the mission story, for in the aftermath of these providential massacres a new enlightened missionary age was inaugurated. "The Arabic Testament just completed," Jessup recalled in 1884, "was ready to be carried . . . all over the land. Schools were in demand. All the leading literary and religious institutions of Syria date back to that era of upheaval and change. Then began in fact a new life of modern Syria. The hand of God was breaking up the old and preparing for the new. Seminaries, colleges, hospitals, printing presses and journals began to appear in the reconstructed towns and cities of that year of massacre and ruin, and the popular mind was awakened from the sleep of ages."[96] The upshot for Jessup was that there was no coexistence in this empire save that which the missionaries enabled through their many American educational institutions. Toleration, which had once been anathema to the American Board missionaries, and so obviously a feature of the Ottoman system to be exploited, had now become a missionary mantra.[97]

సా

Such a self-consciously modern Christian enlightenment of the sort advocated by Jessup was defined most basically in opposition to Oriental Christianity and Islam. From the outset of the Syria mission, Americans had collectively differentiated themselves from the "natives." By Jessup's time, however, this differentiation was represented not simply religiously and culturally, as had first been the case, but racially, scientifically, and above all temporally. The original millennial enthusiasm, which had bound missionaries and heathen together in a race against time rapidly running its course, was superseded by a modern enthusiasm according to which certain advanced races were destined to lead backward races, while other vanquished races were doomed to extinction. The outlook of the missionaries, in other words, was measured not so much in terms of contemporary American theological debates as in juxtaposition abroad with what Jessup regarded as backward, ignorant, and intolerant natives. Issues that most charged domestic American Christians, and that divided liberal Protestants from more conservative ones, revolved around the role of Christianity in national life, biblical literalism, immigration, and the social gospel.[98] These were moot in the multinational, multiethnic, and multireligious setting of late Ottoman Beirut, in which Americans thrived but never dominated.

What was not moot were questions of imperialism and colonialism. In an era of Western empire which often rejected outright the very notion of saving savages, American Protestant missionaries counted themselves the indispensable representatives of an ascendant, exceptional, and benevolent Christian America. They were willing and able to lead the sturdiest of inferior native nations toward modern Protestant civilization and Christianization, which they believed was most gloriously embodied in the United States. For Jessup and others of the Syria mission, this meant rescuing the Arabs from themselves and recasting the significance of the Asʿad Shidyaq affair as a tale of progress, not at the points of bayonets, as was the case in many colonial locales, but by unadulterated benevolent missionary example.

The Shidyaq affair unfolded at a time when the people of Syria, according to Jessup, suffered a native "treatment of the insane [that] was cruel beyond belief. They were beaten, chained, confined in damp, dark dungeons, or given over to priests who professed to exorcise the demons by cruel torture in the dark cavern of the Convent of Kozheiya in Northern Lebanon."[99] Since that time the American Board had sent to Syria medical missionaries, whom Julius Richter, the German chronicler of Protestant missions, describes as "avenging in a noble manner the death of Asad."[100] The evangelically minded Protestant community had also built hospitals and founded, under the direction of the Swiss Protestant Theophilus Waldmeier, the famous Asfuriya hospital for the insane in 1897, on whose executive committee Jessup sat. The hospital was open to all communities and run on the most modern of principles, with an isolation ward, a clinic, and a wash-house in a "salubrious, cheerful, and attractive site." The Maronite Church, which had done so much to stifle the Protestant mission, at length even sent its own to be cured there.[101]

Moreover, during Asʿad's time, Jessup claimed, women were allegedly the stronghold of superstition; now many among them were the transformed objects of missionary feminism. "Mohammedanism," Jessup wrote, "had blighted womanhood."[102] But the axe had been laid at the root of the tree, as missionary Eli Smith said, alluding to Matthew 3:10, and referring specifically to the missionary education of Arab women.[103] Smith's first wife, Sarah, had been instrumental in opening a regular girl's school in 1834 in Beirut. As best as Jessup could see, therefore, across the land women's education in the missions was flourishing, and steadily the cult of domesticity was prevailing. Even Muslims, he noted with smug satisfaction, acknowledged the need for female education. From the first, of course, the missionaries had prided themselves on their emphasis on female education and on the ordered homes that missionary wives kept. But what had been an account of civilization as a process of evangelical trial and hardship in Jessup's hands became a paean to the evangelical work of a racialized national civilization. Doubt was replaced by supreme confidence, which Jessup illustrated in his major treatise on the missionary uplift of "Arab" women titled *Women of the Arabs.*[104]

In it, he extensively praised Sarah Smith and quoted her own words about the pioneering role that "American females" played in the regeneration of their "poor sisters" around the world. But whereas Sarah Smith had complained about the lack of children's literature, the lack of hygiene, the domestic poverty of Syrian families, Jessup boasted about the "great changes" that had since overcome Syria. He provided brief biographies of Syrian women who had been, as he intimated, evangelized and civilized—modern native females who replicated the example set by Sarah Smith and other American missionary wives, and who built homes where "affection, decorum, and Christian refinement" reigned. Sarah Bistany, daughter of Mrs. Smith's native "protégée" who had been taken in by the American and so, gratefully, named her daughter after her, even died a sentimental death. Her sober, dignified funeral was attended by a "great concourse of people of all sects, and the Protestant chapel was crowded."[105] The contrast with Asʿad Shidyaq's fatherless Arab family, in which brother betrayed brother and an uneducated, ignorant, and superstitious mother had raised children in the same vein, could not have been greater. Jessup firmly believed that a "sanctified Christian civilization" was slowly and inevitably going to dissipate the Oriental domestic depravity which had prevailed at the time of the missionaries' first encounter with Asʿad Shidyaq.

The detail with which Jessup could describe the transformation of Arab women was evidence of an increase in the supposedly scientific knowledge of the Orient and of Islam among resident missionaries. Eli Smith had joined Edward Robinson, who had also studied at Andover, in an attempt to make biblical archaeology in Palestine and Syria in the 1830s an objective, dispassionate object of study—a "better guide than any native" one could find on the spot, proclaimed mission apologist Thomas Laurie.[106] And now Jessup and others, such as Samuel Zwemer, tried to do the same for the study of Islam. Jessup became famous in American missionary circles for his knowledge of Islam, and for his commitment to proselytizing Muslims directly.[107] He read the Quran, and he quoted its various verses to prove his own objectivity. The Quran, he insisted, "is a gem of Arab poetry, but like a gem, crystalline and unchanging. . . . Every reform in government, toleration, and material improvement in the Turkish Empire, Persia, and Egypt, is made in spite of the Koran and contrary to its spirit."[108] His recognition of the "element of divine truth which Mohammed derived from the Old and New Testaments, and which runs like a vein of gold through that extraordinary book, the Koran," underscored a more liberal, but not more conciliatory, attitude toward Islam.[109] For Jessup, knowledge of Islam was essential for its systematic undermining, and to bring to a conclusion the epic battle of missionary Christianity against Islam. Exactly like fellow American missionaries James L. Barton and Cyrus Hamlin, he was far more comfortable in the Muslim world, and certainly more intimate with Islam, than his predecessors had been. At the same time, he remained committed to what Barton described as the "Christian conquest of Islam."[110]

๙

By the time Jessup recorded his reminiscences, a far more general American engagement with the Middle East had begun, one that included tourists, most famously Mark Twain, landscape artists, and those who believed in the imminent realization of prophecies centered around the restoration of Jews to Palestine, but, crucially, who exhibited little concern for the presence or welfare of the Arab population of the region. "This Holy Land," Jessup noted wryly, "is the happy hunting-ground of cranks and visionaries of all stripes, Oriental and Occidental."[111] The Syrian Protestant College hosted a regular stream of distinguished American visitors, including Teddy Roosevelt. Jessup was himself nominated to become ambassador to Persia. And Daniel Bliss, who headed the Syrian Protestant College, realized by 1869 how settled the missionaries and their families had become, confessing: "We often wish our boys could be brought up on a farm. There is nothing here for them to do. There is a danger of their becoming in feeling aristocrats. They are so much above the natives about them."[112]

The missionaries, to be sure, still enjoyed the fellowship of British and other European evangelists. They continued to identify with the British

Empire, especially after the British conquest of Egypt in 1882, and in op-position to the "Oriental" world, divided by missionary cartography and reports into Arab and Armenian, Greek and Nestorian, Jewish and Mo-hammedan "races" separated collectively from an increasingly pronounced white "Anglo-Saxon" Protestant race. They also still spoke about light and darkness, Christianity and corruption, evangelism and profanity. But the consistency of missionary rhetoric masked a major shift in the thinking of American missionaries in the later nineteenth century away from the Em-pire of God and toward a fuller embrace of the secular American empire of Anglo-Saxon men and women.[113] Mission work, consequently, was marked by a nearly total and uncritical identification with the United States as it annexed Hawaii, expanded across the West, and subjugated the Philippines.

The missionaries of Syria became far more assertively American. Jessup, for one, hailed the technological progress he claimed Americans introduced into the East, from kerosene oil and lamps to the steam printing press, the camera, iron construction beams, wire nails, sewing machines, parlor organs, the mimeograph, typewriters, dentistry, and the Morse telegraph appara-tus.[114] In *Fifty-Three Years in Syria,* Jessup especially praised and provided il-lustrations of the Syrian Protestant College, which more than any other institution in the empire represented America in its most modern, scientific, and Protestant array. Jessup even made a model of the campus, with its many buildings and its medical school, to represent what America had done for western Asia. He sent it to the 1904 St. Louis World's Fair, which com-memorated the centenary of the Louisiana Purchase. There Jessup's model, in a mahogany and plate glass case, won a gold medal, and vied for atten-tion alongside sculptures that chartered the story of the "disappearance" of the Indian from America and exhibits of "dusky little" Filipino soldiers, whose country had just been the scene of brutal repression by occupying American forces.[115]

The Ely Volume, a massive apologetic for the role of missions in the mod-ern world and their contributions to "scientific" achievement, authored by a onetime missionary to the Nestorians, Thomas Laurie, was typical in this nationalist regard. In a chapter titled "National Regeneration," it reveled in the notion that "American ideas lift up the different races into higher in-telligence, and induce the governments to grant them greater freedoms." But it also pleaded for a better appreciation of the nationalist return on the American missionary investment. "The entire cost of the work of the Board in Turkey, Syria included, up to 1879, was only about $5,000,000, while the subjugation of a handful of Modocs by our government cost one hundred lives and $6,000,000. Do foreign missions pay?" it asked rhetorically.[116] The American missionary resident in Constantinople, James L. Barton, in turn enthusiastically quoted from Lord Cromer and justified missionary work among the "sturdy races" of the Ottoman Empire. "Race survival there was under the law of the survival of the fittest," he wrote, with an oblique reference to a widespread American belief in the inevitability of the eradication of the Indians before a superior white American civilization.[117] And whereas Sarah Smith, who was the principal focus of Jessup's homage to missionary labor among the women of the Arabs, wrote extensively in the mid-1830s about the responsibility of American churches to uplift both Arabs and Indians, and linked national guilt with the guilt of a lost world, Jessup saw little reason to adopt so modest an attitude. The mission to the millions of the "noble" and "vast undying race" of Arabs was the great cause at hand, not to supply the "oracles of God to a few hundreds of islanders upon the Pacific, great as this work may be—nor to Indian tribes fast hastening to extinction."[118] As European and American empires scrambled in the late nineteenth century to lay claim to huge tracts of non-Western lands and peoples and to convert the world in a single generation, Jessup noted not only the "growing power and influence of Christian nations, and the waning power of Paganism and Mohammedanism"—a fantasy that Timothy Dwight had famously indulged in a century earlier—but also what he referred to as an "imperial commission to disciple all nations" for the Gospel.[119]

№

What gave American missionary benevolence in the late Ottoman Empire its peculiar force was its anomalous position relative to Western colonialism. The missionaries operated outside a formal European or American colonial setting but at the same time drew their strength from Western colonialism in America, Africa, and Asia.[120] Unlike in the case of the missionaries who operated in the British Empire, or indeed their own forebears who worked with Indians amidst American expansionism, there was no need for missionaries to burnish their humanism in the face of Western power, no need to reflect as Evarts had once done on the meaning and implication of American settler colonialism, no need to stand as "chaplains and tamers of Western expansion."[121] Jessup and his peers could simply bask in American glory one crucial step removed from its inglorious underpinnings. As Daniel Bliss stated in 1859: "One needs to leave America and compare her with other countries in order to love her. I believe she is the greatest and best country in the world."[122]

Because of this remove, as much ideological as it was physical, the missionaries could represent their vision of a benevolent America to the Arabs virtually unchallenged. They could also contribute greatly to the more scholarly views of Arabs and Muslims in America. Jessup, for example, was invited to speak before the general assembly of the Presbyterian Church at Saratoga in 1884. Against the backdrop of Leopold of Belgium's taking of the Congo and Britain's conquest of Egypt, both of which the missionary applauded in the name of Christian expansion, Jessup declared that the Reformation had been rekindled in America, and that this, in turn, had led to the redemption of a continent, and now the world. The pilgrims, he said, had reached out to the Indians of the "heathen continent of America"; they had built "our own favored and exalted nation"; and they had laid the foundations of an "American church" blessed by a "Christian army" of the greatest mobility and resources, and hence responsibility, in human history.[123] The American Board's William E. Strong echoed these sentiments when he noted that the modern missionary age, which had before it "a world open everywhere save in a few remote corners," represented the "world's last and greatest crusade."[124]

For these men, the Anglo-Saxon burden was a missionary one, mostly felt in America. By 1910, the United States was sending out more missionaries than any other country of the world.[125] The American missionaries in the late Ottoman Empire disputed biological racism but fully accepted and engaged in its more pervasive cultural variant: they discoursed on the national manners, customs, and traits of the Syrians, Turks, Armenians, and Arabs, sometimes sympathetically and sometimes not, but always with the knowledge that theirs was not simply the more righteous civilization but also the most powerful. They were more comfortable in the world, and more comfortable with it. The members of the pioneer generation were also, of course, steeped in racial thinking, but their language of benevolence was far less infused with the chauvinism so evident in the pronouncements and outlook of those missionaries reared in an age of manifest destiny. For the pioneer generation, historical events indicated an approaching millennium and underscored the urgency of mission to the world; for later missionaries, historical events clarified Anglo-Saxon supremacy over the world, and thus validated a hierarchy of nations and their own positions within it. The later missionaries steadfastly avowed the universal nature of Christ, but at the same exact time condemned Islam as a "ritual system based on Oriental ideas and Arab national peculiarities."[126] They were aware of the dangers of presenting Christ as "American" but at the same time believed that America, with what Laurie romanticized as its "New England piety and Puritan ideas," most perfectly resembled a Christian land.[127] They were, in a word, emphatically part of what Jessup recognized as the high point of "Anglo-Saxon power." As such, they were oblivious to, or purposefully silent about, the great dramas, struggles, and injustices under way in the late-nineteenth-century United States.[128]

࿇

As a parable of triumphant American modernity, Jessup's story of mission, including his retelling of the tale of Asʿad Shidyaq, epitomized the degree to which the judgments, knowledge, convictions, and representations of the Orient depended for their coherence on an idealization of America rather than simply an orientalization of the Ottoman Empire. The apotheosis of American exceptionalism thus marked the moment in mission history when American nationalism, racialism, and evangelism fused together in a manner that obviated any further discussion of American shortcomings, and escalated criticisms of those un-American places in the world yet to be saved by American missionaries.

What is most fascinating about the progress so celebrated by Jessup and other late-nineteenth-century missionary figures is not what Jessup condemned in Muslim rule but the assumption that animated the genuine outrage of this condemnation: namely that the United States itself constituted an unproblematic land of liberty, whose empire of manifest destiny had not entailed untold suffering for millions of ex-slaves then living in the shadow of Jim Crow laws, to say nothing of the native Americans quite literally being herded to extinction even as Jessup was writing in the first decade of the twentieth century. That missionaries could sincerely feel that the Ottoman government's treatment of the Armenians in 1895–96—when the Ottomans harshly suppressed an Armenian uprising—was more barbarous than the U.S. treatment of the Indians in the West was an expression of a profound failure of imagination.[129] A mission which had begun with such fiery idealism to redeem America and the world could no longer conceive of them in a single frame. David Brainerd, in effect, gave way to Lord Cromer, the British ruler of Egypt who famously insisted that "reformed Islam is Islam no longer."[130] What such an assumption betrayed was the near total lack of meaningful comparative perspective in what were osten-

sibly comparative judgments of different races and civilizations.
comparative posture is all the more apparent when one consid
that both the Ottoman Empire and the United States, for all t̲.̲.̲.̲.̲ ̲u̲.̲.̲.̲.̲-̲
ences, shared in one respect a common nineteenth-century conundrum:
how to mute, indeed abolish, long-standing discourses and structures of discrimination—religious in the Ottoman case, racial in the American one—
as an integral part of national consolidation.

What is also evident is the degree to which the undeniable passion and
enthusiasm for mission took for granted the natives but not the missionaries' fellow Americans whose pecuniary and moral benevolence they so as-
siduously courted, and to whose criticisms they were clearly attuned. To the
extent that American missionaries engaged in a dialogue of equals, it was
really with those Americans of a more liberal, racist, or secular outlook, but
rarely with the very peoples whose common humanity was the basis of
world mission.

The final, modern American story of Asʿad Shidyaq, which on the face
of it upheld Christian humanism, ultimately confirmed not so much equality as hierarchy, not so much the brotherhood of man as the rising star of
America. It dealt not with the universals of power, cruelty, and material interests, or those of love, betrayal, and sin, but rather with a narrower, less
imaginative indictment of the "East" and a celebration of an exceptional
"America." From such missionaries, ecumenism and Christian humanism
in its fullest flourishing was impossible.

Chapter 7

The Vindication of As'ad Shidyaq

As'ad Shidyaq was most fully vindicated on the eve of the 1860 war in Mount Lebanon. A generation after his persecution, an Arabic version of As'ad's conversion and death was published. The hagiographic account was titled simply *Qissat As'ad al-Shidyaq,* or "The Story of As'ad Shidyaq." Its author was Butrus al-Bustani, who was born in 1819, the same year the American Board mission to Palestine began, and who, like As'ad, had once been a Maronite but willingly embraced Protestantism. Like As'ad, too, he had been condemned by Maronite ecclesiastical authority, but unlike As'ad, he lived and thrived as a famous teacher, encyclopedist, journalist, church elder, and reformer at the intersection of mission and empire.

Three short decades after American missionaries and the Maronite Church had locked themselves into what they believed was an unrelenting, existential war, Bustani engaged in a signal act of defiance. In 130 small pages, printed in a new American Arabic typeface designed by the missionary Eli Smith, Bustani explicitly broke the Ottoman Arab silence that had covered up the tragedy of As'ad Shidyaq. Yet because his criticism emerged out of a genuine sense of belonging to the same native world, not from a sense of superiority to it, Bustani's memoir also repudiated the triumphalist exceptionalism of the American missionaries, and their conviction that without missionary tutelage, local society would always remain a fragile mosaic of antagonistic sectarian parts. Largely and purposefully ignored by the missionaries, the Arabic rehabilitation of Asʿad Shidyaq reflected the historical and literary revolution made possible by the modernization of the Ottoman Empire in which the American missionaries had played a distinct but by no means solitary role.

Bustani was not the first to remember Asʿad Shidyaq in Arabic. As early as 1833 the American missionaries had published the testimony of the convert "persecuted for his witness for truth," at the English Church Missionary Society press in Malta; in 1855 Asʿad's youngest brother, Faris, who had also converted to Protestantism, wrote a withering denunciation of the Maronite Church from his self-imposed exile in Europe, reminding it of the notorious past of the Roman Catholic Church, and of the fact that no amount of time would or could abolish the memory of his brother—no bribes, no tacit understanding, no compromise with what he regarded as the corrupt, violent, and ignorant old regime in Mount Lebanon in which the Maronite Church was implicated. The page could not, he intimated, be turned on this past, nor could the patriarch's reputation be repaired, not so long as "sky remained sky, and the earth, earth."[1] The true significance of Bustani's *Qissat Asʿad Shidyaq* was therefore not its idealization of the Protestant martyr but the deliberate manner in which Bustani used the story of Asʿad to evoke an unprecedented ecumenism, and later a new liberal pluralism as intolerable to American missionaries as it was to the Maronite Church.

Bustani's vision of modern coexistence based on a secular equality of religions and cultures, which he began to explore in his memorial to Asʿad Shidyaq but which he most comprehensively elaborated in the aftermath of the 1860 war, had no corollary in American missionary writings and pronouncements. It had no parallel, either, in the plethora of imperial Ottoman edicts, Islamic juridical rulings, or traditional Christian chronicles of Mount Lebanon. To say that Bustani was before his time is to miss the point entirely: he was a quintessential product of his time. He was shaped by his long and intimate experience with American missionaries; he was, and remained until his death in 1883, a leading member of the Protestant community, but, paradoxically, he also came to embody a secular antithesis to a sectarian age. For many influential American missionaries this was unacceptable. Bustani's vision was also continually contested at a local level, but it was by no means marginal. That is what made his vindication of Asʿad Shidyaq so meaningful, the Maronite denial of Protestantism so anachronistic, and the American missionary narrative of modernity so misleading.

To read Bustani is, in effect, to read Jessup and other American mission-

aries in an entirely different light from that in which the Americans had intended and assumed that their accounts would be read. By their nature and
chronology, coming long before any American missionary would be able to
embrace genuine ecumenism, Bustani's writings fundamentally question the
conceit of progress envisioned in missionary history and in the broader narrative of American and Western impact on the Middle East, which have
routinely viewed liberalism, modernity, and toleration as flowing obviously
and automatically from West to East and from America to an otherwise
stagnant Arab world. Bustani's ecumenism, in reality, was neither indigenous
nor foreign, neither American nor Arab: rather it was a synthesis of elements
from all of these. It did not stream solely from a missionary source but was
strongly shaped by the turbulent currents of Ottoman reform, and by the
proximity in which different faiths had long coexisted in Mount Lebanon.
The events of 1860, which American missionaries such as Jessup saw as confirming the need for a civilizing American impulse to reform a hopelessly
segregated and backward Arab world, Bustani regarded as an ominous national catastrophe. More than anything else, his ecumenism developed as a
reaction to what he regarded as a debilitating and divisive culture of sectarianism in which religious affiliation was made central to modern political
representation, and almost by definition undercut a unifying national imagination in a religiously diverse society. Such a complex genealogy of Arab
liberalism, in its very essence, exposes what Jessup, and a great number of
American historians since, have been wont to deny: that the space opened
by mission did not require American primacy, and modern Arabs were
more than clay molded by benevolent Americans. Bustani's evangelical turn,
however, also exposes what the Ottoman state, as well as Arab Christian and
Muslim apologists and a great many historians of the Middle East since, have
been unable to comprehend: the mission in the East was no simple expression of American imperialism but became an inextricable part of a modern
revolution in which peoples were implicated and through which cultures
were radically changed.

ᘓ

Within the half-century that linked the moment of Asʿad's persecution and
Bustani's account of it, the Ottoman Empire had dramatically reinvented
itself as a "civilized" and "tolerant" state. The desperate nineteenth-century
struggle for survival forced Ottomans into areas they had previously considered beyond their domain. In place of an imperial toleration premised on

the superiority of Muslim over non-Muslim, but which also recognized and afforded a space for the Maronites to thrive, neglected by the Ottomans in Mount Lebanon, and for missionaries to establish themselves in Beirut, imperial authorities scrambled to propose a new order of things that would at once preserve imperial sovereignty and also win the approbation of the "civilized" world. Religious difference between the inhabitants of the empire was no longer to be emphasized and managed but rather neutralized and transcended by a reforming state that now actively claimed to represent all its subjects equally.

The problem of the Protestants, however, remained. The American missionaries were increasingly bold in charting out new areas of the empire to proselytize, but their converts still were without legal recognition, and hence subject to harassment and, often, outright persecution by their former communities. Arab Protestant converts were persecuted in Hasbayya in Mount Lebanon in 1844, as were Armenian Protestants in Istanbul in 1846. Whereas imperial authorities had barely registered the entry of American missionaries in 1820, by the mid-nineteenth century, in the wake of the Greek revolt, a series of spectacular defeats at the hands of Ibrahim Pasha's Egyptian armies in Syria and Anatolia, following the alarm raised by the Eastern churches as American missionaries traveled into the interior of the empire and to Istanbul itself, and the increasingly vociferous complaints made by missionaries and the British government, they assumed a markedly more alert posture.

The standard mid-nineteenth-century Ottoman refrain about American missionaries was that they were "seducing" imperial subjects into abandoning their faith. The Ottomans claimed that the missionaries were corrupting the "foundations of religion"—*kavaid mezheblerini*—in the empire.[2] They also asserted that the American missionaries, "who were spread throughout the world," had "recently arrived in the well-protected imperial domains" to disseminate their seditious doctrines.[3] These accusations against the missionaries, of course, directly echoed those of the Maronite patriarch and other outraged Eastern ecclesiastical authorities. Their opposition to the Protestants remained intense; they continued to insist that converts were the "simpleminded ones," and, finally, they repeatedly reminded the Ottoman government that the danger of the "Biblemen from America" imperiled not just them, lowly Christian subjects, but the entire state.[4]

As much as Ottoman officials in Istanbul grasped the predicament of the Eastern patriarchs, they also realized that religious persecution was now out of place in a world dominated by aggressive European powers monitoring every Ottoman move. The authorities conceded that no matter how many times converts changed sects, they were still protected subjects of the imperial government. The Ottomans also knew that if imperial protection were not forthcoming, British, American, and Prussian pressure would manifest itself, and indeed already had done so. While the government pledged to the Armenian patriarch in Istanbul in 1846, for example, never to recognize the creation of a new Armenian Protestant community in order to protect the age-old "religious order of things," it also made him understand that he, and by implication they, were operating under the "constraints of the day and age."[5]

&

A "sublime and august mandate" in November 1850 formally recognized Protestantism in the Ottoman Empire. The imperial decree, which the missionaries claimed stemmed entirely from the efforts of the powerful, evangelically minded British ambassador Statford Canning, actually followed on a series of concessions to other Christian communities that had broken away from their original Orthodox churches after a century of concerted Catholic missions.[6] It also elaborated on earlier declarations from 1847 that had effectively opened the way for organized native Protestant communities to form.

The sultan let it be known that "my Christian subjects who have embraced the Protestant faith" were under no circumstances to be persecuted, for his imperial benevolence and solicitude "extends to all classes of my subjects." Therefore the sultan decreed that in accordance with his habitual "compassionate will," the Protestant community was henceforth to administer its own affairs and to worship freely, "so that they may live in peace, quiet, and security."[7]

With the stroke of a pen, the Ottoman government legitimated the place of Protestant converts in the empire, and it annulled the logic of the Maronite persecution of As'ad Shidyaq, which had been predicated on the "foreignness" of the Protestants. The ancient language of heresy faltered before the new discourse of "humane interposition."[8]

&

The Ottoman recognition of the Protestant community was a defensive maneuver, a declaration that the empire had now become an integral part of

an enlightened and imperial nineteenth-century age. An imperial concession was thus masked as absolute will. The sublime and sovereign language
recalled a bygone Ottoman era, but also a belated determination to refute
Western assumptions about the lack of tolerance in the empire.[9] The acceptance of Protestantism was soon followed by the revolutionary declaration in 1856, against the backdrop of the Crimean War, of equal treatment
of all subjects regardless of religious affiliation. In his imperial rescript of
1856, one of the ideological centerpieces of the *Tanzimat* reforms, the sultan declared that he desired to establish "a state of things conformable with
the dignity of my empire and the position which it occupies among civilized nations." The imperial decree heralded a "new era" in which the sultan declared his desire "to effect the happiness of all my subjects, who in my
sight are all equal, and equally dear to me, and who are united to each other
by the cordial ties of patriotism."[10]

The official rhetorical and eventually legal transformation of mere vas-
sals into compatriots reflected a radical rereading of the nature of imperial
toleration. Centuries of complex discriminatory rule, in which imperial toleration waxed and waned according to circumstances, were hastily reinter-
preted as proof of an irrefutable history of Ottoman Islamic "tolerance" that
stretched back to the days of Mehmed the Conqueror. In the face of relentless Western criticism, Ottoman officials shot back with a myth of their
own making. They contrasted the "dark ages" of Europe with the empire's
own past and drew what they considered to be the inevitable conclusion.
This was best expressed in a long memorandum to London and Paris from
the imperial foreign minister, in which he argued that the laws of Islam and
the Muslim Ottomans had been "almost unique in history" in their protection and toleration of minorities. No conquered minority had been compelled to convert to Islam; subjects of all faiths had always been free to
worship; and whatever mistakes and errors had been committed would be
quickly rectified, for the reforming Ottoman state was committed to ame-
liorating "the condition of all subjects without distinction to race or religion."[11] The modern Muslim apologetic was born as part and parcel of an
imperial strategy of survival.

⚜

The promise of imperial emancipation signaled a deliberate rupture with a
past now deemed unenlightened. The official change from a policy of discrimination to one of equality was not, perhaps, as momentous for Ottoman

society as was the emancipation of slaves in the United States; the Christians of the Ottoman Empire were simply not oppressed in anything like the systematic and alienating manner that applied to blacks in North America. But it reflected a remarkably similar problem of national integration in enormously diverse polities. Precisely as the abolition of slavery in the United States posed revolutionary, and still unresolved, questions about the relationship between race and politics in America, so too did the Ottoman Empire's formal commitment in 1856 to the equality of treatment between Muslim and non-Muslim pose profound questions about the relationship between religion and politics in the Ottoman domains. There were, of course, enormous differences between the United States and the Ottoman Empire, not least of which was the fact that by this time the United States was expanding rapidly at the expense of the Indians and was far more master of its own destiny than was the empire.

The tragedy of Ottoman emancipation was that it was meant to reclaim subjects from foreign missionaries and states in an era in which the empire's sovereignty was no longer hegemonic. The era of the would-be Ottoman civilizing mission commenced decades after American and Jesuit missionaries had already initiated their own projects to reshape the Ottoman Empire, backed by the respective and increasingly evident power of Britain and France (and, after mid-century, the United States).[12] And it began *after* men and women influenced by the Protestant mission in places like Beirut had already begun to chart their own sense of civilization. Moreover, from its inception, Ottoman emancipation was subverted by aggressive European powers. Algeria had already been conquered by the French in 1830; Balkan independence movements continuously chipped away at the integrity of the empire; and in Mount Lebanon, of course, European, and particularly British and French, interventions in the 1840s had led to an utterly unworkable partition along religious lines which ultimately led to the sectarian debacle of 1860.

✥

Ottoman reform was clearly a fraught process, uneven in elaboration and application. In cities like Beirut it legitimated new "civilized" spaces of empire in which American missionaries and their converts were able to flourish in spite of established orthodoxies. In neighboring rural Mount Lebanon, however, the new Ottoman emphasis on religious equality combined catastrophically with a Western sectarian reading of the land and its

inhabitants. They collectively undermined the foundations of the old regime, which had been based not on religious equality but on social discrimination, and in which great families, not sects, dominated the local landscape.
It was in these overlapping contexts of modernization in Beirut and sectarianism in Mount Lebanon, of Ottoman reform and American mission, that
the Protestant Ottoman subject-citizen in mid-nineteenth-century Beirut
came into his own. In such circumstances as well, the story of Asʿad Shidyaq
was rediscovered and given its most ecumenical and liberal interpretation,
not by American missionaries but by the native Protestant community's
most famous son.

ᴥ

More than any other figure, Butrus al-Bustani integrated American missionary and Ottoman "civilizing" impulses that were so set against each
other. More than any other figure, he also exposed their stark hierarchies,
for each one claimed to rescue allegedly ignorant natives from the other:
those whom the missionaries regarded as oppressed Arab babes in Christ in
need of American tutelage were for the Ottoman state unwitting pawns of
sinister foreigners. Either way, the natives were described and treated as essentially mute subjects who had little sense and certainly no inherent right
of representation. Bustani, however, was a committed evangelical whose
Arab identity illustrated the success of the American mission but also betrayed its racial limits; he was, at the same time, an embodiment of the *Tanzimat,* whose emphasis on independent thinking revealed the hollowness of
Ottoman fears and assumptions that converts were insincere, and that they
drank unthinkingly from the poisoned chalice of American benevolence.
Bustani advocated a freedom of conscience that plainly had evangelical
roots, but at the same time he eloquently pleaded for coexistence as a principal end of his life's work, and not simply as a means to a Christian end or
as a strategy to preserve imperial power.

ᴥ

Bustani was born in a small village near Dayr al-Qamar in Mount Lebanon
in November 1819. He opened his eyes to a Lebanese world dominated by
powerful families who defined the genealogical geography of the land; his
native village lay under the control of the Druze Janbulats. Like Asʿad

Figure 10. Butrus al-Bustani. Source: Special Collections, Yale Divinity School Library, Henry Harris Jessup Papers, RG 117, Box 10/44.

Shidyaq, Bustani had relations who occupied positions high and low in the Maronite Church. Abdullah Bustani was the Maronite bishop of the diocese of Sidon, and he recommended that Butrus, together with his brother's grandson (who would later succeed Abdullah as bishop of Sidon), be educated at the Maronite seminary of ʿAyn Waraqa. There Bustani spent ten years, unwilling to travel to Rome for further religious study out of concern for his widowed mother.

About this period of his life we know remarkably little, save that he eventually knocked on the door of the American missionaries in Beirut seeking employment in late 1840. His motives, like Asʿad's, were initially doubted by the Americans. Although at first the missionaries feared that "we shall perhaps have another Asaad affair," given the similarities of Shidyaq's and Butrus's trajectories, in this era of manifest English power and Ottoman reform, Maronite patriarchal outrage quickly ran its course.[13]

Beirut, center of American missionary operations in Syria, had changed significantly by mid-century, anticipating the birth of the modern city in the decades following 1860 which Henry Harris Jessup so tendentiously celebrated.[14] The military and political upheavals following the British bombardment of Beirut in September 1840 did not prevent the city's expansion. The American missionaries who had left because of the war that saw Ottoman rule restored to Syria returned soon enough. Their schools, including the boys' seminary, were reopened, although the missionaries decided to move it out of the city because it was no longer a "comparatively quiet and retired place."[15] The mission-educated convert Gregory M. Wortabet was more ebullient. "Old Beyrout is like the old town of Edinburgh—black and dingy," he told an audience in Halifax, Nova Scotia, in 1856. "The new town is beautiful—pleasantly situated and embowered amidst mulberry trees."[16] Not only had the city spilled well beyond its ancient walls, but also by 1854, French, Austrian, and English steamers regularly connected Beirut to various ports of call across the Mediterranean and Europe.[17]

An American traveler reflected on how much the city had changed between his two visits in 1841 and 1852, despite the upheavals in Mount Lebanon. He estimated that in this period Beirut's population had doubled to some thirty thousand inhabitants. Its streets, he added, had been repaired, a new suburb had been built, and commerce had increased greatly. The American missionaries lived in fine stone houses which commanded superb prospects, and they also possessed a mission building near the southwestern gate of the city. This structure, close to the American cemetery in which

Pliny Fisk and the former British consul Peter Abbot were buried, housed
a chapel "commodiously fitted up with seats, chiefly by the liberality of the
American consul and other Frank residents," which served as the mission
church, a mission press, and a large upper room on the third floor in which
the work of translating the Scriptures occurred.[18]

Yet the very secular progress of the city and the security and comfort of
the American mission amidst political instability in neighboring Mount
Lebanon failed to resolve the question of conversion. The American Board
and its missionaries still struggled to explain why so few had converted in
Syria while so many had converted in other missions. In 1842, according to
one gloomy missionary, the native congregation in Beirut was made up almost entirely of "domestics, dependents, and expectants," although he acknowledged that Bustani had become "a firm Protestant, and manifests a
tender conscience."[19] A decade later the situation had improved somewhat.
Bustani had taken the lead in the establishment of a separate native Protestant church in the city in 1848 which included nineteen members and four
women.[20] The lands of the Bible were by then covered by thirty primary
schools and nearly nine hundred students. But there were only seventy-five
converts in all of Ottoman Syria and no native pastors.[21]

Moreover, the very transformation of Beirut and the educational opportunities presented by the Americans which had initially attracted Bustani and others to the mission also produced a noticeable anxiety among
some American missionaries. If the Jesuit missionary François Badour
lamented in the early 1850s the disappearance of "Abrahamic costumes" in
favor of Western styles in Beirut, noting that "more than one of our Arabs
has loosened his belt, his tunic, and his *shirwal* to don narrow pants, smoke
cigars, haunt the cafes, and disdain the cares of eternity," he merely echoed
the dismay of the American missionary Samuel Wolcott, who condemned
Beirut for its "exposure to the worst foreign elements."[22] The British
restoration of Ottoman rule had seen several students leave their Beirut
seminary to take up work as translators and guides, or dragomans.[23]

The common fear was not of modernization, which after all facilitated
missionary work as never before, but of its "corrupting" power over natives
who might become, in a word, de-orientalized, who might not act as they
were meant to act in Western eyes, and who might aspire to an equality in
style and substance with the benevolent men and women—as the missionaries saw themselves—who had come from afar to save them. As Rufus Anderson, the influential corresponding secretary of the American Board in
Boston put it, the problem was that until the 1840s the American mission-

Figure 11. View of Beirut (American Mission Church). Source: Blatchford Collection, Archives and Special Collections Department, Jafet Library, American University of Beirut, Ph 1/197.

ary schools had simply and at great expense created secular opportunities for natives who became, in his words, "so *anglified* in their ideas and tastes that they became disgusted with their countrymen, and even with their noble Arabian tongue, and were unfitted in great measure for doing good to their people."[24]

There was a practical aspect to the concern in at least one sense. The mission did not want to waste its precious resources on producing secularized individuals who would not advance the narrowly defined missionary cause. There were also financial considerations to take into account. The American Board was often short of funds relative to its worldwide operations, and Rufus Anderson constantly encouraged economy. But the concern was also palpably racial. Anderson's theory of mission rested on the premise of separate "national" spaces which natives and missionaries were meant to occupy. Secularized education, in which direct preaching of the Word of God was subordinated to the exigencies of practical knowledge, encouraged what

Anderson suspected were "mercenary motives among the native Christians."[25] The great object of mission was not to raise up civilized men and women who coveted equal salaries with the Americans, or at any rate a better standard of living than their "native" condition could bear, but "converting men to God."[26] The ghost of the Foreign Mission School fiasco, when Indian students had caused an uproar by daring to marry white women in the mid-1820s, hovered over the Syria mission in the 1840s and 1850s.

Ottoman subjects such as As'ad Khayyat, John Wortabet, Mikhayil Mishaqa, Butrus al-Bustani, and Faris Shidyaq appreciated their association with missionaries, their schools, and their English-language education.[27] They valued the American mission precisely because it broadened their horizons; they did not see any necessary contradiction between learning English and despising their Arabic culture. Anderson wanted to disillusion these men and make it clear that the American Board simply wanted reliable native informants and assistants to pave the way for a native church. Henceforth, Anderson mandated, only Arabic would be taught in mission schools; English-language instruction was to be curtailed. Christianization had to come before civilization, he insisted, no matter the fact that the missionaries on the ground in Syria knew that it was secular education and foreign languages that students demanded more than anything else.[28] Anderson, in short, criticized the missionaries because, in his estimation, they had relied far too heavily on schools rather than on a "Pauline operation upon the hearts."[29] He demanded the establishment of self-supporting, self-propagating, and self-governing native churches.[30] But with the notable exception of Cornelius Van Dyck, who had joined the Syria mission in 1840, and William and Loanza Benton, almost all the missionaries insisted, in line with their British and American counterparts in virtually every other part of the world, that *natives,* regardless of the acknowledged difference between a Sandwich Islander and a Syrian, were as a whole not ready enough, not evangelical enough, and not yet civilized enough to be trusted with independence.[31]

Part of this disagreement over the viability of an independent native pastorate was theoretical, and much of it was sincerely debated, with examples from Saint Paul to Luther to the Half-Way Covenant. All of it, however, was part of an essentially closed conversation between an American Board and American missionaries about the nature and mechanics of a mission and about the deficiencies of "native" spirituality that juxtaposed Syrians and Sandwich Islanders. As much as Anderson supported Arabic-language instruction, his perspective on the Syrian converts was inherently conde-scending. As natives, they were to be content with their subordinate station in life. They were not to aspire, or be encouraged to aspire, to any position beyond that which was deemed suitable for them by a benevolent Ameri-can Board. He wanted them to love their Arabic language, which he did not know, but he wanted them also to realize that at the end of the day, Arabs were not Americans.

He thus devoted a single meeting to the local Protestants during his tour of Beirut on the evening of 21 March 1844. Bustani was there. He urged Anderson not to forget the small native congregation, but to write letters to them and furnish them with the means for instructing the laity in the way of preaching. He also told Anderson that what gave his fellow Protes-tants hope was that others in distant lands prayed for them and that this direct tie to the outside world was crucial for the sustenance of the con-gregation. Anderson replied that the "native brethren"—a qualifier the Americans habitually added to undercut any lurking equality in the mis-sionary brotherhood of Christ—were to continue to work for Christ, but they could have no immediate connection with the American Board. They were to deal only with the resident missionaries. There were hierarchies to be maintained in this benevolent empire. Christian universalism did not im-ply, let alone mean, equality.[32]

❧

Butrus al-Bustani worked in the 1840s for $300 a year. An American mis-sionary usually was paid at least twice as much, and often several times as much, a year.[33] As a translator in the third-floor room of the mission house, a copyist, a teacher first in Beirut and then in the village of Abeih, and an unordained evangelist, he intimated to his erstwhile missionary patron Eli Smith his dissatisfaction with his low salary and remarked that he "was de-termined to have it increased." He even told the American missionary that he believed Smith had deliberately blocked "him from earning more in time past."[34] By 1851, with Van Dyck's support, he became the first dragoman at the U.S. consulate, effectively doubling his salary.

The native convert was beginning to recognize just how deep ran the paternalism that characterized Anderson and most of his American mis-sionaries, but his outlook on the mission remained positive. Not privy to the stream of confidential American communications about "avarice and ambition of the native heart," he still worked on the translation of the Scriptures which Smith had commenced in 1847, and at the mission press, which had been revitalized by Smith.[35]

Bustani, like Faris Shidyaq before him, took advantage of the intersection of imperial reform and missionary endeavor. Unlike the American Board and missionaries, who believed in a stringent dichotomy between themselves—as white American evangelists—and the "natives," Arab subjects of the mid-century Ottoman Empire did not think so much in racial terms as in religious ones. With the exception of Algeria, Arabs had not been directly colonized by Europeans. No overt segregation, and no outraged humanity, of the kind evident in a European colony or the post-Reconstruction American South existed in Ottoman Syria that would or could produce intellectuals in the mold of W. E. B. Du Bois.

There was no need for Bustani to define himself in stark opposition to the Americans, only in relation to them. In 1844 he helped establish a Protestant congregation in the town of Hasbayya in southeastern Mount Lebanon.[36] For a short period in 1846–1847 Bustani worked intensely beside the missionary Van Dyck at the relocated seminary in the village of Abeih, in the Druze-dominated area of Mount Lebanon. The experience was formative because Van Dyck was one of the few American missionaries (together with Smith) who had mastered Arabic, was the American most open to the idea of a genuine Christian brotherhood, and was also extremely taken with the importance of secular scientific learning.[37]

Bustani, with Van Dyck, participated enthusiastically in a new organization independent of the American mission called the Syrian Society of Arts and Sciences, which was founded in Beirut in 1847 and which met regularly until 1852. This society was composed mostly of natives, but its presidents were American missionaries, first William Thomson and then Eli Smith. It ran regular monthly meetings on questions of arts and sciences but significantly refused to delve into questions of "religious rites and doctrines."[38] Its constitution reflected the signs of the times: it affirmed new secular spaces in Beirut where American and Arab men of different backgrounds could meet, essentially repudiating Rufus Anderson's philosophy of mission, the overt spiritual crusade of the first generation of missionaries, and the Maronite Church's violent rejection of missionaries and their converts.

Bustani's involvement with this avowedly "scientific" society reflected the unmistakable stamp of the American evangelicals. Bustani recognized that he had grown enormously in the shadow of the mission. He still believed in collaborating with those men such as Van Dyck, Smith, and Thom-

Figure 12. Dr. Cornelius Van Dyck. Source: Special Collections, Yale Divinity School Library, Henry Harris Jessup Papers, RG 117, Box 10/44.

son who, Anderson's strictures on secular education notwithstanding, acknowledged the reality of, and perforce interacted with, a local world outside the mission. He had married Rahil ʿAtta, who had herself been raised and educated by Sarah Smith, Eli's first wife. Together the Bustanis embodied an almost ideal "native" couple: an educated, literate, professing Protestant in the service of the mission wedded to a pious literate women for whom building an evangelical home and raising her Christian family were her primary responsibilities.

Not surprisingly, therefore, Bustani's discourse on women's education, which he presented as a lecture to the Syrian Society in 1850, conformed utterly to a gendered missionary view of the idealized Christian family. Women had to be raised by pious men out of their state of ignorance; their education was crucial if they were to raise proper children, to keep a tidy house, to cook, to clean, to sew, and to be saved and to save others. Bustani urged his male audience to consider the fact that no society could advance without the proper education of its women, and men could not be considered to have knowledge, and implicitly to be free, without having their women share in this knowledge and freedom.[39] Yet the boldness of Bustani's argument about the necessity of women's education, stated well before the Egyptian Qasim Amin's more famous treatise, *Tahrir al-marʾa* (The Liberation of Women), published in 1899, which argued that the gradual emancipation of women was not incompatible with Islam, revealed the degree to which he reproduced an American missionary framework that segregated the world into advanced and backward nations and tribes. Bustani, for example, praised British colonialism in India because it ostensibly liberated women from *sati* (widow immolation). He made it clear that he considered the women of Syria to be at a halfway point between the "civilized" women of Europe and the "barbarians" of the world, by which Bustani lumped together the women of India, Africa, and native America.[40]

Bustani's advocacy of a renaissance of Arab civilization, beginning with women but extending to all branches of society, mirrored a mid-century American Board discovery of the "Arabs." The *Missionary Herald,* for example, proclaimed in 1844 that the "Arabs are a wonderful people. They have the elements of a noble character."[41] Eli Smith rounded out this description by explaining to an American audience six years later why the "Arab race is my favorite": they had literature and poetry, "the soul of sublimity," a record of achievement in science, mathematics, philosophy, and history, and an Arabic language that made English sink "into insignificance before its beauty and force."[42] Smith, in fact, reminded members of his Arab audience, which must have included Bustani, at a meeting of the Syrian Society in 1852 that they had the capacity to become modern. "As for your Arab ancestry," he said, "its literature is a connecting link between the ancient world, adorned with Roman and Grecian sciences, and the modern, adorned with the sciences of Europeans and their thorough research."[43] When in 1859 Bustani dwelt on the glories of the medieval Abbasid Arab past to rouse his countrymen to a nineteenth-century "awakening," when he took pride in his native Arabic language but lamented the decline of the Arabs, when he compared their present pitiable condition to the science and progress of the Europeans, he painted an unabashedly positivist sketch for Arab reform on a missionary canvas.[44]

〜

On the face of it, then, Bustani was a quintessential native informant. He facilitated missionary labor and legitimated and reproduced missionary discourse. But Bustani's significance, as A. L. Tibawi, the most important historian of the Syria mission, recognized decades ago, lay in his exemplification of a process of conversion that would take an unanticipated secular route which the missionaries could not control and refused to sanction.[45] His work, in short, must be read alongside that of his missionary interlocutors as a riposte to their evangelical challenge but also as a response to other, more obvious and more local sectarian developments. Both the missionaries and their convert celebrated the "Arab race"; both spoke about "barbarism"; both were evangelical; both believed in freedom of conscience, in education, in literacy; but their pieties had vastly different political implications.

The missionaries' celebration of the "Arab" was predicated on their abandonment of the "Indian" at home, for to speak as Jessup did in 1884 of the "undying" race of Arabs was to affirm and naturalize, without seriously questioning, the extermination of the "dying" races that was going on in the United States and in various European colonies in the second half of the nineteenth century. More immediately, when Thomson told Anderson in 1844 that there was a foundation among "these people for taking care of themselves. Greater than in the Sandwich Islands, or Africa," he was not assuming the equality of Arab to American but was presupposing the tutelage of Arabs by the American mission.[46]

Bustani's evangelism, by contrast, was constructed on the unfulfilled promise of native agency. His call for an Arab cultural "awakening" generalized and secularized the deeply personal struggle with faith that awakened an evangelically minded person from so-called spiritual death and the challenge to prevailing orthodoxies that it entailed. In both instances, awakening required sustained self-reflection. It demanded agency. And it depended on freedom of thought, or *huriyyat al-fikr,* which Bustani juxtaposed with enslaved thought, or *al-fikr al-mustaʿbad,* for it allowed one to situate oneself honestly and self-critically in relation to God and to others, and therefore to evaluate correctly and remedy one's position in the world.[47] The avowedly evangelical Christian, therefore, articulated a broadly defined notion of Arab culture, one that bound Muslim and Christian together through a common Arabic language and a shared protracted history of rise and decline which had brought the "Arab race" into the nineteenth century far behind its "civilized" European counterparts.

The pride Bustani took in the Arabic language and in the medieval Arab past clearly underscored his idea that Arabs had been the creators and not simply the recipients or transmitters of culture.[48] Although this narrative of ancient glory and current stagnation was borrowed directly from the missionaries, Bustani's plea for "the generation of the nineteenth century" to initiate its own renaissance did not entail the dilution of very different religious pieties, the subordination of Arabs to the West, or of Christians to Muslims. It was thus a genuinely revolutionary liberalism in the multireligious world he inhabited in the shadow of Western hegemony.

The awakening of the "Arabs" that Bustani called for in 1859 would be possible not through devotion to Protestant doctrines, but through an explicit and deliberate appreciation by his Muslim and Christian *compatriots* of a unique nineteenth-century moment that brought, in Bustani's view, benevolent American missionaries together with a reforming Ottoman sultan.[49] Because his interaction with the missionaries had opened horizons for him as it had for Asʿad and Faris Shidyaq, he insisted that the encounter with the foreign and the unfamiliar through physical or mental exploration was essential for an Arab *re*-acquisition of knowledge and science.

Bustani therefore ridiculed those who spurned Western thought simply because it was Western. He also lambasted those whom he called *mutafarnijin,* or those intoxicated with the West, for heedlessly adopting Western costume and language at the expense of their own "noble language."[50] Again, strong echoes of Rufus Anderson and Eli Smith permeated Bustani's discourse. But at the heart of all Bustani's missionary-derived language of culture and authenticity was a plea for cultural dialogue, itself made possible by a convert's self-conscious and, as it turned out, subversive *liberalization* of an inflexibly hierarchical, and insidiously racialized, mid-century American missionary piety.

Like the first missionaries who set foot on Ottoman shores, he saw cultural difference as an indication of a common humanity realized to different degrees. But unlike the first missionaries and most of their successors,
he believed that true evangelism required an openness to others, and that
the moral and scientific gap that existed between the "civilized" Western
nations and the "Arabs" did not portend a struggle between "Christianity"
and "Mohammedanism" in which one must vanquish the other. Rather,
Bustani regarded the obvious technological and educational disparity between his missionary patrons and his own Eastern world as evidence of a
historical condition produced by the fateful decisions of Arabs themselves.
Their advancement and salvation ultimately depended on themselves and
not on the charity or benevolence of others, although he readily acknowledged a role for that benevolence.

As^cad Shidyaq was therefore seized upon by Butrus al-Bustani as a glorious yet tragic figure: the first flower to emerge from the rich soil of cross-
cultural encounter, rudely plucked before its time. Shidyaq's death had not
been inevitable; therein, thought Bustani, lay his tragedy. Bustani memori-
alized As^cad Shidyaq in 1860 just before sectarian events devastated Mount
Lebanon and radically transformed Butrus al-Bustani.[51]

Bustani confided to Rufus Anderson his object in reviving the story of
Shidyaq in a rare letter written in English at the beginning of 1860. His goal
was

> to publish a full work of his life in the Arabic language for the benefit of
> my countrymen, and especially the Maronites who cannot help being in-
> terested and benefitted [sic] by the exampel [sic] of one who once belonged
> to their church. I flatter myself to have succeeded in finding many things
> relating to the life of this wittness [sic] to the truth and if I am not too san-
> guine I think that his life is one of the most valuable evidences to the power
> of the grace of God in the hearts of men.[52]

In his Arabic introduction, Bustani elaborated his perspective on the affair. "It is undeniable," read his opening words,

> that many natives and foreigners have heard of the name of As^cad Shidyaq
> and have been familiar with facets of his story. These have come mostly

from his partisans or his detractors, both of whom have not had the opportunity to dwell on the truth. Many false allegations and fabrications have been inserted into his chronicle which by their nature would severely castigate his persecutors, attributing to them actions they did not commit and ambitions they did not have. These [allegations] would also describe and ascribe to him actions and intentions that had no basis in reality.[53]

Bustani's account was assuredly hagiographic. Its basic narrative was sketched from multiple sources including letters from As'ad and his brothers Faris and Tannus. Faris had five years earlier, in 1855, published in Paris a brilliantly witty and, in style, composition, and form, revolutionary autobiographical work, *Al-Saq 'ala al-saq fi ma huwa al-Farayaq aw ayyam wa shuhur wa a'wam fi 'ajm al-'arab wa al-a'jam,* or "The Leg over the Leg Concerning What Is Faryaq, or Days, Months, and Years Spent in Trying Arabs and Non-Arabs," in which he sarcastically, if bitterly, recounted As'ad's persecution as part of a wider narrative of his travels in and commentaries on Europe, Malta, and Egypt.[54] Tannus had published in Beirut in 1859 a major history of Mount Lebanon called *Kitab akhbar al-a'yan fi Jabal Lubnan.* Bustani used both accounts, but also relied on missionary documents and As'ad's Arabic testament of faith, which had been printed at the Church Missionary Society press in Malta in 1833, and which Bustani now reproduced in full. His narrative emphasized As'ad's struggle with his faith, his embrace of Protestantism, and his persecution, and it underscored the deliberate individual choices made by both As'ad and his Maronite contemporaries, some of whom took pity on him, others of whom hardened their hearts and closed their minds toward their former student, friend, colleague, and brother. But Bustani's vindication of As'ad Shidyaq, more than anything else, was a bold declaration of the possibilities of the new nineteenth-century "age" of knowledge, reform, light, and liberation which he had extolled the year before in his speech on the culture of the Arabs. He described the essence of As'ad's story in the following terms:

Unquestionably, freedom of conscience cannot be bestowed by the rulers of this world. And even if all the forces of this earth and hell joined together, they would not be able to wrest [freedom] from the heart that owns it. Nor can oppression, tyranny, and prisons restrain it. For once any person has tasted the sweetness of this divine freedom there is no way to return him to slavery. It is a freedom that has descended from above, granted to humanity after it had been purchased and solidly sealed by the blood of the

Lord Jesus Christ. And through it God, the Controller of all, whose words cannot be changed, granted a covenant made secure by a strong vow and an unshakable promise. Exert yourself [independently, *ijtahid*], dear reader, to gain and safeguard this freedom earnestly.[55]

The very act of empathetically narrating the forbidden history of Asʿad Shidyaq was an explicit repudiation of the forms and ways of the old regime. Ironically, these had been given full expression just a year before by Asʿad's older brother Tannus, whose massive history of Mount Lebanon was, with Bustani's assistance and editing, published at the American press in Beirut.[56]

Whereas Bustani focused on a dissident individual, Tannus took refuge in the orthodoxies of the old regime. He thus rendered the history of Mount Lebanon largely a chronicle of the established Druze and Maronite families, their genealogies, their feuds, their wars, their alliances, and their relationship to Ottoman governors. To the extent that the commoners were included in this history, they were simply passive props in the struggles of great men, marched in and out of history as the narrative demanded. Tannus explicitly stated that he intended his to be a definitive history. All the more noticeable, then, was his silence on his brother's fate, and his embrace of the very men and families, such as the Hubayshes and the Shihabs, who had oppressed his own brother. Asʿad was mentioned in the genealogy of the Shidyaqs, but Tannus wrote not a single word about Asʿad's conversion or his persecution, nor of the American missionaries for whom Tannus himself had once worked.[57]

This willful omission was not out of hatred for the brother Tannus had tutored and enrolled at ʿAyn Waraqa, only to see him fall into what he had regarded as Protestant heresy and then die what he believed to have been an utterly unnecessary death. Tannus had in fact tried to save Asʿad, but was not willing to break openly with the Maronite Church or risk further stigmatizing of his family. He became complicit instead in expunging his brother's memory for the coherence of the "truthful" history that he narrated. Asʿad's evangelism and his emphasis on the imperative of living faith contradicted, and was very much out of place in, a story of inherited and unquestioned lineages. His emphasis on a decisive turning point inherent in conversion, its absolute rupture with what he considered an immoral and unchristian past, could not easily be fitted into a chronicle whose structure was not simply chronological but cyclical as well. The great men whose lives he recounted lived in the shadow of Ottoman toleration that waxed and waned in an almost perpetual cycle of punishment and forgiveness, and of expulsion and integration into the "domain of favor."[58] The only certainty of the world evoked by Tannus's history was the seemingly eternal division of men of rank from commoners, and the plurality of religions that informed but did not preclude the interdependence of the ruling families.

Although As'ad was effectively erased from Tannus's history, Yusuf Hubaysh was remembered in the pages of the chronicle as a noble man who desperately sought to prevent the sectarian skirmishes in 1841, which Tannus clearly blamed on the "arrogant" attitude of the Christians of Dayr al-Qamar who "forsook the commands of their [Druze] Nakadi shaykhs."[59] The portrayal of the Maronite patriarch as a true leader of the Maronites, while the Druze desire for revenge led to all-out war, constituted the climax of Tannus's account: the moment when the old regime was, by his own admission, collapsing, when even the language of his own narrative becomes jarringly sectarian, and far more urgent in tone, emphasizing for once not the elite politics of families and households but rather the "betrayal" of the Maronites of the Shuf by their erstwhile leaders at their hour of greatest need.[60] Through the medium of print, and against the backdrop of an unraveling old regime and its ideology of elite politics and religion, Tannus published his paean to a passing age.

Through exactly the same medium of print and mechanical reproduction of American mission printing fonts, Bustani, however, revealed the absurdity of the crude, and in Tannus's case tragic, Maronite attempt to obliterate As'ad Shidyaq's tale. The narration of As'ad's story from Beirut and the appeal to an educated, anonymous "reader" expressed an outright rejection of the relationship between power and knowledge that defined the old regime. Like Faris Shidyaq's earlier *Al-Saq,* but with the primary audience he had in mind before him in Beirut, Bustani's explicit evocation of As'ad's fate, his refusal to forget, to let bygones be bygones, his deliberate publication of a scandal for all to read, marked more than a revolution of print over scribal culture, and more than the advent of a modern subject in an imagined community of Arabic readers that reached far beyond confessional identity.[61] It marked a fundamental break with the temporality of the old regime which had sustained a certain form of toleration and a certain form of coexistence as an integral part of the hegemony of the few over the many. The ability, in other words, of Ottoman governors at one juncture to unmask infidels and, at another, to embrace them, of local secular elites alternately to rebel against and submit to imperial authority, and of ecclesiastical leaders to perceive at one moment a world of dangerous heretics and, at another, one of fellow notables, to celebrate the Shidyaqs but obliterate As'ad, to terrorize and to forgive, was bound up with a play of politics. This politics depended on the willingness of both the governors and the governed to return to the status quo ante, to resume their proper place in an elaborate hierarchy, to forget what had to be forgotten in a world of slaves and masters, lords and servants, patriarchs and flocks.

To refuse categorically to play the part of the obedient subject or the faithful Maronite, and to be explicit where silence had been the rule, was in effect to repudiate the hegemony of the old regime which had enjoined religious and political quiescence in a multireligious world. But whereas the self-consciously worldly Faris had heaped opprobrium on the patriarch for his narrow defensive mentality, Bustani was more concerned with extracting a single moral lesson from what he described as the unjust persecution of an individual. His vindication signified an attempt to supplant the genealogical geography that had dominated the landscape of Mount Lebanon. Rather than propose a sectarian reading of the land and its inhabitants (as the Europeans, the Americans, and the Maronite Church were doing at this time), Bustani proposed an individualized, critical reading of the land and its people.

But as much as Bustani's primary reason for publishing a memoir of Asʿad Shidyaq was to provoke rational Maronites into reconsidering what had transpired against an innocent individual in their collective name, he refused to accept the American missionaries' understanding of the tragedy, even as he copied some of their words verbatim. Bustani's Shidyaq could not be reconciled with the various American representations of the same martyr. The American missionary sensibility had first forced the figure of "Asaad esh Shidiak" into a generic pantheon of "native" martyrs that included the Cherokee Catherine Brown and the Hawaiian Henry Obookiah. After 1860 it transformed his tribulations into a justification for avowedly modern missionary labor among the Arabs. Both the early evangelical and later, modern versions of the story were calculated to translate American moral, spiritual, and cultural superiority over the East, presumably felt by American readers, into continued support for the missionary enterprise to the East. They were based on the assumption that the Maronite Church was unremittingly despotic, a metaphor for a general Oriental condition, and an encapsulation of Roman Catholic bigotry.

In Bustani's hands, the parable of Asʿad Shidyaq, "son of Yusuf, known as Abi Husayn, son of Mansur al-Shidyaq, son of Jaʿfar, son of Fahd, son of Shahin son of Ja'far, son of Raʿd the Hasruni Lebanese Maronite," was rendered in a far more locally rooted narrative.[62] In place of the stock characters and stereotypes of the American stories, Bustani humanized the major protagonists. Hence the first chapter of Bustani's *Qissat* narrated As'ad's life in details and with poetry penned by As'ad that had not found their way into the American biographies. And hence his portrayal of the Maronite patriarch as genuinely perturbed by As'ad's crisis of faith showed him as one who nevertheless ultimately decided—who *chose*—to try to force As'ad into submission but was ultimately unable to break the convert's will.

Like the missionaries, Bustani severely reproached the Maronite Church. He refuted Maronite assertions that As'ad had converted because he was insane, or that he had been bribed by the American missionaries. Instead, Bustani drew a portrait of a man moved by genuine spiritual and intellectual engagement with Protestant principles, cruelly treated and eventually abandoned to his fate as a martyr. Bustani wanted to make As'ad's story an example of what he regarded as "real" faith, as opposed to blind obedience to dogma. This evangelical faith was crucial to Bustani's liberal perspective and was tied not to specific Protestant principles but to a more general belief in the universal freedom of the individual to believe without compulsion, to search and to enquire after truth regardless of the physical obstacles and communal strictures. He thus concluded his narrative by declaring that Shidyaq's punishment was not only morally and ethically wrong but unjust as well, for the patriarch had no legitimate power to compel As'ad into obedience:

> It is undeniable that this punishment was bestowed upon him simply because of belief and not because he committed an abomination or a crime against neighbor, lord, or the state. For had he done that he should have been tried before a legitimate judge. *All are in agreement* that the patriarch's coat is stained with the blood of As'ad, regardless of how As'ad ultimately died. And given that the patriarch has departed to the world of justice, there is no need for us to dwell on this thought, except to say that the patriarch was condemned by the wise men of his and other sects whose vision was not blinded by prejudice nor their understanding debased by blind obedience. The patriarch's ill treatment of As'ad was indeed ill treatment of the person of the sultan under whose shade As'ad reposed. And if the patriarch had desired to take one dirham from As'ad's house, he had no right because both are equal in rights; so how is it permissible for him to take As'ad's soul.[63]

The conclusion is striking because it was clearly inspired by Faris Shidyaq's withering denunciation of the Maronite Church. Indeed, parts of it were copied directly from *Al-Saq*.[64] Bustani's criticism, however, was more carefully framed to allow for reconciliation, and as a result, in place of the brilliant sarcasm, fury, and even despair evident in Faris's recollection of his brother's miserable fate, Bustani's narrative substituted a more ponderous didacticism that defined Bustani's style. He left space in his account for dissenting Maronite and other Eastern voices, and his narrative was peppered with instances of Maronite clergymen who had urged the patriarch to rethink his imprisonment of As'ad.[65] That details he provided may have been exaggerated, or, as at least once later critic insisted, invented, was hardly the point.[66] His insistence that "all are in agreement" about the Maronite patriarch's culpability did not so much soften the criticism of the patriarch as make it more amenable to the broader reform project of the Arab "race" to which Bustani was committed.

In a word, Bustani greatly altered the implications of As'ad Shidyaq's death. Rather than simply recounting a Protestant martyrology that heaped opprobrium on enemies of the faith, he salvaged As'ad's own assertion that he could be both evangelical and Maronite. Bustani, after all, was himself almost a second incarnation of As'ad Shidyaq. But Butrus had survived where As'ad had not—and not just survived but thrived in a now protected, legalized, dissident evangelical space engendered by the intersection of American mission and Ottoman reform. He thus overlaid his account of As'ad Shidyaq with his own belief that religious diversity, rather than being a threat to be contained and managed, could become a basis for a new kind of liberal coexistence in which church and state could and should be separated.

Bustani recognized that the missionaries had opened up the possibility for As'ad Shidyaq, and more generally speaking for the East, to relate to authority in a new way. By insisting that an individual should of his own free will read and be convinced of the veracity of Protestant belief, the missionaries privileged direct intellectual engagement over physical compulsion and demanded scriptural "evidence" in order to justify specific religious practices. There is no denying that at the level of individuals such as Shidyaq and Bustani there was something powerfully attractive (which missionary opponents insisted was beguiling) in this missionary religiosity. But Bustani transformed a missionary message of exclusionary Protestant salvation predicated on the destruction of all other forms of religious belonging into an inclusivist message of salvation that could, in Bustani's mind at least, accommodate multiple forms of religiosity.

Whereas both the missionaries and Bustani aspired to a society without masters and slaves, the missionaries believed that such a society must emulate their quite idealistic vision of the United States—the way women dressed, the way people ate, the furniture they used, and above all the Protestant God to whom they prayed— and conform to their own racialized vision of the world upon which the benevolent United States unilaterally acted. Bustani, by contrast, proposed a model of coexistence for Muslims and Christians alongside Western cultures but not subordinate to them.

ʾ2.

The secular implications of Bustani's biography of Asʿad Shidyaq became explicit only after the catastrophic sectarian violence of 1860 in Mount Lebanon and Damascus, which left thousands of Ottoman Christian subjects dead and thousands more refugees crowding the missionary-inhabited suburbs of Beirut. The sectarian strife also left the previously hegemonic social order in tatters. It revealed, finally, a deep sectarian imprint clearly inscribed on the bloodied landscape. The war of 1860 was seared into the local consciousness as deeply as the U.S. Civil War was seared into the American national consciousness. For those caught up in its maelstrom, it cut their nineteenth century in half just as sharply as the Civil War partitioned American history for Americans. In this context Butrus al-Bustani again put pen to paper as Druzes and Maronites engaged in bitter recriminations about the fighting in Mount Lebanon, while in Damascus, Christians remained terrified of Muslims, who in turn were confronted in the later months of 1860 with the violent retribution of an embarrassed Ottoman Empire.

As Western consuls and missionaries comforted themselves with the belief that the events signaled the "the dying struggles of the fierce Moslem tiger," the Ottomans had hastened with a modern army to Syria to defend the honor of "civilized" Islam at the point of imperial bayonets.[67] The subsequent state terror saw the execution of scores of alleged Muslim rioters in Damascus after the most perfunctory of investigations, as well as the utter pacification of Mount Lebanon, most of whose Druze lords were condemned to death, and all of whose established families were stripped of their ancient tax privileges and immunities. Having satisfied themselves and their European counterparts that the violence in Mount Lebanon was an "age-old" eruption of tribal fanaticism, Ottoman officials finally declared in 1861 that all traces of the recent events had been forever uprooted.[68]

From the ruins of his Lebanese world Bustani knew better. The sectarian horrors could not simply be banished by imperial proclamation, and certainly not by imperial force alone. Under the pseudonym "A patriot," Bustani outlined a new secular and egalitarian basis for coexistence in a series of eleven broadsheets titled *Nafir Suriyya,* or the "Syrian Clarion," which he printed between 29 September 1860 and 22 April 1861. In them Bustani addressed his "compatriots," those who he said lived in the same land, spoke the same language, and had the same manners and customs regardless of their different faiths, the sons of "Syria" he wished to awaken. His local, Arabic–speaking, active, individual, anonymous secular figure of the "patriot" stood in sharp contrast to the official Ottoman invocation of the sultan as the embodiment of an Ottoman nation made up of various obedient communities. Bustani urged his compatriots, therefore, not to forget the events that had devastated the region, or wash their hands of them, but to confront the reasons for the violence. He wanted them to understand, once and for all, that there could be no progress, no civilization, no catching up with Europe, no revival of past glory unless a "firm barrier" were placed between religious and secular authority. He called for the self-deliverance of men and women from the thrall of "sectarian, communal, and familial interests," and for a fundamental realization that religion provided a moral but not a political basis for nineteenth–century nationhood. *Hubb al-watan min al-iman,* "the love of the nation comes from faith," declared Bustani, quoting a saying attributed to the Prophet Muhammad, in order to draw a clear distinction between an ennobling religion and its antithesis, a degrading sectarianism.[69]

Bustani dismissed those "who are prejudiced" against the "people of Syria," those who insinuated that the Syrians were not intellectually or morally capable of effecting their own renaissance.[70] This oblique criticism of the foreign missionaries confirmed the extent to which Bustani had broken with the limited and paternalistic sphere of missionary work. To be sure, Bustani acknowledged in *Nafir Suriyya* his continued debt to American missionary discourse; he alluded to the classic missionary tropes of the "heathen" of India and the "savages" of Africa in order to situate the Syrians midway between the poles of barbarism and civilization. But for Bustani, such descriptions were literary devices to help clarify an Arab predicament, not discourses rooted in the experience and practice of racial discrimination and domination.

വ

In 1863 Bustani embarked on his own civilizing mission.[71] He founded his celebrated "National School" in a new suburb of Beirut, where he sought to inculcate the values of ecumenical nationalism in a new generation of students drawn from diverse backgrounds: to respect religious difference, not to broach "sectarian" matters; to specifically reject religious proselytization; and to make a unifying patriotism the very basis of modern life through rigorous education.[72] The Arabic curriculum of the boarding school, whose students outnumbered those in the American mission's two schools in Beirut, covered literary and scientific materials. Students also learned English, French, Greek, Latin, and Turkish. Even William and Loanza Benton, who had been expelled from the mission because of their defiant independence, sent their two children to Bustani's school, "although there were not but Arab boys there."[73] Underscoring his break with American missionary philosophy, Bustani insisted that "moderate" religious belief, rather than evangelical Christianity per se, was essential for proper education. Therefore, he made sure that students of different faiths—Muslims, Druzes, and Christians of various sects—were to be separately instructed in their respective religions.[74]

ଯୁ

Bustani was honored by the Ottoman state for his late work, for his school, for a massive encyclopedia he began to write, and for a new Arabic dictionary which he dedicated to the Ottoman sultan Abdul-Aziz. Despite the tired Ottoman mantra about the hypocrisy of converts, imperial officials granted him a monetary prize and an imperial decoration.[75] This rapprochement could not, however, conceal a basic difference that would continue to divide the imperial state from liberal subjects such as Bustani, and Bustani from contemporary reformers who regarded themselves as guardians of unbroken religious traditions. For the Ottoman state, the nineteenth century was an age of anxiety and defensiveness: imperial reformation was never intended, obviously, to liberate subjects, but rather to bind them more tightly to central power.[76] For Bustani, the nineteenth century was one of possibility despite, or perhaps because of, the 1860 war; as much as he was able to free himself from the inherently triumphal religiosity of the American mission, he never denied his debt to it or his friendship with missionaries such as Cornelius Van Dyck. In this he differed substantially from many major reformist intellectuals of the era who were galvanized by the educational accomplishments of the missionaries but whose primary concern lay not with a general secular advancement but with a far narrower preoccupation with their own communities.[77] The well-known Muslim reformist intellectual Muhammad Rashid Rida, for instance, issued a *fatwa* specifically forbidding students from attending mission schools, and what he described as secular schools, because they threatened to de-Islamify them—an ironic and utterly unappreciated echo of Rufus Anderson's racialist conceit of "denationalizing" natives, and of course of the Maronite patriarch's original encyclical against the American missionaries in 1823.[78] Whereas most reformers in the late empire dealt with issues of civilization, backwardness, and reform, Bustani advocated a liberal national project that hoped to transcend religious difference. Self-consciously Muslim reformers and the Maronite, Greek Catholic, and Orthodox churches could only propose modern projects that affirmed religious difference, and hence opened parochial schools to rival those of the missionaries but not, in any secular sense, to supersede them.

As the founder of the first genuinely ecumenical, if not secular, school in the Ottoman Empire, Bustani entertained a modern vision which departed most significantly from that projected by the Syrian Protestant College (SPC), a new institution of higher education which American missionaries had opened on property they had rented from Bustani, adjacent to his own school, in 1866. The SPC was independent of the American Board in large part because of a pronounced missionary desire to be liberated from Anderson's prohibition of worldly education and his emphasis on native agency. The college's Christian idealism and missionary character were nevertheless refracted through a mid-century American racialist reading of the world. As its first president, Daniel Bliss, put it so succinctly: "We open its doors to the members of the most advanced and most backward of races. As for me, I would admit the Pigmies of Central Africa in the hope that after a lapse of a few thousand years some of them might become leaders of Church and State. Why not? For hath not God made of one blood all nations of men for to dwell on all the face of the earth?"[79]

The well-funded college, the precursor to today's American University of Beirut, inevitably dwarfed Bustani's own solitary effort. At first Bustani's school served as a preparatory department for the college, but such collaboration was untenable, given the markedly different goals the respective institutions cherished. The American institution soon moved to a new campus on the undeveloped outskirts of town. "This College," said Bliss famously on 7 December 1871, as the cornerstone was laid of the main college building, designed in New York and built of the best grade of sandstone with cheap local labor, "is for all men without regard to colour, nationality, race, or religion. A man white, black, or yellow; Christian, Jew, Mohammedan or heathen, may enter and enjoy all the advantages of this institution for three,

Figure 13. Dr. Daniel Bliss in 1905, aged 82. Source: Henry H. Jessup, *Fifty-Three Years in Syria* vol. 1 (New York: Fleming H. Revell Company, 1910), 711a (opposite 711).

four or eight years; and go out believing in one God, in many Gods, or in no God. But it will be impossible for any one to continue with us long without knowing what we believe to be the truth and our reasons for that belief."[80] This was a remarkable sentiment uttered by a committed Protestant missionary. This sentiment was also uniquely American. Bliss invoked racial categories of white, black, and yellow (but not, crucially, red) that were meaningless in an Ottoman context but that, nevertheless, revealed how far the American mission had come in four decades: from the "flying of time" that marked the millennial exuberance of the first assault on the "empire of sin" to an impatient accommodation to its complex reality. The founding generation of American missionaries were unmistakably part of a broader effort to stave off the total dispossession of American Indians. They were replaced by a new generation of missionaries committed to the gradual paternalistic building up of other inferior races, which did not appear doomed as the Indians were made out to be, but which were nevertheless subordinated to American men and women.

ॐ

Bustani tried to persuade the missionaries to support his own school in its non-Protestant and nonsectarian course, and as a result he was deemed by several influential Americans, including Bliss, to be selfish, proud, and excessively vain. When Bustani wrote an article criticizing foreign schools in March 1874 after the American mission press had printed an attack on the founder of the Maronite Church, the patrician Bliss wrote of the native Protestant church's most famous son that he was "a bad, bold man— a stumbling block."[81] In his prejudice the American missionary was outdone only by David Stuart Dodge, a founding donor, English-language teacher at the college, and eventually chairman of its board of trustees in New York, who lambasted Bustani as a tricky and underhanded child of the East. "He must be assigned a place and be kept there," wrote Dodge spitefully, "and never be regarded as one whom we can fully trust in any particular."[82]

Bustani had become the unwanted apostle for an ecumenical humanism which the American mission had never intended. The Syrian Protestant College, tellingly, put in place an entire system that privileged white Anglo-Saxon professors over the very people whom they had come to save. The college commenced with Arabic as its language of instruction and with a solemn vow to turn over its faculty to full native control in the shortest possible time. By 1884, following the British occupation of Egypt and a crisis over Darwinism that decimated the ranks of the more liberal professors, English, the language "imbued with the spirit of progress," as the college put it, was made the language of education. This is still the case today, as is American control over what would in 1920 become the American University of Beirut. Compulsory religious service was the norm until finally the Young Turk revolution in 1908, and a student rebellion the following year, forced the American administration to relax its grip, but never let go, of the institution. Natives were systematically excluded from the professorial ranks until 1895, and differential pay scales and race-based appointments would continue until after the Ottoman Empire collapsed.[83]

But in Bustani, the initially violent intersection of different American and Arab histories had thrown up, by no means inevitably, an eloquent advocate for dialogue *within and across* cultures. A cultural clash had, in a word, produced its antithesis. It was this that the American missionary Cornelius Van Dyck recognized most plainly and significantly. Having already resigned his medical professorship at the Syrian Protestant College after Bliss had led a crackdown on liberal views and on native employment at the institution following the crisis over the teaching of Darwin in 1882, Van Dyck attended Bustani's funeral a year later in 1883 and there delivered a eulogy in Arabic to "my brother and beloved."[84] Bustani, as he himself recognized only too well, was the privileged product of a transitional age, an age of progress claimed by all but owned by none. But as he also knew, he was neither this age's only prophet nor its most powerful one.

⁂

There is, in the end, an instructive comparison to be drawn between the figure of Butrus al-Bustani, who anonymously printed pamphlets urging his compatriots away from the sectarian precipice, and Jeremiah Evarts, the head of the American Board, who had in the late 1820s authored a series of pamphlets under the pseudonym "William Penn" in the vain attempt to prevent the expulsion of Cherokee Indians from Georgia.

In both instances, two evangelically minded, idealistic men sought to impress on their compatriots the urgency and moral imperatives of the great issues of their respective times: racial tolerance in America, religious tolerance in the Ottoman Empire. Both sought to wrest the future of their respective nations away from those who took an altogether narrower view of human nature. There were, to be sure, obvious differences between the two. Evarts consorted with powerful men, and was fully committed to an aggressive missionary posture premised on the inevitable elimination of Indian and all other heathen cultures, but not the extermination of Indians. He had to contend with, and failed to soften, the racist depravity of the vast majority of his fellow citizens. Bustani also had to exhort his own compatriots to forsake religious fanaticism, and in this he was only partially successful. The Protestant convert turned ecumenical educator was confronted, in addition, with the chauvinism of Evarts's missionary heirs.

As divergent as their paths were, and as dissimilar their locations in their respective societies, they both insisted on the capacity of human beings to overcome their temporary differences and unite around their essential sameness. Bustani therefore articulated a seminal plea for the practice of liberalism that was neither derived from, nor fully independent of, the context of mission and empire. His belief in the political equality of Muslim and Christian and of West and East was anathema not only to American missionaries but also to many of his own Arab contemporaries. His refusal to allow the Maronite suppression of As̒ad Shidyaq's story, or the American monopoly over it, indicated both the possibilities and limits of his nineteenth-century world. He helped construct and embody notions—East and West, sectarianism and patriotism, culture and civilization, progress and barbarism—that consumed him for the rest of his life, and that set the tone for the next century and into the present one. Like As̒ad and Faris Shidyaq, Butrus al-Bustani was willing to borrow from foreign cultures, and to rethink the basis of his own.

In the end, the Protestant convert struggled to redefine coexistence from a strategy of empire, or a tactic of mission, to a way of life. From a condition of resignation to the fact of long and intimate proximity to others of different faiths, and from an intricate series of signs and codes that structured a manifestly unequal society, coexistence might yet become something far bolder: a self-conscious, explicit, articulated identification by individuals as equal, civilized subjects in a political community greater than the sum total of its various religious parts.

There was, and remains, a price to be paid for this kind of coexistence. Idealistic and didactic, it encouraged and still encourages a certain kind of self-censorship, a hesitancy, if not an outright inability, to delve seriously into history's darker moments that might impinge on its sustaining ecumenical notion. But there is a far greater price to be paid for sectarianism. And, of course, for racism.

Epilogue

Daniel Bliss's son Howard succeeded his father as president of the Syrian Protestant College just after the turn of the twentieth century. Two decades later, in 1920, he proclaimed the advent of the "Modern Missionary," that is, one who accepts "ungrudgingly and gratefully" that Christianity is not "the sole channel through which divine and saving truth has been conveyed." Indeed, confessed Bliss, such a missionary "comes to supplement, not solely to create. He prays for all men with a new sympathy—for all mosques and temples and synagogues as well as for all churches."[1]

Howard Bliss's remarkable essay came exactly a century after the American Board had begun its mission to the Ottoman Empire, hoping to replace what it believed to be the edifices of false piety that oppressed the Holy Land with "pure" Christian churches. It came, also, sixty years *after* Butrus al-Bustani first vindicated As'ad Shidyaq and advocated a liberal vision of coexistence as a modern way of life—akin to what is called "multiculturalism" in America today. Following the collapse of the Ottoman Empire, American missionaries finally and openly reconciled themselves to an ecumenical reality they had for so long labored against. In that same year the Syrian Protestant College changed its name to the American University of Beirut.

My point here is not so much that Bustani was an exceptional figure but rather that he was an exemplary liberal product of the commingling of American and Arab histories that legitimated new identities, allowed for new histories, and made possible new, and often contradictory, conceptions of the modern world. After all, the same nineteenth-century intersection of American mission and Ottoman Empire that created the liberalism of Bustani also wrought, as we have seen, the modern belligerence of Henry Harris Jessup and the modern defensiveness of Ottoman and Arab nationalist reformers who routinely equated missionaries with imperialism.[2] Neither Bustani's nor Howard Bliss's liberalism was inevitable. Certainly neither was self-evident at the outset of the missionary project in the region: they were both produced—with different implications and elisions, to be sure—as a result of a long cross-cultural engagement. To appreciate this basic fact is to move one step away from fundamentalist and nationalist sensibilities unable and unwilling to grasp the subtleties of history; it is also to draw attention to the larger history of American involvement with the region of which this particular story of American missionaries and their failed conquest of the Middle East is but a part. This larger history, I believe, is in need of serious revision.

This book will contribute, I hope, to a fundamental overturning of the seductive language of American or Islamic exceptionalism which has so often invoked essential values and temperaments that have in reality changed radically over time. The self-portrait first painted by Jessup has proven remarkably enduring precisely because its initial evangelical form has been able to take more secular expression. The idea of American missionaries as pioneers required that the Ottoman Empire be seen as an extension of the fabled American frontier, a semi-barbarous landscape in need of colonization and enlightenment by rugged "American" individualism, liberal education, and above all religious toleration. Such a view depended—and still depends—on idealizing America as much as it depends on orientalizing the Arab world. It sees in the former what it refuses to see in the latter; it engages in comparative work without fair comparison, and it does so in order to validate preconceived ideas, not in order to understand self and other better. It relies, furthermore, on a notion of modernity that is described as if it were an American gift to be given to the people "sitting in darkness," people whose only choice is to reject or to adapt to forms alien to their history and culture.[3] Such representations are the source of contemporary notions of an age-old struggle between an advanced, tolerant "Judeo-Christian West" and its intolerant Islamic antithesis; they rationalize, in turn, the modern conceit of a "clash of civilizations," and its requisite reduction of diverse, vibrant, contradictory multireligious cultures, into essential monolithic religious blocs.[4]

This book disputes such essentialist propositions not by denying the violence of history, or the reality of cultural confrontation, but by studying them historically, that is to say, by maintaining a distinction between the irregular unfolding of history and the narratives of it that do indeed sweep smoothly across huge spans of time. Cultures are not caricatures to be set in irreconcilable opposition to one another. To acknowledge the contingency of Bustani's liberalism is not simply to reverse the sequence of an established, and still powerful, narrative of American benevolence toward an illiberal Middle East in order to claim that the "Arabs" were first and the Americans second in their liberalism. There could have been no Bustani without the American mission—*or* without the Ottoman and Arab context that defined its application.

To speak and make judgments about the problems, and evident limits, of liberalism in the Arab world is perfectly valid; to speak about them by assuming that liberalism is a completed, uncomplicated, and uncontested problem in America, or the West more generally, is not.[5] Rather than compare Arab and American cultures as if they were plotted on a single evolutionary line in which America (or "the West") leads—or should abandon the attempt to lead—a recalcitrant Middle East into a uniquely Western modernity, it seems far more reasonable and truthful to undertake a history that reveals the different but simultaneous emergence of modernity in both locations and that tries to understand the uneven relationship between them. "America and the world" presupposes not two spheres to be separately analyzed but one.

ℛ

Yet in embarking on this kind of new history as I have done, however imperfectly, I do not overlook the ties that bind our present condition to the nineteenth-century past with which this book is primarily concerned. Whatever one chooses to call it, American imperialism exists, and it exists nowhere more obviously than in the Arab world. But I have deliberately resisted the idea of labeling the American missionaries to that world "cultural imperialists."

As I have tried to explain in this book, even though American missionaries became ever more explicitly racist as the nineteenth century progressed, and were increasingly determined to distinguish themselves from the very natives they converted and educated, they were not, properly speaking, cultural imperialists. They could not coerce directly, nor could they hope to rely on the coercive context of a colonial state to facilitate their establishment as their Puritan forebears had done in early America. The founding of their most enduring and famous institution in the Middle East, the Syrian Protestant College, was not so much an act of cultural imposition as it was a final recognition of the futility of direct evangelism in deeply multireligious lands, and also an accommodation to a local demand for secular education. When David S. Dodge expressed relief upon the resignation of the Armenian Protestant medical doctor John Wortabet from the Syrian Protestant College in 1886 by writing to Daniel Bliss, "What a blessing to be rid of the last of the half-hearted, half-educated (in the best sense), unwilling, un-American, missionary line of Professors," he was reflecting not cultural imperialism but anxiety about its absence.[6] A half-century of sustained trial and error, of rebuff and frustration, and above all of mutual transformation of American missionaries and their Arab environment, had finally yielded an institution whose underlying secular emphasis would have been unimaginable to the founders of the American mission, and ultimately was unacceptable to men like Dodge and Daniel Bliss. Their disparaging of natives was indeed an indication of the racial currents of the late-nineteenth-century United States; but it drew just as greatly on a real fear that "their" college, which was located in one of the few significant corners of the world net yet formally colonized by Western powers, might well slip from their control.

It is for this reason that facile comparisons between the nineteenth-century mission and what America is doing in and to the Middle East today are so unsatisfying. The politics of oil and Israel, and of course the occupation of Iraq, mark not a continuity with but a radical rupture from previous American involvement. Many Americans today, of course, still use the rhetoric of converting the world to democracy or freedom. Still others firmly believe in a new and apocalyptic version of millennialism, particularly so-called Christian Zionism; but these are incommensurable with the American Board's mission to the Ottoman Empire, whose work was *overwhelmingly* focused on the Eastern Christians and Muslims of the region, and whose agents, as we have seen, abandoned millennial enthusiasm for the much harder task of accommodating themselves to foreign realities. Many Arabs and Muslims, for their part, subscribe to the rhetoric of repulsing the "crusaders," and in this they recall (albeit unknowingly) the anathemas of the Maronite patriarch against the encroaching, satanically inspired missionaries. But between these sentiments, these continuities of form and expression, there are also two centuries of complex history, and of dramatic changes of context which have fundamentally remade both America and the Arab world.

Institutions such as the American University of Beirut still, of course, retain palpable reminders of their missionary past, most concretely in the buildings that bear the names of the founding missionaries and their evangelical patrons. But far more obviously, the American University of Beirut has struggled to adapt to the extraordinary militarization of the modern Middle East in the aftermath of the Arab-Israeli conflict and as a result of the cold war, in which the United States clearly marked the oil-rich region as a sphere of paramount importance. For instance, in the aftermath of the events of September 11, the president of the university, John Waterbury, wrote in *Foreign Affairs* that the American University of Beirut was a supreme example of the "soft power" of the United States, and hence a formidable ideological asset to America in the region. In repudiating the idea that only the demonstration of overwhelming American military might could subdue the Middle East, Waterbury was compelled to admit an overt relationship to U.S. strategic power that the founders of the Syrian Protestant College, for all their racism, would not have recognized or necessarily accepted.[7]

※

Today, Bustani's dream of coexistence is needed more than ever, but not as he first tried to realize it, or as many liberal and secular Arab nationalists, who adopted his kind of thinking, promoted it for much of the twentieth century. Bustani's distinction between "real" religion, which was tolerant and affirmative, and "false" religion, which was intolerant and belligerent, reflected his preoccupation with the 1860 war in Mount Lebanon and his determination to educate his compatriots away from the sectarian precipice. In the process, however, he anticipated a central concern of Arab nationalist thought which mythologized coexistence by reinforcing the very religious categories it was trying to transcend.

Lebanon, which was established as a republic by the French as part of a European colonial partition of the Arab world following the First World War, has strictly prohibited "sectarian agitation" and strongly proclaims coexistence between different faiths as an essential element in political life. Like other Arab states such as Syria, Iraq, and Egypt, and indeed like the nineteenth-century Ottoman Empire from which all these countries issued, Lebanon saw in coexistence a unifying nationalist ethos to justify its independence from foreign tutelage. Yet despite Bustani's plea to separate decisively religion from politics, the opposite occurred. Religion was made, and remains, the defining feature of the sectarian political system in Lebanon. In Lebanon, as in the wider Arab world to which it belongs, coexistence has become a mantra rather than part of a credible historical narrative; it is something to be proclaimed defiantly and defensively in the face of foreign detractors and sectarian ideologues at home but not seriously or historically investigated.

Admittedly, nationalist scholars in the Arab world have been writing in a hostile environment, marked by colonialism, the loss of Palestine, wars, military coups, and revolutions largely unimaginable to their counterparts in the United States. They are deeply reluctant, if not altogether unwilling, to investigate the meaning of past episodes of sectarian strife, or to discuss candidly the nature of imperial Islamic discrimination, or to take seriously the Christian character of formidable figures such as Bustani or Faris Shidyaq (who is known and celebrated today as *Ahmad* Faris Shidyaq because of his conversion to Islam). Bustani's optimism has, practically speaking, vanished. Although Arab history is a source of immense pride and identity, it has also become a field carefully navigated lest, as in Iraq, its repressed, but not forgotten, divisive narratives be suddenly and violently resurrected. As real and as understandable as such fears are, they have effectively demarcated much of Arab history as a forbidden no-man's land.

This apologetic sensibility has again condemned Asʿad Shidyaq to obscurity in his own homeland. The evidence of Asʿad's fate has lain in the Maronite archives, not hidden, but not explored either. His conversion and persecution were assumed to be significant only to the politically marginal community of Protestants of Lebanon. His tale was considered, moreover, to be an embarrassment to the Maronites. To judge by the near total silence on his case and on the history of early American involvement in the Arab world which gave it meaning, it was a story best not told; or perhaps it was a story that nobody quite knew how to tell, because it simply does not conform to prevailing notions of coexistence and the simplistic identification of American missionaries with imperialism. But as the enormously kind Maronite archivist at Bkirke told me as he knowingly handed document after document that "incriminated" the Maronite Church to a person he thought of as a Protestant and whose nineteenth-century ancestors had been converted by American missionaries, it is high time that all communities, including the Maronites, acknowledge and openly come to terms with the difficult moments in their past.

We are, in the end, all implicated in one another's histories.

Notes

Introduction

1. Although I am well aware of the vexed history of the term "native," I use the terms "local," "native," and "indigenous" interchangeably. I do, however, assume a sufficiently clear distinction between the condescending missionary use of the term "native" and my own meaning of a locally rooted person.

2. I use the term "Indians" rather than "Native Americans" because that is the term used by missionaries.

3. The phrase "clash of civilizations," popularized by Samuel Huntington in his essay "The Clash of Civilizations?" *Foreign Affairs* 72 (Summer 1993): 22–49, was first used in the context of Islam and the West by Bernard Lewis in his essay "The Roots of Muslim Rage," *Atlantic Monthly* 266 (September 1990): 47–60.

4. William Carey, *An Enquiry into the Obligations of Christians, to use Means for the Conversion of the Heathens* (London, 1792); Gordon Hall and Samuel Newall, *The Conversion of the World: Or the Claims of Six Hundred Millions and the Ability and Duty of the Churches Respecting Them*, 2nd ed. (Andover, Mass.: Flagg and Gould, 1818).

5. Studies of American mission still deal overwhelmingly with missionaries and not with converts. See, for example, Wilbert R. Shenk, ed., *North American Foreign Missions, 1810–1914: Theology, Theory, and Policy* (Grand Rapids: Eerdmans, 2004).

6. For instance, in Eric Foner and John A. Garraty, eds., *The Reader's Companion to American History* (Boston: Houghton Mifflin, 1991), the ABCFM does not even merit an entry. The relative marginalization of nineteenth-century American mission work in the historiography is made obvious by the vibrancy of the debates around missionaries and Indian-white relations in the colonial period, as attested by works such as Alden T. Vaughn, *New England Frontier: Puritans and Indians, 1620–1675*, 3rd ed. (1965; Norman: University of Oklahoma Press, 1995); Francis Jennings, *The Invasion of America: Indians, Colonialism, and the Cant of Conquest* (New York: Norton, 1975); and later James Axtell, *The Invasion Within* (New York: Oxford University Press, 1985). Richard White's pioneering work *The Middle Ground: Indians, Empires, and Republics in the Great Lakes Region, 1650–1815* (Cambridge: Cambridge University Press, 1991), stands out here.

7. Especially for the study of America and the Middle East, Ian Tyrrell's admonition about a comparative history that fails to transcend the boundaries of nationalist historiography still rings

very true. See Ian Tyrrell, "American Exceptionalism in an Age of International History," *American Historical Review* 96 (1991): 1031–55.

8. The contrast with the British case is instructive. Jean and John L. Comaroff's justly famous two-volume account of nonconformist British missionaries among the southern African Tswana insisted that a missionary encounter must be studied as a "complex dialectic of challenge and riposte, domination and defiance," and as a "long conversation, the drawn out process of colonization, that was to follow," in which the natives had to engage on intrinsically unfavorable terms. See Jean Comaroff and John L. Comaroff, *Of Revelation and Revolution,* vol. 1, *Christianity, Colonialism, and Consciousness* (Chicago: University of Chicago Press, 1991), 12, 171, 213; and vol. 2, *The Dialectics of Modernity on a South African Frontier* (Chicago: University of Chicago Press, 1997). There is also a rich history of Indian Christianity and missionaries, including Susan Bayly, *Saints, Goddesses, and Kings: Muslims and Christians in South Indian Society, 1700–1900* (Cambridge: Cambridge University Press, 1989), and Gauri Viswanathan, *Outside the Fold: Conversion, Modernity, and Belief* (Princeton: Princeton University Press, 1998).

9. In the broader North American context, Allan Greer, working mainly through French Jesuit sources, is a notable exception in his *Mohawk Saint: Catherine Tekakwitha and the Jesuits* (Oxford: Oxford University Press, 2005). Daniel Richter, *Facing East from Indian Country: A Native History of Early America* (Cambridge: Harvard University Press, 2001), makes an effort to rethink what American history might have looked like from various Indian vantage points, although he is limited by the preponderance of English archives and the totality of Indian defeat.

10. Marshall Sahlins, *Islands of History* (Chicago: University of Chicago Press, 1985), 72.

11. William R. Hutchison, *Errand to the World: American Protestant Thought and Foreign Missions* (Chicago: University of Chicago Press, 1987), is the most obvious example of this exclusive focus on American missionaries in telling the story and significance of American missionary history. James A. Field Jr., *America and the Mediterranean World, 1776–1882* (Princeton: Princeton University Press, 1969), is also typical in this respect regarding American involvement in the Levant. The most interesting recent work on Americans in the Middle East has come not from historians but from scholars of literature and American studies such as Timothy Marr, *The Cultural Roots of American Islamism* (Cambridge: Cambridge University Press, 2006); Melani McAlister, *Epic Encounters: Culture, Media, and U.S. Interests in the Middle East, 1945–2000* (Berkeley: University of California Press, 2001); and Hilton Obenzinger, *American Palestine: Melville, Twain, and the Holy Land Mania* (Princeton: Princeton University Press, 1999), but even these do not take up any but American archives.

12. See Aron Rodrigue, "Difference and Tolerance in the Ottoman Empire: Interview by Nancy Reynolds," *Stanford Humanities Review* 5, no. 1 (1995): 81–92, in which he enjoins scholars to forgo the misleading language of post-Enlightenment majority and minority in the Ottoman Empire.

13. A. L. Tibawi, *American Interests in Syria, 1800–1901: A Study of Educational, Literary, and Religious Work* (Oxford: Clarendon Press, 1966), is the classic study of this mission. The pendulum is beginning to swing again in the direction of the vastly understudied array of missionary encounters in the Ottoman Empire. See, for example, Ussama Makdisi, "Reclaiming the Land of the Bible: Missionaries, Secularism, and Evangelical Modernity," *American Historical Review* 102 (1997): 680–713; Samir Khalaf, *Cultural Resistance: Global and Local Encounters in the Middle East* (London: Saqi Books, 2001), 105–197; Eleanor Tejirian and Reeva Simon, eds., *Altruism and Imperialism: Western Cultural and Religious Missions in the Middle East* (New York: Middle East Institute, Columbia University, 2002); and Jeremy Salt, *Imperialism, Evangelism, and the Ottoman Armenians, 1878–1896* (London: F. Cass, 1993); for Egypt, see Heather Sharkey, "Arabic Antimissionary Treatises: Muslim Responses to Christian Evangelism in the Modern Middle East," *International Bulletin of Missionary Research* 28 (2004): 98–104, and her "Empire and Muslim Conversion: His-

torical Reflections on Christian Missions in Egypt," *Islam and Christian-Muslim Relations* 16 (2005): 43–60; see also Paul Sedra, "Textbook Maneuvers: Evangelicals and Educational Reform in Nineteenth-Century Egypt" (Ph.D. diss., New York University, 2005).

14. See the work of Jens Hanssen, *Fin-de-Siècle Beirut: The Making of an Ottoman Provincial Capital* (Oxford: Clarendon Press, 2005); Bruce Masters, *Christians and Jews in the Ottoman Arab World: The Roots of Sectarianism* (Cambridge: Cambridge University Press, 2001); Benjamin Fortna, *Imperial Classroom: Islam, the State, and Education in the Late Ottoman Empire* (New York: Oxford University Press, 2002); and Eugene L. Rogan, *Frontiers of the State in the Late Ottoman Empire: Transjordan, 1850–1921* (Cambridge: Cambridge University Press, 1999). The same cannot be said for Jesuit history, which has seen the remarkable work of Bernard Heyberger, *Les Chrétiens du Proche-Orient au temps de la réforme Catholique: Syrie, Liban, Palestine, XVIIe–XVIIIe siècles* (Rome: École française de Rome, 1994), and *Hindiyya: Mystique et criminelle* (Paris: Auber, 2001), for which there is no comparable English-language work.

15. The indefatigable missionary apologist Andrew Porter has pointed this out on more than one occasion. See his "'Cultural Imperialism' and Protestant Missionary Enterprise, 1780–1914," *Journal of Imperial and Commonwealth History* 25 (1997): 367–391; see also Ryan Dunch, "Beyond Cultural Imperialism: Cultural Theory, Christian Missions, and Global Modernity," *History and Theory* 41 (2002): 301–325. And see also David J. Bosch, *Transforming Mission: Paradigm Shifts in Theology of Mission* (Maryknoll, N.Y.: Orbis Books, 1991), 291–313; and Stephen Neill, *Colonialism and Christian Missions* (London: Lutterworth Press, 1966), 412–425, for attempts to grapple with, and yet ultimately to justify, the relationship between Western missionaries and colonialism.

16. The phrase "pre-modern accommodations of difference" is one that Sugata Bose and Ayesha Jalal suggest for Indo-Islamic cultures before the arrival of the British as an alternative to either an anachronistic sense of liberal multiculturalism or an ahistorical sense of age-old communalism or sectarianism. See Sugata Bose and Ayesha Jalal, *Modern South Asia: History, Culture, Political Economy* (London: Routledge, 1998), 23–34.

17. American Board missions to China are a fascinating counterpoint in a far more belligerent context. Although they began a decade after the mission to the Middle East, both the American Board and the later American Presbyterian missions expanded significantly following the Chinese defeat during the 1840 Opium War and the harsh Treaty of Nanking signed in its aftermath. See G. Thompson Brown, *Earthen Vessels and Transcendent Power: American Presbyterians in China, 1837–1952* (Maryknoll, N.Y.: Orbis Books, 1997), and William Ellsworth Strong, *The Story of the American Board* (1910; New York: Arno Press, 1969).

18. See in this regard C. L. Higham, *Noble, Wretched, and Redeemable: Protestant Missionaries to the Indians in Canada and the United States, 1820–1900* (Albuquerque: University of New Mexico Press, 2000), 110–117; for British missionaries, see Andrew Porter, *Religion versus Empire? British Protestant Missionaries and Overseas Expansion, 1700–1914* (Manchester: Manchester University Press, 2004), 283–292.

19. Norman Etherington's introduction to his *Mission and Empire* (New York: Oxford University Press, 2005), 7, presumes to vindicate Christian missions from the charge of cultural imperialism simply because the agents of conversion in many parts of the British Empire were local people.

20. For the notion of fundamental egalitarianism, see Porter, "'Cultural Imperialism' and Protestant Missionary Enterprise," 384, and Lamin Sanneh, *Translating the Message: The Missionary Impact on Culture* (Maryknoll, N.Y.: Orbis Books, 1989), 125. For assumptions about imperialism, see Mustafa Khalidi and ʿUmar Farrukh, *Al-tabshir wa al-istiʿmar fi al-bilad al-ʿarabiyya* (Missionaries and Colonialism in the Arab World), 2nd ed. (1953; Beirut: Al-maktaba al-ʿasriyya, 1957); see also the analysis by Sharkey, "Empire and Muslim Conversion," 54–56.

21. Bernard Heyberger has called for exactly such a reevaluation of connected nineteenth-

century Middle East histories artificially cloistered by twentieth-century historiography. See his "Pour une 'histoire croisée' de l'occidentalisation et de la confessionnalisation chez les chrétiens du Proche-Orient," *MIT-Electronic Journal of Middle East Studies* 3 (2003): 36–49.

1. Mather's America

1. Cotton Mather, *Magnalia Christi Americana; or, The Ecclesiastical History of New-England; From Its First Planting, In The Year 1620, Unto The Year Of Our Lord 1698. In Seven Books,* 2 vols. (1702; Hartford: Silas Andrus and Son, 1855).

2. Ibid., 1:55.

3. Ibid., 1:26–27; see also Theodore Dwight Bozeman, *To Live Ancient Lives: The Primitivist Dimension in Puritanism* (Chapel Hill: Institute of Early American History and Culture, Williamsburg, Va., by the University of North Carolina Press, 1988).

4. Quoted in Perry Miller, *Orthodoxy in Massachusetts, 1630–1650: A Genetic Study* (Cambridge: Harvard University Press, 1933), 225.

5. *The Book of the General Laws and Libertyes Concerning the Inhabitants of the Massachusetts,* reprinted in William H. Whitmore, ed., *The Colonial Laws of Massachusetts* (Boston, 1889), 160. See also William G. McLoughlin, *New England Dissent, 1630–1833: The Baptists and the Separation of Church and State,* 2 vols. (Cambridge: Harvard University Press, 1971), 1:15.

6. Mather, *Magnalia,* 1:51 based on Ps 44:1–3.

7. Ibid., 56.

8. Royal charter cited ibid., 557.

9. Ibid., 558.

10. Ibid., 529.

11. Ibid., 556.

12. These sources, many of which were published in the 1640s and 1650s, were carefully scripted as part of an ongoing struggle between supporters and detractors of Puritan New England as noted by most historians of this period. Missionary activity or lack thereof figured prominently in the efforts to discredit or uphold the Puritan commonwealth in Massachusets and its relationship to royal authority. See Michael P. Clark, ed., *The Eliot Tracts with Letters from John Eliot to Thomas Thorowgood and Richard Baxter* (Westport, Conn.: Praeger, 2003).

13. Daniel Richter has tried to reconstruct an alternative Indian perspective on John Eliot's mission in *Facing East from Indian Country: A Native History of Early America* (Cambridge: Harvard University Press, 2001), 111–129. See also Colin G. Calloway, *New Worlds for All: Indians, Europeans, and the Remaking of Early America* (Baltimore: Johns Hopkins University Press, 1997).

14. Francis Jennings, *The Invasion of America: Indians, Colonialism, and the Cant of Conquest* (New York: Norton, 1975), 235–241.

15. Quoted in Alden Vaughn, *New England Frontier: Puritans and Indians, 1620–1675,* 3rd ed. (1965; Norman: University of Oklahoma Press, 1995), 294.

16. Richard W. Cogley, *John Eliot's Mission to the Indians before King Philip's War* (Cambridge: Harvard University Press, 1999), 245–246. For an elaboration on the range of Indian perspectives, see Dane Morrison, *A Praying People: Massachusett Acculturation and the Failure of the Puritan Mission, 1600–1690* (New York: Peter Lang, 1995), 22–25.

17. John Eliot, *A Further Account of the Progress of the Gospel Amongst the Indians in New England* (London, 1660), reprinted in Clark, *The Eliot Tracts,* 387.

18. Richter, *Facing East,* 95–96.

19. Thomas Shepard (?), *The Day-Breaking if not the Sun-Rising of the Gospell with the Indians in New-England* (London, 1647), reprinted in Clark, *The Eliot Tracts,* 92.

20. Quoted in Cogley, *John Eliot's Mission to the Indians,* 7.

21. Quoted in Neal Salisbury, "Red Puritans: The "Praying Indians" of Massachusetts Bay and John Eliot," *William and Mary Quarterly,* 3rd ser., 31 (1974): 32.

22. Mather, *Magnalia*, 1:557.

23. "The Letter of Mr. Eliot to T.S. concerning the late work of God among the Indians," in Thomas Shepard, *The Clear Sunshine of the Gospel Breaking Forth Upon the Indians in New-England* (London, 1648), reprinted in Clark, *The Eliot Tracts*, 124.

24. Henry W. Bowden and James P. Ronda, eds., *John Eliot's Indian Dialogues: A Study in Cultural Interaction* (Westport, Conn.: Greenwood Press, 1980), 40. It is not clear how Eliot distributed his translated Bibles or how they were read. See Cogley, *John Eliot's Mission to the Indians*, 121.

25. See Clark, *The Eliot Tracts*, 2–3, 93, 138–139, for examples of anti-Catholic mission apologetics.

26. Mather, *Magnalia*, 1:572–573.

27. Ibid., 573.

28. Ibid., 560.

29. Cogley, *John Eliot's Mission to the Indians*, 230–232; James D. Drake, *King Philip's War: Civil War in New England, 1675–1676* (Amherst: University of Massachusetts Press, 1999), 62.

30. Bowden and Ronda, *John Eliot's Indian Dialogues*, 80.

31. Ibid., 60.

32. On Roanoke, see Edmund S. Morgan, *American Slavery, American Freedom: The Ordeal of Colonial Virginia* (New York: Norton, 1975), 44.

33. Richard Slotkin and James K. Folsom, eds., *So Dreadfull a Judgment: Puritan Responses to King Philip's War, 1676–1677* (Hanover, N.H.: Wesleyan University Press, 1978), 38–39; Jill Lepore, *The Name of War: King Philip's War and the Origins of American Identity* (New York: Vintage, 1999), 159; Louise A. Breen, *Transgressing the Bounds: Subversive Enterprises among the Puritan Elite in Massachusetts, 1630–1692* (Oxford: Oxford University Press, 2001), 165–167.

34. Jennings, *The Invasion of America*, 324–325. See also Drake, *King Philip's War*, 175. Recent scholarship has also emphasized the persistence of Indians and their resistance despite the nineteenth-century New England evolution of the myth of the "vanishing Indian." See Colin G. Galloway and Neal Salisbury, eds., *Reinterpreting the New England Indians and the Colonial Experience* (Boston: Colonial Society of Massachusetts, 2003). See also Jean M. O'Brien, *Dispossession by Degrees: Indian Land and Identity in Natick, Massachusetts, 1650–1790* (Cambridge: Cambridge University Press, 1997), 3–12, and Amy E. Den Ouden, *Beyond Conquest: Native Peoples and the Struggle for History in New England* (Lincoln: University of Nebraska Press, 2005).

35. Quoted in Cogley, *John Eliot's Mission to the Indians*, 232; see also Lepore, *The Name of War*, 160.

36. Mather, *Magnalia*, 1:566.

37. The covenant provided "halfway" status for baptized descendants of church members unable to profess a conversion narrative. See Alan Simpson, *Puritanism in Old and New England* (Chicago: University of Chicago Press, 1955), 35–36; see also McLoughlin, *New England Dissent*, 1:43–44.

38. McLoughlin, *New England Dissent*, 1:107.

39. Kenneth Silverman, *The Life and Times of Cotton Mather* (New York: Welcome Rain Publishers, 1984), 302, 405. See also Perry Miller, *The New England Mind: From Colony to Province* (Cambridge: Belknap Press, 1953), 128–129, although the argument is made therein that Mather was compelled to accept a fait accompli. See McLoughlin, *New England Dissent* 1:109–110.

40. Sidney H. Rooy, *The Theology of Missions in the Puritan Tradition: A Study of Representative Puritans, Richard Sibbes, Richard Baxter, John Eliot, Cotton Mather, and Jonathan Edwards* (Grand Rapids: Eerdmans, 1965), 246.

41. Mather, *Magnalia*, 1:574.

42. Ibid., 556.

43. Ibid., 574.

44. Cotton Mather, *India Christiana: A Discourse Delivered unto the Commissioners for the Propagation of the Gospel among the American Indians* (Boston: Green, 1721), 29, 40, 46−47.

2. "The Grammar of Heresy"

1. There are several extant manuscripts of Istifan Duwayhi's *Tarikh al-azmina*. I am using the edition published by Butrus Fahd (Beirut: Dar Lahd Khater, n.d.), which is based on manuscript no. 215 from the Syriac section of the Vatican Library.

2. See Bruce Masters, *Christians and Jews in the Ottoman Arab World: The Roots of Sectarianism* (Cambridge: Cambridge University Press, 2001), 16−40, for more details on the Ottoman rulers' treatment of and attitude toward Christians and Jews in their empire.

3. *Encyclopedia of Islam*, new ed., s.v. "Dhimma." For more information on the Pact of ʿUmar, see Mark R. Cohen, *Under Crescent and Cross: The Jews in the Middle Ages* (Princeton: Princeton University Press, 1994), 54−65.

4. For further elaboration, see Gottfried Hagen, "Ottoman Understandings of the World in the Seventeenth Century," afterword to Robert Dankoff, *An Ottoman Mentality: The World of Evliya Çelebi* (Brill: Leiden, 2004), 242.

5. As the Orientalist A. S. Tritton has observed in regard to the Muslim treatment of *dhimmis*, "Laws were made, observed for a time, and then forgotten till something brought them to the remembrance of the authorities." A. S. Tritton, *The Caliphs and their Non-Muslim Subjects: A Critical Study of the Covenant of ʿUmar* (London: Oxford University Press, 1930), 229.

6. Tijana Krstic "Trampling on the Turban: Conversion to Islam, Apostasy, and Martyrdom in Ottoman Rumeli (15th−17th Centuries)," paper presented at a workshop, "Beyond the Clash of Civilizations: Missionaries, Conversion, and Tolerance in the Ottoman Empire," held at Rice University, April 2004.

7. Ray Jabre Mouawad, "Qui sont les Maronites Blancs?" in Charles Chartouni, ed., *Histoire sociétés et pouvoir aux Proche et Moyen Orients*, 2 vols. (Paris: Geuthner, 2001), 1:123−135.

8. Quoted in Abdul-Rahim Abu-Husayn, *The View from Istanbul: Lebanon and the Druze Emirate in the Ottoman Chancery Documents, 1546−1711* (London: Centre for Lebanese Studies and I. B. Tauris, 2004), 35.

9. Ussama Makdisi, *Culture of Sectarianism: Community, History, and Violence in Nineteenth-Century Ottoman Lebanon* (Berkeley: University of California Press, 2000), 28−50; Stefan H. Winter, "Shiite Emirs and Ottoman Authorities: The Campaign against the Hamadas of Mt. Lebanon, 1693−1694," *Archivum Ottomanicum* 18 (2000): 201−245.

10. Yusuf al-Dibs, *Al-Jamiʿ al-mufassal fi tarikh al-mawarina al-muʾassal* (Beirut: Lahd Khater, 1987), 234−237.

11. Kamal Salibi, *Syria under Islam: Empire on Trial, 634−1097* (Delmar, N.Y.: Caravan Books, 1977), 28−31.

12. Ray J. Mouawad, "Recherches sur la vallée de la Qadisha," *Proche-Orient Chrétien* 50 (2000): 5−13.

13. Kamal Salibi, *Maronite Historians of Medieval Lebanon* (1959; Beirut: Naufal, 1991); Ray Jabre Mouawad, *Lettres au Mont-Liban d'Ibn al-Qilaʿi (XVème siècle)* (Paris: Geuthner, 2001).

14. Mouawad, *Lettres au Mont Liban d'Ibn al-Qilaʿi*, 246. All translations into English are my own unless otherwise stated.

15. Quoted ibid., , 220.

16. Quoted in Salibi, *Maronite Historians of Medieval Lebanon*, 83.

17. Butrus al-Jumayyil, ed., *Zajaliyyat Jibraʾil ibn al-Qilaʿi* (Beirut: Dar Lahd Khater, 1982), 90.

18. Mouawad, *Lettres au Mont-Liban d'Ibn al-Qilaʿi*, 212.

19. Bernard Heyberger, *Les Chrétiens du Proche-Orient au temps de la réforme Catholique: Syrie, Liban, Palestine, XVIIe−XVIIIe siècles* (Rome: École française de Rome, 1994), 139, 185−208.

20. Mouawad, *Lettres au Mont-Liban d'Ibn al-Qilaʿi*, 71.

21. Duwayhi, *Tarikh al-azmina,* 10.

22. Ibid., 322–323. In another edition of *Tarikh al-azmina* edited by Rashid al-Chartouni, published as *Tarikh al-ta'ifa al-maruniyya* (Beirut: al-matba'a al-kathulikiyya, 1890), 129, Duwayhi adds a brief description of the burning of Patriarch Hajula in the same year.

23. Nasser Gemayel, *Al-batriyark Istifanus al-Duwayhi: hayatuhu wa mu'allafatuhu* (Beirut, 1991), 219.

24. Ibid., 208.

25. Duwayhi, *Tarikh al-azmina,* 456, 506.

26. Ibid., 395–396.

27. Ibid., 354.

28. Ibid., 353–355

29. Ibid., 361–371.

30. Gemayel, *Al-batriyark Istifanus al-Duwayhi,* 280–281.

31. The most complete and important work on Ottoman statecraft and local realities in the seventeenth- and eighteenth-century Ottoman Arab world is Stefan Helmut Winter, "The Shiite Emirates of Ottoman Syria (Mid-17th–Mid-18th Century)" (Ph.D. diss., Department of History, University of Chicago, 2002).

32. Girolamo Dandini, *A voyage to Mount Libanus: wherein is an account of the customs, manners, &c. of the Turks: also a description of Candia, Nicosia, Tripoly, Alexandretta, &c.: with curious remarks upon several passages re[l]ating to the Turks & Maronites* (London: J. Orme, 1698), 45.

33. Heyberger, *Les Chrétiens du Proche-Orient,* 71.

34. Duwayhi, *Tarikh al-azmina,* 571.

35. Ibid., 505.

36. Winter, "Shiite Emirs and Ottoman Authorities," 213, 217.

37. David Urquhart, *The Lebanon: (Mount Souria) A History and a Diary,* 2 vols. (London: Thomas Cautley Newby, 1860), 1:208.

38. Heyberger, *Les Chrétiens du Proche-Orient,* 431.

3. The Flying of Time

1. Joseph W. Phillips, *Jedidiah Morse and New England Congregationalism* (New Brunswick, N.J.: Rutgers University Press, 1983), 204.

2. See "An Address to the Christian Public on the Subject of Missions to the Heathen and Translations of the Scriptures" of 10 November 1812, by Jeremiah Evarts, Jedidiah Morse, and Samuel Worcester, who talked about a "new era in the history of the American churches," in *Report of the American Board of Commissioners for Foreign Missions; Compiled from Documents Laid Before the Board, at the Third Annual Meeting, Which Was Held at Hartford, September 16, 1812* (Boston: Samuel T. Armstrong, 1812), 29.

3. ABCFM, *First Ten Annual Reports of the American Board of Commissioners for Foreign Missions, with Other Documents of the Board* (Boston: Crocker and Brewster, 1834), 67.

4. For more details, see Sam Haselby, "The Origins of American Religious Nationalism, 1787–1832" (Ph.D. diss., Columbia University, 2006).

5. As expressed by the title of Oliver Wendell Elsbree's account, *The Rise of the Missionary Spirit in America, 1790–1815* (Philadelphia: Porcupine Press, 1980).

6. For British influence, see Clifton Jackson Phillips, *Protestant America and the Pagan World: The First Half Century of the American Board of Commissioners for Foreign Missions, 1810–1860* (Cambridge: East Asian Research Center, Harvard University, 1969), 26; see also A. L. Tibawi, *American Interests in Syria, 1800–1901: A Study of Educational, Literary, and Religious Work* (Oxford: Clarendon Press, 1966), 4–5; for the influence of Pietism on British and American evangelism, see Andrew F. Walls, *The Cross-Cultural Process in Christian History* (Maryknoll, N.Y.: Orbis, 2002), 202–203.

7. ABCFM, *First Ten Annual Reports,* 27:"If not so much can be said of the missions of Eliot and Brainerd [as of Ziegenbalg at Tranquebar, who allegedly converted eighty thousand pagans], it is to be considered, that their labors were among a people scattered in the wilderness, and that men of a like spirit were not found to succeed them in their work, and prosecute their pious design. Still, however, there were precious fruits of their labors, which will remain for joy and praise, in the kingdom of the Redeemer, when this world shall be no more. The general history of such missions as have at any time been conducted on Christian principles, and with a real regard to the salvation of the heathen, affords abundant encouragement to proceed with vigor, in the same glorious cause."

8. Haselby, "The Origins of American Religious Nationalism," 193–196, 237.

9. William R. Hutchison, *Errand to the World: American Protestant Thought and Foreign Missions* (Chicago: University of Chicago Press, 1987), 49.

10. Quoted in E. C. Tracy, *Memoir of the Life of Jeremiah Evarts* (Boston: Crocker and Brewster, 1845), 67. See Leonard Woods, *A Sermon Delivered at the Tabernacle in Salem, Feb 6 1812, on Occasion of the Ordination of the Rev. Messrs. Samuel Newell, A.M. Adoniram Judson, A.M. Samuel Nott, A.M. Gordon Hall, A.M. and Luther Rice, A.B. Missionaries to the Heathen in Asia, Under the Direction of the Board of Commissioners for Foreign Missions* (Boston: Samuel T. Armstrong, 1812), 18.

11. Cotton Mather, *Magnalia Christi Americana; or, The Ecclesiastical History of New-England; From Its First Planting, In The Year 1620, Unto The Year Of Our Lord 1698. In Seven Books,* 2 vols. (1702; Hartford: Silas Andrus and Son, 1855), 1:40.

12. Gordon Hall and Samuel Newall, *The Conversion of the World: Or the Claims of Six Hundred Millions and the Ability and Duty of the Churches Respecting Them,* 2nd ed. (Andover, Mass.: Flagg and Gould, 1818), 55.

13. ABCFM, *First Ten Annual Reports,* 27.

14. J. A. De Jong, *As the Waters Cover the Sea: Millennial Expectations in the Rise of Anglo-American Missions, 1640–1810* (Kampen: J. H. Kok, 1970), 123, refers to a "renaissance in missions" in the eighteenth century, not so much in terms of results as in the number of full-time ordained men in Anglo-American missionary ranks.

15. Phillips, *Jedidiah Morse and New England Congregationalism,* 204.

16. *Report of the American Board of Commissioners for Foreign Missions; Compiled from Documents Laid Before the Board at the Eighth Annual Meeting Which Was Held at Northampton, Mass. Sept. 18, 19, and 20, 1817* (Boston: Samuel T. Armstrong, 1817), 18.

17. For more on the politics of expansion, missionaries, and race, see John A. Andrew III, *From Revivals to Removal: Jeremiah Evarts, the Cherokee Nation, and the Search for the Soul of America* (Athens: University of Georgia Press, 1992). For a more general treatise, see Reginald Horsman, *Expansionism and American Indian Policy: 1783–1812* (1967; Norman: University of Oklahoma Press, 1992).

18. Papers of the American Board of Commissioners for Foreign 85.9, Special Topics, Box 10.

19. Joseph A. Conforti, *Jonathan Edwards, Religious Tradition, and American Culture* (Chapel Hill: University of North Carolina Press, 1995), 63–65.

20. Ibid., 69; for the wider theological and international impact of Jonathan Edwards's memoir of David Brainerd, and for the significant difference in the way Edwards saw Brainerd and the way the missionaries saw him, see Andrew F. Walls, "Missions and Historical Memory: Jonathan Edwards and David Brainerd," in David W. Kling and Douglas A. Sweeney, eds., *Jonathan Edwards at Home and Abroad: Historical Memories, Cultural Movements, and Global Horizons* (Columbia: University of South Carolina Press, 2003), 248–265.

21. Leonard Woods, *History of the Andover Theological Seminary* (Boston: James R. Osgood and Company, 1885), 169; Daniel O. Morton, *Memoir of Rev. Levi Parsons, Late Missionary to Palestine*

(Poultney, Vt.: Smith and Shute, 1824), 237. Alvan Bond, *Memoir of the Rev. Pliny Fisk* (1828; New York: Arno Press, 1977), 68, 93.

22. Sereno Edwards Dwight, ed., *Memoirs of the Rev. David Brainerd; Missionary to the Indians on the Borders of New-York, New-Jersey, and Pennsylvania Chiefly Taken from His Own Diary by Rev. Jonathan Edwards, of Northampton* (New Haven: S. Converse, 1822), 433; see also Jonathan Edwards, *The Life of David Brainerd,* ed. Norman Petit (New Haven: Yale University Press, 1985), 501–502; Conforti, *Jonathan Edwards,* 78.

23. Morton, *Memoir of Rev. Levi Parsons,* 105.

24. Dwight, *Memoirs of the Rev. Brainerd,* 129–134.

25. Ibid., 342.

26. Sidney E. Morse, *A New System of Modern Geography, or a View of the Present State of the World* (Boston: George Clark, 1822), 95.

27. Morton, *Memoir of Rev. Levi Parsons,* 162.

28. Edwards, *Life of Brainerd,* 579. See also George M. Marsden, *Jonathan Edwards: A Life* (New Haven: Yale University Press, 2003), 390, for a description of how broken the Indians were, and how their children were encouraged by Edwards to live with English families to be "civilized."

29. Edwards, *Life of David Brainerd,* 574–575, 580.

30. Ibid., 572–573.

31. ABCFM, *First Ten Annual Reports,* 48.

32. As Hall and Newall put it in the title of their missionary tract, *The Conversion of the World.*

33. Andover Theological Seminary, *The Constitution and Associate Statutes* (Andover, Mass.: Flagg and Gould, 1817), 9.

34. Nathan O. Hatch, *The Democratization of American Christianity* (New Haven: Yale University Press, 1989), 18–19.

35. Woods, *History of Andover Theological Seminary,* 27.

36. Ibid., 234–236, for a copy of the constitution of the seminary and expected curriculum.

37. Ibid., 160. John H. Sailhamer, "Johann August Ernesti: The Role of History in Biblical Interpretation," *Journal of the Evangelical Theological Society* (June 2001): 193–206.

38. Woods, *History of Andover Theological Seminary,* 235, 236. The *Catalogue of the Library Belonging to the Theological Institution in Andover* (Andover, Mass.: Flagg and Gould, 1819) lists simply an 1801 London edition of George Sale's two-volume translation of the Quran at Andover, and a copy of Joseph Simonius Assemani's *Bibliotheca Orientalis Clementino-Vaticana* published in Rome 1719–1728.

39. Morton, *Memoir of Rev. Levi Parsons,* 18.

40. Ibid., 19.

41. Bond, *Memoir of Fisk,* 16.

42. N. Bouton to William Thompson, 1 September 1858, Yale Divinity School Library, Special Collections, Eli Smith Family Papers, RG 124, Box 2/7.

43. E. D. G. Prime, *Forty Years in the Turkish Empire; Or, Memoirs of Rev. William Goodell, D.D.* (New York: Robert Carter and Brothers, 1876), 40.

44. Andrew Walls makes the point that the evangelicalism that emerged from British and American revivals was a highly successful "Christian adaptation to the European Enlightenment." See Walls, *Cross-Cultural Process,* 201.

45. Society of Inquiry Respecting Missions, *Memoirs of American Missionaries, Formerly Connected with the Society of Inquiry Respecting Missions in the Andover Theological Seminary: Embracing a History of the Society, etc.* (Boston: Peirce and Parker, 1833), 17. Ruth H. Bloch, *Visionary Republic: Millennial Themes in American Thought, 1756–1800* (Cambridge: Cambridge University Press, 1985), 220–222.

46. Bloch, *Visionary Republic,* xiii–xiv; Phillips, *Protestant America and the Pagan World,* 8–9; Alan Frederick Perry, "American Board of Commissioners for Foreign Missions and the London

Missionary Society in the Nineteenth Century: A Study of Ideas" (Ph.D. diss., Washington University, 1974), 347; De Jong, *As the Waters Cover the Sea*, 199–227. For more recent evaluations of the millennialist thesis in relation to American missions, see Richard Lee Rogers, "'A Bright and New Constellation': Millennial Narratives and the Origins of American Foreign Missions," in Wilbert R. Shenk, ed., *North American Foreign Missions, 1800–1914: Theology, Theory, and Policy* (Grand Rapids: Eerdmans, 2004), 39–60.

47. ABCFM, *First Ten Annual Reports*, 28.

48. Timothy Dwight, *A Sermon, Delivered in Boston Sept. 16, 1813, Before the American Board of Commissioners for Foreign Missions at their Fourth Annual Meeting*, 2nd ed. (Boston: Samuel T. Armstrong, 1813), 25–27.

49. For Morse, see Ira V. Brown, "Watchers for the Second Coming: The Millenarian Tradition in America," *The Mississippi Valley Historical Review* 39 (1952): 450; for Hopkins, see De Jong, *As Waters Cover the Sea*, 209.

50. Jedidiah Morse, *The American Universal Geography, or, A View of the Present State of All the Kingdoms, States, and Colonies in the Known World*, 2 vols., 7th ed. (Boston: Lincoln and Edmands, 1819), 74–76.

51. John H. Livingston, *A Sermon, Delivered Before the New-York Missionary Society, at their Annual Meeting, April 3*, 1804 (New York: T. and J. Swords, 1804), 7.

52. Dwight, *Memoirs of Brainerd*, 92. See Pliny Fisk, "The Holy Land an Interesting Field of Missionary Enterprise: A Sermon, Preached in the Old South Church Boston, Sabbath Evening, Oct. 31, 1819, Just Before the Departure of the Palestine Mission," reprinted in *Holy Land Missions and Missionaries* (New York: Arno Press, 1977), 38–39; Jonas King, "A Sermon delivered at Paris," Misc. Mss., vol. 17, 33, Archives and Special Collections, Williams College.

53. Livingston, *Sermon*, 6. See also William R. Hutchison, "New England's Further Errand: Millennial Belief and the Beginnings of Foreign Missions," in *Proceedings of the Massachusetts Historical Society* 94 (1982): 49–64.

54. Society of Inquiry Respecting Missions, *Memoirs of American Missionaries*, 366. Phillips, *Protestant America and the Pagan World*, 93–96.

55. ABCFM, Minutes of Prudential Committee, 24 September 1818, American Board Archives, Congregational House, Boston.

56. ABCFM, *First Ten Annual Reports*, 229–230.

57. ABCFM, *Instructions from the Prudential Committee of the American Board of Commissioners for Foreign Missions, to the Rev. Levi Parsons and the Rev. Pliny Fisk, Missionaries designated for Palestine. Delivered in the Old South Church Boston, Sabbath Evening, Oct. 31, 1819* (Boston, 1819), 4.

58. Alan Perry, *Study of Ideas*, 182.

59. Woods, *Sermon*, 11; see also ABCFM, *Instructions to the Missionaries About To Embark for the Sandwich Islands; and to the Rev. Messrs. William Goodell, and Isaac Bird, Attached to the Palestine Mission Delivered by the Corresponding Secretary of the American Board of Commissioners for Foreign Missions* (Boston: Crocker and Brewster, 1823), 8, 14.

60. Marsden, *Jonathan Edwards*, 385–390.

61. ABCFM, *Instructions to Goodell and Bird*, 18.

62. ABCFM, *Instructions to Parsons and Fisk*, 10, 1.

63. ABCFM, *Instructions to Goodell and Bird*, 15.

64. ABCFM, *Instructions to Parsons and Fisk*, 6.

65. Fisk, "The Holy Land an Interesting Field of Missionary Enterprise," 32.

66. Ibid., 26. See also Morse, *American Universal Geography*, 79. For more on anti-Islamic polemics, see Norman Daniel, *Islam and the West: The Making of an Image* (1960; Oxford: Oneworld Publications, 1993). For a more recent work on the place of Islam in early American culture, see Timothy Marr, *The Cultural Roots of American Islamicism* (Cambridge: Cambridge University Press, 2006). See also Thomas S. Kidd, "'Is it Worse to Follow Mahomet than the Devil?' Early American Uses of Islam," *Church History* 72 (2003): 766–790.

67. William Jowett, *Christian Researches in the Mediterranean from 1815 to 1820 in furtherance of the Objects of the Church Missionary Society*, 3rd ed. (London: L. B. Seeley and Son, 1824), 253.

68. Fisk, "The Holy Land an Interesting Field of Missionary Enterprise," 26.

69. For more general early American attitudes toward Islam, see Marr, *The Cultural Roots of American Islamicism*, 21. As much as recent scholars have commented on the Barbary Wars, however, and as much as these conflicts captured the imagination of a nascent American public, as noted by Marr, there is remarkably little discussion of the wars in American Board literature of the era; see also Samir Khalaf for a discussion of what he calls "Protestant Orientalism" in his *Cultural Resistance: Global and Local Encounters in the Middle East* (London: Saqi Books, 2001), 105–125.

70. Timothy Marr, "'Drying up the Euphrates': Muslims, Millennialism, and Early American Missionary Enterprise," in Abbas Amanat and Magnus T. Bernhardsson, eds., *The United States and the Middle East: Cultural Encounters* (New Haven: Yale Center for International and Area Studies, 2002), 133. See also Kidd, "Is It Worse to Follow Mahomet?" 778–781; see also Block, *Visionary Republic*, 145.

71. Marr, *The Cultural Roots of American Islamicism*, 112.

72. Marr, "Drying up the Euphrates," 134–138.

73. King, "Sermon delivered at Paris," 10–11.

74. Morton, *Memoir of Parsons*, 303.

75. Fisk, "The Holy Land an Interesting Field of Missionary Enterprise," 27.

76. Morton, *Memoir of Parsons*, 223.

77. King, "Sermon delivered at Paris," 18.

78. Levi Parsons, "The Dereliction and the Restoration of the Jews. A Sermon Preached in Park-Street Church Boston, Sabbath, Oct. 31, 1819, Just Before the Departure of the Palestine Mission" (Boston: Samuel T. Armstrong, 1819), reprinted in *Holy Land Missions and Missionaries* (New York: Arno Press, 1977), 8. See also Hall and Newall, *The Conversion of the World*, 38.

79. Fisk, "The Holy Land an Interesting Field of Missionary Enterprise," 26; Parsons, "The Dereliction and Restoration of the Jews," 8.

80. Parsons, "The Dereliction and Restoration of the Jews," 17.

81. Dwight, *Memoirs of Brainerd*, 13.

82. Here a substantial difference existed between those members of the board who had a direct interest in Indian affairs such as Jeremiah Evarts and the missionaries to Palestine. See ABCFM, *First Ten Annual Reports*, 27.

83. Fisk, "The Holy Land an Interesting Field of Missionary Enterprise," 32.

84. Morse, *American Universal Geography*, 212–213.

85. Lion G. Miles, "The Red Man Dispossessed: The Williams Family and the Alienation of Indian Land in Stockbridge, Massachusetts, 1736–1818," in Alden T. Vaughan, ed., *New England Encounters: Indians and Euroamericans, ca. 1600–1850* (Boston: Northeastern University Press, 1999), 295.

86. Morton, *Memoir of Parsons*, 217–218. See also Electa F. Jones, *Stockbridge, Past and Present* (Springfield, Mass.: Samuel Bowles and Company, 1854), 95–96. For Edwards's words, see Marsden, *Jonathan Edwards*, 385.

87. Prime, *Memoirs of Rev. William Goodell*, 69.

88. Rufus Anderson, *Memoir of Catharine Brown, a Christian Indian of the Cherokee Nation*, ed. William Stanley Hoole (1825; University, Ala.: Confederate Publishing Company, 1986), 58. Society of Inquiry Respecting Missions, *Memoir of American Missionaries*, 364.

89. *Journals and Letters of the Rev. Henry Martyn*, ed. Samuel Wilberforce, 1st American ed. (New York: M. W. Dodd, 1851), 453–456. See also *Memoir of the Rev. Henry Martyn*, 7th ed. (London, 1822), 364.

90. Fisk, "The Holy Land an Interesting Field of Missionary Enterprise," 32, 28.

91. Morton, *Memoir of Rev. Levi Parsons*, 257.

92. Tibawi, *American Interests,* 14–15.

93. Morton, *Memoir of Rev. Parsons,* 297.

94. Ibid., 292.

95. A common missionary theme; see Samuel Worcester, *Paul on Mars Hill: Or, a Christian Survey of the Pagan World. A Sermon, Preached at Newburyport, June 21, 1815, at the Ordination of the Reverend Messrs. Samuel J. Mills, James Richards, Edward Warren, Horatio Bardwell, Benjamin C. Meigs, and Daniel Poor, to the Office of Christian Missionaries* (Andover, Mass.: Flagg and Gould, 1815); see also Livingston, *Sermon.*

96. Morton, *Memoir of Rev. Parsons,* 264.

97. ABCFM, *Instructions to Goodell and Bird,* 20.

4. The Artillery of Heaven

1. Alvan Bond, *Memoir of the Rev. Pliny Fisk, A.M., Late Missionary to Palestine* (1828; New York: Arno Press, 1977), 264. The initial encounter occurred in Egypt in 1822 while Emir Bashir was temporarily exiled.

2. Ussama Makdisi, *Culture of Sectarianism: Community, History, and Violence in Nineteenth-Century Ottoman Lebanon* (Berkeley: University of California Press, 2000), 35–37; John Lewis Burkhardt, *Travels in Syria and the Holy Land* (1822; London: Darf Publishers, 1992), 197.

3. Burckhardt, *Travels in Syria and the Holy Land,* 21; Başbakanlık Devlet Arşivi, Istanbul, HH 20022-6 15 L 1247 (18 March 1832).

4. Nasif Yaziji, *Risala tarikhiyya fi ahwal jabal lubnan al-iqtaʿi,* ed. Muhammad Khalil al-Basha and Riyad Husayn Ghannam (Beirut: Dar Maʿn, 2002), 67. These are estimates for the male population, and like almost all statistics from this period about this region are to be taken as loose approximations.

5. Hananiyya al-Munayyir, *Al-Durr al-marsuf fi tarikh al-Shuf* (Beirut, 1984) 130–131.

6. Yaziji, *Risala tarikhiyya,* 22. Naʾila Taqi al-Din Qaidbey, ed., *Al-imara al-Shihabiyya wa al-iqtaʿiyyun al-Duruz: sirat al-usra al-Nakadiyya li-katibiha Nasib Said Nakad* (Beirut: Dar al-Nahar, 2004), 55–56.

7. See chapter 2, "The Grammar of Heresy." .

8. Makdisi, *Culture of Sectarianism,* 28–50; Stefan Helmut Winter, "The Shiite Emirates of Ottoman Syria (Mid-17th–Mid-18th Century)" (Ph.D. diss., University of Chicago, 2002), 176–236.

9. Winter, "Shiite Emirates of Ottoman Syria," 197–201.

10. Yaziji, *Risala tarikhiyya,* 23–24.

11. The information about the Shidyaq family is derived from Tannus al-Shidyaq, *Kitab akhbar al-aʿyan fi Jabal Lubnan,* ed. Fouad E. Boustany, 2 vols. (1859; Beirut: Publications de l'Université Libanaise, 1970), 1:110–119.

12. Nasser Gemayel, *Les échanges culturels entre les Maronites et l'Europe: Du Collège Maronite de Rome (1584) au Collège de ʿAyn-Warqa (1789)* 2 vols. (Beirut: Imprimerie Y. and Ph. Gemayel, 1984), 1:1003. Nasser Gemayel, *Madrasat ʿAyn Waraqa fi al-dhikra al-miʾawiyya al-thaniyya li-taʾsisiha* (Beirut: Matbaʿat Dakash, 1989).

13. Bernard Heyberger, *Les Chrétiens du Proche-Orient au temps de la réforme catholique* (Rome: École Française de Rome, 1994), 433–451; Bernard Heyberger, *Hindiyya: Mystique et criminelle* (Paris: Auber, 2001), 92–98.

14. Ghassan al-ʿAyyash, *Majmaʿ al-Luwayza* (Beirut: al-Markaz al-watani lil-maʿlumat wa al-dirasat, 1991). See also Ilyas al-Zinati, *Qawanin al-majmaʿ al-lubnani* (Beirut: al-matbaʿa al-kathulikiyya, 1926). The resolutions of this council were not substantially put into effect into well into the nineteenth century, and even then local family politics continued to be evident.

15. Bernard Heyberger, "L'autorité cléricale chez les Maronites: myths, politique et dispositif social," in Denise Aigle and Sabrina Mervin, eds., *Autorités religieuses entre charisme et hiérarchie* (Turnhout: Bibliothèque de l'École des Hautes Études Sciences Religieuses, forthcoming).

16. Bruce Masters, *Christians and Jews in the Ottoman Arab World: The Roots of Sectarianism* (Cambridge: Cambridge University Press, 2001), 111–115.

17. Bernard Heyberger, "Individualism and Political Modernity: Devout Catholic Women in Aleppo and Lebanon between the Seventeenth and Nineteenth Centuries," in Amira El-Azhary Sonbol, ed., *Beyond the Exotic: Women's Histories in Islamic Societies* (Syracuse: Syracuse University Press, 2005), 71–89.

18. Cited in Heyberger, *Hindiyya,* 7–8. Charles Henry Churchill, *Mount Lebanon: A Ten Years' Residence from 1842 to 1852 Describing the Manners, Customs, and Religion of its Inhabitants with a Full & Correct Account of the Druse Religion and Containing Historical Records of the Mountain Tribes from Personal Intercourse with their Chiefs and other Authentic Sources,* 3rd ed., 3 vols. (1853; London: Garnet Publishing, 1994), 1:78–85. Heyberger, *Hindiyya,* 253–268, provides details of the nature and manner of the torture to which Hindiyya's opponents were subjected.

19. Heyberger, "Individualism and Political Modernity," 84.

20. Ibid., 84.

21. Heyberger, *Hindiyya,* 285; for a contemporary Maronite rebuke of Maronite "ignorance," see Butrus Fahd, *Batarikat al-mawarina wa asaqifatuhum, al-qarn 18* (Beirut: Dar Lahd Khater, 1985), 361.

22. Bulus ʿAbbud Ghustawi, *Basaʾir al-zaman* (Beirut: Sabra, 1911), 205.

23. Gemayel, *Madrasat ʿAyn Waraqa,* 13–23. Much of my description of the establishment of ʿAyn Waraqa is derived from Nasser Gemayel's account.

24. Gemayel, *Madrasat ʿAyn Waraqa,* 28–29. Gemayel, *Les échanges culturels entre les Maronites et l'Europe,* 2:1043–45. All students enrolled at ʿAyn Waraqa were to take the vow; those who were already sixteen when they enrolled were to wait six months; those not yet sixteen were to take the vow immediately upon turning sixteen.

25. Fahd, *Batarikat al-mawarina, al-qarn 18,* 361–362.

26. The early-nineteenth-century account by Rufaʾil Karama, *Hawadith Lubnan wa Suriyya min sanat 1745 ila sanat 1800* (Tripoli: Jarrus Press, 1983), details the remarkable spread of Greek Catholic monasteries belonging to the Basilite order of Shwayr in the second half of the eighteenth century.

27. Butrus Fahd, *Tarikh al-rahbaniyya al-lubnaniyya, bi farʿayha al-halabi wa al-lubnani,* 3 vols. (Juniya, 1963), 1:85–86 and 2:32–33.

28. Bond, *Memoir of Pliny Fisk,* 328. Burckhardt, *Travels in Syria and the Holy Land,* 21–22. Qannubin was restored in 1811 by Patriarch Yuhanna al-Hilu. See Butrus Fahd, *Batarikat al-mawarina wa asaqifatuhum, al-qarn 19,* 2 vols. (Beirut: Dar Lahd Khater, 1986), 1:126.

29. This was especially true of the Khazin family in the eighteenth century, as it had been of the Shiʿa Hamade family earlier, but it was always contested, particularly by Latinizing reformers within the Maronite ecclesiastical community. See Richard Van Leeuwen, *Notables and Clergy in Mount Lebanon: The Khazin Sheiks and the Maronite Church (1736–1840)* (Leiden: E. J. Brill, 1994), 101–147; see also Ilya F. Harik, *Politics and Change in a Traditional Society* (Princeton: Princeton University Press, 1968), 87–93, 118–126.

30. The information about Yusuf Hubaysh is taken from an unpublished typeset version of a manuscript by Bulus Qaraʾli titled "Tarjama mukhtasara lil-batriyark Yusuf Hubaysh 1823–1845" kindly put at my disposal by Hiyam Mallat (Beirut).

31. Fahd, *Batarikat al-mawarina, al-qarn 19,* 1:204–205. There were also accusations that Hubaysh had not achieved the necessary two-thirds majority vote to legitimize his election. See Mikhaʾil A. Ghibraʾil, *Kitab Tarikh al-kanisa al-antakiyya al-siryaniyya al-maruniyya,* 2 vols. (Baʿabda: al-Matbaʿa al-lubnaniyya, 1904), 2:757–758.

32. Cited in Qaraʾli, "Tarjama," 10.

33. For the continuing fear of Hindiyya, see Archivo Storico, "Sacra Congregatio de Propaganda Fide," Vatican (hereafter SCPF), Fondo SC Maroniti 18 (1823–1827), Butrus Karam to Propaganda Fide, no. 129, n.d. but probably 1824.

34. Qara'li, "Tarjama," 12.

35. Kamal Salibi and Yusuf K. Khoury [Khuri], eds., *The Missionary Herald: Reports from Ottoman Syria, 1819–1870* (hereafter MHROS), 5 vols. (Amman: Royal Institute for Interfaith Studies, 1995), 1:368. The original reference to the "artillery of heaven" in the *Missionary Herald* from July 1826 was to the ancient Eastern Christian churches which Satan had seized and turned to the defense of his kingdom. The missionaries were thus the latest weapons of God, a new kind of heavenly artillery.

36. A. L. Tibawi, *American Interests in Syria, 1800–1901: A Study of Educational, Literary, and Religious Work* (Oxford: Clarendon Press, 1966), 18–26.

37. MHROS, 1:367.

38. Papers of the American Board of Commissioners for Foreign Missions deposited at Houghton Library, Harvard University, Cambridge, Mass. (hereafter ABC), ABC 16.6, Mission to the Jews, 1824–1831, 3 vols., Palestine Mission, vol. 1, Jonas King Journal, Thursday 17 July 1823.

39. Lady Hester Stanhope to B. Barker, Esq., 9 June 1824, copied in Isaac Bird, Journal 1824 May–1830 October, Box 2/24, Isaac Bird Papers, Manuscripts and Archives, Yale University Library.

40. Heyberger, *Hindiyya,* 266–267.

41. Archives of the Maronite Patriarchate, Bkirke, Lebanon (hereafter AB), drawer of Yusuf Hubaysh, Hanna Marun to Propaganda Fide, n.d.

42. ABC 16.6, Palestine Mission, vol. 1, Pliny Fisk Journal, Monday, 6 October 1823.

43. Tibawi, *American Interests,* 27.

44. ABC 16.6, Palestine Mission, vol. 1, Pliny Fisk Journal, 15 October 1823.

45. Ibid., 12 October 1823.

46. Ibid., Journal of Jonas King, 10 August 1823.

47. Ibid., Journal of William Goodell and Isaac Bird, 16–17 November 1823; Tibawi, *American Interests,* 31–32.

48. ABC 16.6, Palestine Mission, Vol. 1, Journal of Goodell and Bird, 16–17 November 1823.

49. MHROS, 1:233.

50. MHROS, 1:401.

51. ABC 16.6, Palestine Mission, vol. 1, Goodell to Jeremiah Evarts, 24 January 1824; see also E. D. G. Prime, *Forty Years in the Turkish Empire; Or, Memoirs of Rev. William Goodell, D.D.* (New York: Robert Carter and Brothers, 1876), 79; for trade, see Henri Guys, *Beyrouth et le Liban,* 2 vols. (1850; Beirut: Dar Lahd Khater, 1985), 1:37–38. The missionaries also carried, of course, passports from the Commonwealth of Massachusetts. See Eli Smith Papers, ABC 60, V/135, Houghton Library, Harvard University.

52. MHROS, 1:233; Tibawi, *American Interests,* 31.

53. Goodell to Fisk, King, and Bird, 20 February 1824, MS-556, American Missionaries in the Near East and Malta, 1822–1865, Special Collections, Dartmouth College Library (hereafter Dartmouth Papers).

54. Daniel Temple to Ann Bird and Abagail Goodell, 1826, Dartmouth Papers.

55. ABC 16.6, Palestine Mission, vol. 1, Goodell to Evarts, 24 January 1824; Bird to Goodell, 20 February 1832, Dartmouth Papers. For a description of missionary life, see Prime, *Memoirs of Rev. William Goodell,* 80.

56. ABC 16.6, Palestine Mission, vol. 1, Journal of Pliny Fisk, 12 October 1823.

57. For example, see Tannus al-Haddad to Isaac Bird, 28 August 1833, letters to Rev. and Mrs. Isaac Bird, 1822–1835, Archives and Special Collections, Mount Holyoke College.

58. MHROS, 1:243; for more on missionary attitudes toward female education in Lebanon and the impact they had, see Ellen Fleischmann, "The Impact of American Protestant Missions in Lebanon on the Construction of Female Identity, c. 1860–1950," *Islam and Christian-Muslim Relations* 13 (2002): 411–425.

59. Tibawi, *American Interests,* 32–33.

60. "Brief Sketch of the Life and Labours of Jonas King," Misc. MSS, vol. 35, 57 (oversize), Archives and Special Collections, Williams College.

61. ABC 16.6, Palestine Mission, vol. 1, Journal of Jonas King, 4 September 1823.

62. MHROS, 1:331.

63. ABC 16.6, Palestine Mission, vol. 1, Journal of Jonas King, 21 August 1823. The journal does not spell out the actual verses but refers directly to them; all biblical citations from King James Version.

64. Ibid., vol. 3, Journal of Jonas King, 6 June 1824.

65. King to Bird, 24 June 1824, Dartmouth Papers.

66. King to Bird, 19 August 1824, Isaac Bird Papers, Special Collections, Leyburn Library, Washington and Lee University.

67. ABC 16.6, Palestine Mission, vol. 3, Journal of Jonas King, 18 May 1825. King's journal is compressed here, unlike his earlier journals, and says simply that he arrived in Beirut on 18 May and spent about a month there before going to Dayr al-Qamar, where he spent six weeks, "four of which were spent in the study of Syriac."

68. "A Prayer Composed by Rev. King and copied in Arabic by Asaad esh Shidiak," MS Arab 67.1, Arabic Manuscripts, Houghton Library, Harvard University. It is not clear whether this prayer was corrected by Shidyaq or simply copied by him.

69. Mikhayil Mishaqa, *Al-Jawab ʿala iqtirah al-ahbab* (A Response to a Proposition by Beloved Ones), translated into English by Wheeler M. Thackston under the unfortunate title *Murder, Mayhem, Pillage, and Plunder: The History of the Lebanon in the 18th and 19th Centuries* (Albany: State University of New York Press, 1988), 146.

70. For copies of the document, quoted here and below, see Archives of the Near East School of Theology (hereafter NEST), MS AK-2-b; see also AB, drawer of Yusuf Hubaysh, and SCPF, Fondo SC Maroniti, vol. 18 (1823–1827), no. 208, which reproduces and dates Patriarch Hubyash's anathema against Biblemen. For another English translation published by the missionaries in the *Missionary Herald,* see section titled "Order of the Maronite Patriarch against the Scriptures," in MHROS, 1:480–482.

71. Antoine Rabbath, ed., *Documents inédits pour servir a l'histoire du Christianisme en Orient,* 2 vols. (1905–1911; New York: AMS Press, 1973), 1:546–547. For the earlier *firman* of 1690 which legitimated missionary activity among Greek, Armenian, and Coptic subjects of the empire, see Masters, *Christians and Jews,* 84.

72. Masters, *Christians and Jews,* 81.

73. The *fatwa* was issued in response to a Greek Catholic petition; the ruling made clear that the Muslim state could not compel Greek Catholics to submit to their Greek Orthodox hierarchy because a Muslim ruler could not willingly refer any of his subjects to practice *kufr* or unbelief. The *fatwa* is reproduced in Haydar Ahmad al-Shihabi, *Lubnan fi ʿahd al-umaraʾ al-shihabiyyin,* ed. Asad Rustum and Fouad E. Boustany, 3 vols. (1933; Beirut: Editions St. Paul, 1984), 1:57–58.

74. ABC 16.6, Palestine Mission, vol. 1, Fisk and Bird to Evarts, 28 February 1824; MHROS, 1:291.

75. Arabic copy of the *firman* found in Box 2/24 of the Isaac Bird Papers, Manuscripts and Archives, Yale University Library.

76. Isaac Bird, *Bible Work in Bible Lands* (Philadelphia: Presbyterian Board of Publication, 1872), 153.

77. King to Bird, 19 August 1824, Isaac Bird Papers, Special Collections, Leyburn Library, Washington and Lee University.

78. MHROS, 1:482–485. See also the unedited Arabic version, "Surat radd ʿala hadha al-manshur," MS AK-2-b, NEST.

79. King to Isaac and Isabel Bird, 17 June 1824, Dartmouth Papers.

80. ABC 16.6, Palestine Mission, vol. 3, Journal of Jonas King, 9 June 1824.

81. Ibid.

82. See an English version in Jonas King, *The Oriental Church and the Latin* (New York: John A. Gray & Green, 1865). I cite the English version, checked against an Arabic version, "Wada' Yunus Kin ila ahiba'ihi fi Filastin wa Suriyya," 5 September 1825, MS Arab 67, Arabic Manuscripts, Houghton Library, Harvard University. See also Tibawi, *American Interests,* 36–37, who misdates the letter as 5 April.

83. King, *The Oriental Church and the Latin,* 24.

84. Of course, the massacre in 1572 of the French Protestants was committed not by the Roman Church but by the French court of Charles IX.

85. *The Missionary Register for 1827 containing the principal transactions of the various institutions for propagating the gospel with the proceedings at large of the Church Missionary Society,* vol. 15 (London: L. B. Seeley & Sons, 1827), 334.

86. King, *Oriental Church and the Latin,* 32.

5. An Arab Puritan

1. Archives of the Maronite Patriarchate, Bkirke (hereafter AB), drawer of Yusuf Hubaysh, As'ad Shidyaq's Arabic Statement of Faith, March 1826. The Maronite archives are organized serially by patriarchs. As'ad's writings are not otherwise classified. In the following references I therefore provide descriptive titles for these documents within brackets. Another Arabic copy of the testament in two distinct handwritings can be found in the personal library of Nasser Gemayel, 'Ayn al-Kharruba, Lebanon. Butrus al-Bustani reproduced As'ad's Arabic statement verbatim in his *Qissat As'ad al-Shidyaq* (1860; Beirut: Dar al-Hamra', 1992), 22–39. An English translation by Isaac Bird under the title "Public Statement of Asaad Shidiak" can be found in Kamal Salibi and Yusuf K. Khoury [Khuri], eds., *The Missionary Herald: Reports from Ottoman Syria, 1819–1870* (hereafter MHROS), 5 vols. (Amman: Royal Institute for Interfaith Studies, 1995), 1:408–421.

2. Papers of the American Board of Commissioners for Foreign Missions, deposited at Houghton Library, Harvard University (hereafter ABC), 16.6, Mission to the Jews, 1824–1831, 3 vols., Palestine Mission, vol. 2, Bird to Evarts, 22 May 1826 and specifically note under journal entry for 10 August 1825; see also Isaac Bird, Journal 1824 May–1830 October, Box 2/24, Isaac Bird Papers, Manuscripts and Archives, Yale University Library (hereafter Isaac Bird Papers).

3. ABC 16.6, Palestine Mission, vol. 2, Bird to Evarts, 22 May 1826.

4. Bustani, *Qissat,* 14–15.

5. Tannus al-Shidyaq, *Kitab akhbar al-a'yan fi Jabal Lubnan,* ed. Fouad E. Boustany, 2 vols. (1859; Beirut: Publications de l'Université Libanaise, 1970), 1:120.

6. Bustani, *Qissat,* 15.

7. Mikhayil Mishaqa, *Al-Jawab 'ala iqtirah al-ahbab* (A Response to a Proposition by Beloved Ones), trans. Wheeler M. Thackston, *Murder, Mayhem, Pillage, and Plunder: The History of the Lebanon in the 18th and 19th Centuries* (Albany: State University of New York Press, 1988), 146.

8. Haydar Ahmad al-Shihabi, *Lubnan fi 'ahd al-umara' al-shihabiyyin,* 3 vols., ed. Asad Rustum and Fouad E. Boustany (1933; Beirut: Editions St. Paul, 1984), 3:785; 'Isa Iskandar Ma'luf, *Dawani al-qutuf fi tarikh bani al-Ma'luf,* 2 vols. (Damascus: Dar Hawran, 2003), 1:308–309; Ibrahim al-'Awra, *Tarikh wilayat Sulayman Basha al-'adil 1804–1819* (Beirut: Dar Lahd Khater, 1989), 392. For As'ad's pay, see Isaac Bird, Journal 1824 May–1830 October, Box 2/24, Isaac Bird Papers. The missionaries, by contrast, had drafts ranging from $800 to $1,000 a year to draw on for the first three years of the mission. In a letter from Shidyaq to the patriarch in the personal library of Nasser Gemayel, undated but probably from 1824 or 1825, As'ad puts the patriarch on notice that he needs work and cannot simply sit in his home waiting for the patronage of the bishop of Beirut.

9. ABC 16.6, Palestine Mission, vol. 3, Journal of Jonas King, 18 May 1825.

10. Isaac Bird, Journal 1824 May–1830 October, Box 2/24, Isaac Bird Papers. The appendix of Bird's journal lists Tannus as a copyist of several tracts at two piasters per tract.

11. Mishaqa, *Jawab ʿala iqtirah al-ahbab,* 146.

12. ABC 16.6, Palestine Mission, vol. 2, Bird to Evarts, 22 May 1826.

13. Ibid., vol. 3, Journal of Jonas King, 18–26 September 1825.

14. All quotations are from Hubaysh to Shidyaq, 16 October 1825, Box 4/45, Isaac Bird Papers.

15. An incident about which the historical record is otherwise silent, but to judge from another letter written by the bishop of Beirut which refers to Asʿad's path of deviance that began in "Acre and Tripoli," this may well be a reference to his discussion with Muslims and the rumors of his conversion to Islam that Bustani refers to in *Qissat,* 14.

16. ABC 16.6, Palestine Mission, vol. 2, Bird to Evarts, 22 May 1826.

17. Karam to Shidyaq, 16 October 1825, Box 4/45, Isaac Bird Papers.

18. Ibid.

19. Archivo Storico, Sacra Congregatio de Propaganda Fide, Vatican (hereafter SCPF), Fondo SC Maroniti 18 (1823–1827), Butrus Karam to Propaganda Fide, no. 129, n.d. but probably 1824.

20. AB, drawer of Yusuf Hubaysh, Karam to Propaganda Fide, n.d. but estimated to be from 1827.

21. ABC 16.6, Palestine Mission, vol. 2, Bird to Evarts, 22 May 1826; see also MHROS, 1:440–441.

22. AB, drawer of Yusuf Hubaysh, [Shidyaq Arabic Statement of Faith], 30.

23. Ibid., 3.

24. Ibid., 33–34.

25. Başbakanlık Devlet Arşivi, Istanbul, Mesail-i Muhimme 967, 12 Ra. 1262 (15 April 1846).

26. AB, drawer of Yusuf Hubaysh, [Shidyaq Arabic Statement of Faith], 9.

27. Ibid., 24. For more on notions of insanity in Islamic societies, see Michael W. Dols, *Majnun: The Madman in Medieval Islamic Society* (Oxford: Clarendon Press, 1992), 117, 123–124; for an English perspective on the Maronite treatment of the insane in Mount Lebanon in this period, see Charles Henry Churchill, *Mount Lebanon: A Ten Years' Residence from 1842 to 1852 Describing the Manners, Customs, and Religion of its Inhabitants with a Full & Correct Account of the Druse Religion and Containing Historical Records of the Mountain Tribes from Personal Intercourse with their Chiefs and other Authentic Sources,* 3rd ed., 3 vols. (1853; London: Garnet Publishing, 1994), 1:64–68.

28. AB, drawer of Yusuf Hubaysh, [Shidyaq Arabic Statement of Faith], 29.

29. This information is derived from evidence provided in MHROS, 1:443.

30. Shihabi, *Lubnan fi ʿahd al-umaraʾ al-shihabiyyin,* 3:780–781.

31. MHROS, 1:446.

32. MHROS, 1:457.

33. AB, drawer of Yusuf Hubaysh, Asʿad Shidyaq to Yusuf Hubaysh, n.d. but clearly written while he was at Isaac Bird's house.

34. MHROS, 1:447–448.

35. See Mansur al-Shidyaq's discussion with Isaac Bird in MHROS, 1:514.

36. MHROS, 1:445.

37. Istifan Farayha al-Bishʿalani, "Tanassur al-amir ʿAbdullah al-Lamʿi," *Al-Machreq* 19 (1921): 271–277.

38. MHROS, 1:457.

39. MHROS, 1:379.

40. AB, drawer of Yusuf Hubaysh, [Fragments of Journal of Asʿad Shidyaq], April 1826.

41. Ibid., prayer from Monday 10 April 1826.

42. As'ad Shidyaq to Isaac Bird, 27 March 1826, Box 2/24, Isaac Bird Papers.

43. For more information on theories of illness in Islamic societies, see Dols, *Majnun,* 52–53; see also Butrus al-Bustani, *Muhit al-muhit,* rev. ed. (Beirut: Librarie du Liban, 1993), 439.

44. AB, drawer of Yusuf Hubaysh [Fragments of Journal of As'ad Shidyaq, April 1826].

45. For the introduction of Latin forms of confession in Aleppo, see Bernard Heyberger, "Morale et confession chez les melkites d'Alep d'après une liste de péchés (fin XVIIe siècle)," in Geneviève Gobillot and Marie-Thérèse Urvoy, eds., *L'Orient chrétien dans l'empire musulman: Hommage au professeur Gérard Troupeau* (Versailles: Éditions de Paris, 2005), 283–306.

46. AB, drawer of Yusuf Hubaysh, [Fragments of Journal of As'ad Shidyaq, April 1826].

47. Ibid., [Register of Correspondence from the Sacred Congregation to Yusuf Hubaysh], no. 26, 7 October 1826.

48. Ibid., [Fragments of Journal of As'ad Shidyaq], April 1826.

49. The missionary narrative, based largely on Isaac Bird's journals, reports that As'ad was sent to Quzhayya sometime in late May or early June. Butrus al-Bustani's narrative, however, does not mention Quzhayya. Because of the allegations of demonic possession, it is possible that As'ad was indeed sent to the monastery then famous for its treatment of the mentally ill and those possessed, but Hubaysh makes no mention of this, and moreover, given the importance of the case, and the fact that Quzhayya was not under the patriarch's direct control but rather under a monastic order, it is equally plausible that As'ad was not sent there but confined at Qannubin in a similar manner to the way that the putatively insane were at Quzhayya. The patriarch in a letter to Rome on 5 January 1827 claims that As'ad escaped three times. See AB, drawer of Yusuf Hubaysh, [Register of Correspondence sent by Yusuf Hubaysh to the Holy Congregation], no. 28, 5 January 1827.

50. Bustani, *Qissat,* 54–56. AB, drawer of Yusuf Hubaysh, Yusuf Hubaysh to Propaganda Fide, 5 January 1827.

51. Bustani, *Qissat,* 55. An undated letter in the Maronite archives from As'ad Shidyaq to Yusuf Hubaysh, likely in 1826, has him pleading with the patriarch to stop his "humiliation and coercion," for he has fully repented.

52. AB, drawer of Yusuf Hubaysh, Yusuf Hubaysh to Propaganda Fide, 5 January 1827.

53. See Dols, *Majnun,* 124–125; Churchill, *Mount Lebanon,* 1:67; Eugene Rogan, "Madness and Marginality: The Advent of the Psychiatric Asylum in Egypt and Lebanon," in Eugene Rogan, ed., *Outside In: On the Margins of the Modern Middle East* (London: I. B. Tauris, 2002), 110.

54. From an Arabic letter copied by Isaac Bird, Yusuf Hubaysh to Emir A., 26 June 1826, Box 2/24, Isaac Bird Papers.

55. Bernard Heyberger, "Individualism and Political Modernity: Devout Catholic Women in Aleppo and Lebanon between the Seventeenth and Nineteenth Centuries," in Amira El-Azhary Sonbol, ed., *Beyond the Exotic: Women's Histories in Islamic Societies* (Syracuse: Syracuse University Press, 2005), 84.

56. Bernard Heyberger, *Hindiyya: Mystique et criminelle* (Paris: Auber, 2001), 197–199; see also 255–256 for details of how two nuns who opposed Hindiyya were locked away in a cell in 1777, deprived of light and nourishment, and severely beaten and tortured; Bulus 'Abbud Ghustawi, *Basa'ir al-zaman* (Beirut: Sabra, 1911), 141–145.

57. AB, drawer of Yusuf Hubaysh, Yusuf Hubaysh to the Propaganda Fide, 5 January 1827.

58. See entry under 16 July 1826, Journal 1824 May–1830 October, Box 2/24, Isaac Bird Papers.

59. MHROS, 1:464.

60. See Asad Rustum, *Bashir bayn al-sultan wa al-'aziz,* 2 vols. (Beirut: Publications de l'Université Libanaise, 1966) 1:5; Henri Guys, *Beyrouth et le Liban,* 2 vols. (1850; Beirut: Dar Lahd Khater, 1985), 2:93; Dols, *Majnun,* 439.

61. "Nubdha tarikhiyya fi tanassur ba'd al-umara' al-Lam'iyyin," *al-Machreq* 28 (1930): 496–500.

62. For more on conversion in Aleppo, see Bruce Masters, *Christians and Jews in the Ottoman Arab World: The Roots of Sectarianism* (Cambridge: Cambridge University Press, 2001), 95–97; see also R. M. Haddad, "Conversion of Eastern Orthodox Christians," in Michael Gervers and Ramzi Jibran Bikhazi, eds., *Conversion and Continuity: Indigenous Christian Communities in Islamic Lands, Eighth to Eighteenth Centuries* (Toronto: Pontifical Institute of Medieval Studies, 1990), 455.

63. Bustani, *Qissat,* 54–55. In their appeal to Emir Bashir, Ghalib and Antun Shidyaq simply state that the patriarch refused to release As'ad to Tannus and his mother because he claimed As'ad was sick. Ghalib and Antun Shidyaq to Bashir Shihab, n.d. but around 26 October 1826, Box 2/24, Isaac Bird Papers.

64. Bustani, *Qissat,* 56–57.

65. AB, drawer of Yusuf Hubaysh, [As'ad Shiydaq's vision, his appeal, and Maronite Church response], n.d. but probably in 1826; Bustani, *Qissat,* 58.

66. AB, drawer of Yusuf Hubaysh, Yusuf Hubaysh to Propaganda Fide, 5 January 1827.

67. Ibid., [Encyclical against the Biblemen], 15 December 1826.

68. Goodell to Bird, 7 August 1827, in MS-556, American Missionaries in the Near East and Malta, 1822–1865, Special Collections, Dartmouth College Library (hereafter Dartmouth Papers).

69. Emir Bashir to Consul Abbot, n.d., Box 2/24, Isaac Bird Papers.

70. MHROS, 2:86; see also Goodell to Bird, 7 August 1827, Dartmouth Papers.

71. MHROS, 2:119.

72. Yusuf Hubaysh's letter to the Dahir shaykhs, 9 August 1827, Box 2/24, Isaac Bird Papers; see also MHROS, 2:87.

73. AB, drawer of Yusuf Hubaysh, Hubaysh to Propaganda Fide, 4 October 1827.

74. MHROS, 2:93–95.

75. Goodell to Bird, 7 September 1827, Dartmouth Papers.

76. There are at least two distinct letters written by Wolff, a shorter one addressed and apparently delivered to the patriarch directly and a longer one addressed to the entire Maronite "nation" which also found its way to the patriarchate. Copies of the latter can be found undated in the Maronite archives, AB, drawer of Yusuf Hubaysh; "Surat tahrir Yusuf al-Inkilizi," the Arabic papers of Eli Smith, ABC 50/Box 3; and in ABC 16.5, Bird to Goodell, 14 June 1830. The shorter version in Arabic, and possibly an original in the hand of Joseph Wolff, is to be found in "Letters of Isaac Bird and his wife, Ann Parker Bird, Missionaries in the Levant, 1822–1836," Collection of Arabic and Oriental manuscripts, ca. 1799–ca. 1830, Library of the Boston Athenaeum. I am grateful to Eleanor Doumato for informing me about this collection. Bird's English translation of this letter can be found in the Isaac Bird Papers at Yale University.

77. From the Arabic version in "Letters of Isaac Bird" in the Library of the Boston Athenaeum.

78. AB, drawer of Yusuf Hubaysh, "Surat tahrir Yusuf al-Inkilizi." See ABC 16.5, Communications for the Mediterranean, 1817–1837, vol. 1, for an English copy of the letter translated by Bird in his letter to Goodell of 14 June 1830, filed under letters from Joseph Wolff.

79. ABC 16.5, Communications for the Mediterranean, 1817–1837, vol. 1, Bird to Goodell, 14 June 1830.

80. Ibid., extracts of a letter from Bird to Goodell, 22 July 1830, filed under letters from Joseph Wolff.

81. Quoted in Bustani, *Qissat,* 60.

82. AB, drawer of Yusuf Hubaysh, [Confession of As'ad Shidyaq], n.d., probably 1829.

83. Ibid.

84. SCPF, Fondo SC Maroniti, vol. 19 (1823–1827), no. 208, Yusuf Hubaysh to Propaganda

Fide, 23 December 1831; see also AB, drawer of Yusuf Hubaysh, Hubaysh to Rome, 23 December 1831.

85. AB, Drawer of Yusuf Hubaysh, Francis Muhasib to the Propaganda Fide, 1 May 1830. This report is in Italian. I thank Dr. Ombretta Frau for her help and translation.

6. The Apotheosis of American Exceptionalism

1. Henry Harris Jessup, *Syrian Home Life,* compiled by Isaac Riley (New York: Dodd and Mead, 1874), 360–361.

2. For more on this, see David S. Heidler and Jeanne T. Heidler, *Indian Removal* (New York: Norton, 2007). For a moving account of Jeremiah Evarts's battle to prevent the deportation, see John A. Andrew III, *From Revivals to Removal: Jeremiah Evarts, the Cherokee Nation, and the Search for the Soul of America* (Athens: University of Georgia Press, 1992).

3. Kamal Salibi and Yusuf K. Khoury [Khuri], eds., *The Missionary Herald: Reports from Ottoman Syria, 1819–1870* (hereafter MHROS), 5 vols. (Amman: Royal Institute for Interfaith Studies, 1995), 1:405–406.

4. Papers of the American Board of Commissioners for Foreign Missions, deposited at Houghton Library, Harvard University, Mission to the Jews, 1824–1831, 3 vols. (hereafter ABC), 16.6, Palestine Mission, vol. 1, Fisk to Van Lennep, 19 August 1823.

5. MHROS, 1:407.

6. Temple to Bird and Goodell, 31 May 1826, MS-556: American Missionaries in the Near East and Malta, 1822–1865, Special Collections, Dartmouth College Library (hereafter Dartmouth Papers).

7. ABC 1.01, preliminary series, letters 1812–1839, vol. 5, Anderson to Bird, 5 April 1825.

8. Ibid., Vol. 6, Evarts to King, 24 June 1825.

9. Sam Haselby, "The Origins of American Religious Nationalism, 1787–1832" (Ph.D. diss., Columbia University, 2006), 316; John A. Andrew III, *Rebuilding the Christian Commonwealth* (Lexington: University of Kentucky Press, 1976), 123.

10. Cited in John Salliant, "Missions in Liberia and Race Relations in the United States, 1822–1860," in Daniel H. Bays and Grant Wacker, eds., *The Foreign Missionary Enterprise at Home: Explorations in North American Cultural History* (Tuscaloosa: University of Alabama Press, 2003), 16.

11. See Andrew, *Rebuilding the Christian Commonwealth,* 81–83, 128–129, for criticisms of overseas ventures. For criticism of ABCFM Indian policy, see Andrew, *From Revivals to Removal.*

12. Evarts cited in Andrew, *From Revivals to Removal,* 135; John A. Andrew III, "Educating the Heathen: The Foreign Mission School Controversy and American Ideals," *Journal of American Studies* 12 (1978): 331–342.

13. On Jackson in comparison with the American Board and what Haselby refers to as "national evangelists," see Haselby, "The Origins of American Religious Nationalism," 385–392; Andrew, *From Revivals to Removal,* 169–198.

14. MHROS: 1:388

15. Goodell to Bird, 27 June 1824, Dartmouth Papers.

16. Temple to Bird and Goodell, 28 October 1826, Dartmouth Papers.

17. Eli Smith, *Missionary Sermons and Addresses* (New York: Saxton and Miles, 1842), 51–52.

18. Ibid., 63.

19. Ibid., 18.

20. MHROS, 1:429.

21. Eli Smith, *Missionary Sermons,* 62.

22. MHROS, 1:368.

23. MHROS, 2:70.

24. MHROS, 1:429.

25. ABC 16.6, Palestine Mission, vol. 2, Bird to Evarts, 6 January 1826.

26. Ibid., Bird to Anderson, 14 March 1826.

27. ABC 16.5, Communication for the Mediterranean, 1817–1837, Goodell to Evarts, 15 September 1826; Isaac Bird, *Bible Work in Bible Lands; Or, Events in the History of the Syria Mission* (Philadelphia: Presbyterian Board of Missions, 1872), 196–197.

28. Temple to Bird and Goodell, 28 October 1826, Dartmouth Papers.

29. MHROS, 1:407.

30. ABC 16.6, Palestine Mission, vol. 3, Journal of Jonas King, 18 May 1825; MHROS, 1:404.

31. MHROS, 1:467.

32. ABC 1.01, preliminary series, letters 1812–1839, vol. 5, Anderson to Bird, 4 October 1825.

33. *Report of the American Board of Commissioners for Foreign Missions Compiled from Documents Laid Before the Board at the Nineteenth Annual Meeting* (Boston: Crocker and Brewster, 1828), 40–44.

34. MHROS, 1:436; ABC 2.01, preliminary Series, vol. 3, Anderson to Bird, 20 June 1828.

35. Isaac Bird, Journal, 12 November 1830, Box 2/24, Isaac Bird Papers, Manuscripts and Archives, Yale University Library.

36. MHROS, 2:292–293.

37. MHROS, 2:321.

38. MHROS, 2:331.

39. Archives of the Maronite Patriarchate, Bkirke, Lebanon, drawer of Yusuf Hubaysh, Robert Tod to Faris Shidyaq, n.d.

40. MHROS, 2:323.

41. Joseph Tracy, *History of the American Board of Commissioners for Foreign Missions compiled chiefly from the published and unpublished documents of the board,* 2nd ed. (New York: M. W. Dodd, 1842), 180.

42. Jonas King, *Extraits d'un ouvrage écrit vers la fin de l'année 1826 et au commencement de 1827, sous le titre de Coup d'Oeil sur la Palestine et la Syrie, accompagné de quelques reflexions sur les missions évangeliques par Jonas King* (Athens: C. Nicolaidès Philadelphien, 1859), 182.

43. Rufus Anderson, *History of the Missions of the American Board of Commissioners for Foreign Missions to the Oriental Churches,* 2 vols. (Boston: Congregational Publishing Society, 1884), 1:71.

44. This is the title of the memoir I consulted; see ABCFM, *A Memoir of Asaad Esh Shidiak; An Arab young man of the Maronite Roman Catholic Church, in Syria,* Missionary Paper no. 7 (Boston: Crocker and Brewster, n.d.), which was itself the third edition with a print run of three thousand. It was based almost entirely on materials already published in the *Missionary Herald.* The first edition was published in 1827 under the title *A brief memoir of Asaad Shidiak: an Arab young man, of the Maronite Catholic Church in Syria.* The punctuation, spelling, and exact wording of the title varied from edition to edition, but the basic text remained the same.

45. Leonard Woods, *A Sermon Delivered at the Tabernacle in Salem, Feb 6 1812, on Occasion of the Ordination of the Rev. Messrs. Samuel Newell, A.M. Adoniram Judson, A.M. Samuel Nott, A.M. Gordon Hall, A.M. and Luther Rice, A.B. Missionaries to the Heathen in Asia, Under the Direction of the Board of Commissioners for Foreign Missions* (Boston: Samuel T. Armstrong, 1812), 18.

46. ABC 16.6, Palestine Mission, vol. 2, Bird to Anderson, 14 March 1826; William M. Thomson, *The Land and the Book or Biblical Illustrations Drawn from the Manners and Customs, the Scenes and Scenery, of the Holy Land,* vol. 3, *Lebanon, Damascus, and Beyond Jordan* (Hartford: S. S. Scranton, 1910), 129; Isaac Bird, *The Martyr of Lebanon* (Boston: American Tract Society, 1864); Jessup, *Syrian Home Life,* 360–361. As'ad's story also made its way into Amos Blanchard's *Book of Martyrs or, A History of the Lives, Sufferings, and Triumphant Deaths of the Primitive and Protestant Martyrs*

from the Introduction of Christianity, to the Latest Periods of Pagan, Popish, Protestant, and Infidel Perse-cutions (Kingston, C.W.: N. G. Ellis, 1844), 390–439, which was itself compiled from Foxe's *Book of Martyrs* and "other authentic sources."

47. MHROS, 1:439.

48. ABC 16.6, Palestine Mission, vol. 2, Bird to Anderson, 20 September 1825; Paul William Harris, *Nothing But Christ: Rufus Anderson and the Ideology of Protestant Foreign Missions* (New York: Oxford University Press, 1999), 40, discusses the memoirs of Henry Obookiah and Catherine Brown.

49. Samuel Spring, "The Charge," appended to Woods, *Sermon Delivered at the Tabernacle in Salem,* 34. This is a biblical reference from 1 Peter 2:2–3.

50. Tracy, *History of the American Board,* 174.

51. Jeremiah Evarts, *Cherokee Removal: The "William Penn" Essays and Other Writings,* ed. Francis Paul Prucha (Knoxville: University of Tennessee Press, 1981), 211.

52. For more information on this, see Andrew, *From Revivals to Removal;* see also Edwin A. Miles, "After John Marshall's Decision: *Worcester v. Georgia* and the Nullification Crisis," *Journal of Southern History* 39 (1973): 519–544.

53. Andrew, *From Revivals to Removal,* 153; Joshua David Bellin, "Apostle of Removal: John Eliot in the Nineteenth Century," *New England Quarterly* 69 (1996): 3–32; Indian missions did not altogether end, but never again was there as intense a moment of confrontation between the American Board and white racism. Indeed, as the American frontier continued to expand, so too did missionaries set up new missions west of the Mississippi, only to end eventually in failure as Indian lands were relentlessly confiscated and Indians decimated and herded into reservations. See, in this regard, C. L. Higham, *Noble, Wretched, and Redeemable: Protestant Missionaries to the In-dians in Canada and the United States, 1820–1900* (Albuquerque: University of New Mexico Press, 2000), 175–176; 213; Harris, *Nothing But Christ,* 23.

54. Harris, *Nothing But Christ,* 94.

55. Harris, *Nothing But Christ,* provides the most complete account of Rufus Anderson. The next chapter will detail the implications of Anderson's mission philosophy on the ground in the Syria mission.

56. Rufus Anderson, "The Work of Missions to be Progressive. A Sermon on the Present Crisis in the Missionary Operations of the American Board of Commissioners for Foreign Missions," 2nd ed. (Boston: Crocker and Brewster, 1840), 4.

57. Harris, *Nothing But Christ,* 77–95; Charles A. Maxfield III, "The 1845 Organic Sin De-bate: Slavery, Sin, and the American Board of Commissioners for Foreign Missions," in Wilbert R. Shenk, ed., *North American Foreign Missions, 1810–1914* (Grand Rapids: Eerdmans, 2004), 86–115.

58. *Report of the American Board of Commissioners for Foreign Missions Presented at the Thirty-Third Annual Meeting* (Boston: Crocker and Brewster, 1842), 117.

59. A. L. Tibawi, *American Interests in Syria: A Study of Educational, Literary, and Religious Work* (Oxford: Clarendon Press, 1966), 76–95.

60. *Report of the American Board of Commissioners for Foreign Missions Presented at the Meeting Held at Boston, Mass.* (Boston: T. R. Marvin and Son, 1860), 72.

61. See, in regard to American exceptionalism, Rob Kroes, "American Empire and Cultural Imperialism: A View from the Receiving End," in Thomas Bender, ed., *Rethinking American His-tory in a Global Age* (Berkeley: University of California Press, 2002), 295–297.

62. Tracy, *History of the ABCFM,* 1, 2–3.

63. Ibid., 7.

64. Ibid., 267.

65. Ibid., 21.

66. See Joseph A. Conforti, *Imagining New England: Explorations of Regional Identity from the*

Pilgrims to the Mid-Twentieth Century (Chapel Hill: University of North Carolina Press, 2001), 124, for an elaboration of what he describes as "New England's antebellum national regionalism."

67. Tracy, *History of the ABCFM*, 22–23.

68. Tannus al-Shidyaq, *Kitab akhbar al-ʿayan fi jabal lubnan,* ed. Fouad E. Boustany, 2 vols. (Beirut: Publications de l'Université Libanaise, 1970), 2:476; for more details, see Ussama Makdisi, *The Culture of Sectarianism: Community, History, and Violence in Nineteenth-Century Ottoman Lebanon* (Berkeley: University of California Press, 2000), 59–78.

69. Tracy, *History of the ABCFM*, 440, 443.

70. Anderson, *History of the Missions of the American Board of Commissioners for Foreign Missions to the Oriental Churches,* 1:277.

71. *Missionary Herald* 34 (1838): 397–398; MHROS, 3:145. This sympathy was not, however, shared by every missionary, some of whom confidentially described the Druzes as a "truculent and deceitful race" because of their refusal to convert. See ABC 16.5, vol. 3, Near East, 1828–1842, Miscellaneous Letters, Samuel Wolcott to Anderson, 1 June 1842.

72. Anderson, "The Work of Missions to be Progressive," 8.

73. Tracy, *History of the ABCFM,* 442–443.

74. Loanza Benton, "The Diaries, Reminiscences, and Letters of Loanza Goulding Benton (Mrs. William Austin Benton) and William Benton, Missionaries to Syria, 1847–1869" (hereafter Loanza Benton, "Diaries"), 30. This diary is a facsimile of an unpublished typeset manuscript kindly put at my disposal by Marjorie Benton.

75. Ibid., 45.

76. Edward W. Hooker, *Memoir of Sarah L. Huntington Smith, Late of the Syria Mission,* 3rd ed. (New York: American Tract Society, 1845), 294.

77. Loanza Benton, "Diaries," 22; Benton to Lathrop, 12 April 1858, Box 11, Folder 2, William A. Benton Papers, Department of Special Collections, Joseph Regenstein Library, University of Chicago.

78. Loanza Benton, "Diaries," 87. For China, see Jane Hunter, *The Gospel of Gentility: American Women Missionaries in Turn-of-the-Century China* (New Haven: Yale University Press, 1984), 129.

79. Loanza Benton, "Diaries," 248.

80. ABC 16.8.1, Syrian Mission, vol. 7, 1860–1871, pt. 2, Thomson to Anderson, 23 May 1860.

81. Ibid., pt. 1, Eddy to Anderson, 5 June 1860.

82. Ibid., Jessup to Anderson, 1 June 1860.

83. Ibid., Jessup to Anderson, 5 June 1860.

84. See Makdisi, *Culture of Sectarianism,* 118–145, for more details on the sectarian violence itself; and Ussama Makdisi, "Reclaiming the Land of the Bible: Missionaries, Secularism, and Evangelical Modernity," *American Historical Review* 102 (1997): 680–713, for more on American missionary reactions to the 1860 events.

85. ABC 16.8.1, Syrian Mission, vol. 7, pt. 1, Jessup to Anderson, 29 August 1860.

86. Ibid., vol. 6, Benton to Anderson, 11 October 1860.

87. Ibid., Loanza Benton to Anderson, 24 July 1860.

88. See, in regard to Beirut, Jens Hanssen, *Fin-de-Siècle Beirut: The Making of an Ottoman Provincial Capital* (Oxford: Clarendon Press, 2005); Malek Sharif, "The Ottoman Municipal Laws and the Municipality of Beirut (1860–1908)" (Ph.D. diss., Free University, Berlin, 2004); May Davie, *Beyrouth et ses faubourgs (1840–1940): Une integration inachevée* (Beirut: CERMOC, 1996); as for the transfer of the ABCFM Syria mission to the Presbyterians in 1870, see Tibawi, *American Interests in Syria,* 191–192.

89. Julius Richter, *A History of Protestant Missions in the Near East* (New York: Fleming H. Revell, 1910), 201.

90. Henry Harris Jessup, *Fifty-Three Years in Syria,* 2 vols. (1910; Reading, U.K.: Garnet Publishing, 2002), 2:641, 651.

91. Ibid., 1:35, 40.

92. Ibid., 44. Edward Peters, *Inquisition* (New York: Free Press, 1988), 155–156, has suggested that the notion of the Inquisition was largely an Enlightenment invention based on Reformation-era myths. In Samir Khalaf, *Cultural Resistance: Global and Local Encounters with the Middle East* (London: Saqi Books, 2001), 162–168, Khalaf describes Jessup as a "quintessential Protestant Orientalist." Khalaf also accuses Jessup of having a "medievalist mindset" which I think fundamentally misses the point of Jessup's departure from previous missionary narratives of the East.

93. Cyrus Hamlin, *Among the Turks* (New York: R. Carter and Brothers, 1878), 26.

94. James L. Barton, *Daybreak in Turkey* (Boston: Pilgrim Press, 1908), 52.

95. Henry Harris Jessup, *Sermon Delivered at the Opening of the General Assembly of the Presbyterian Church in the United States of America at Saratoga, May 15th, 1884* (n.p.: Friends of Foreign Missions, 1884), 25

96. Ibid., 25.

97. Eli Smith, *Toleration in the Turkish Empire* (Boston: T. R. Marvin, 1846), is an example of how missionaries before 1860 saw Ottoman toleration as something to be exploited.

98. William R. Hutchison, *Religious Pluralism in America: The Contentious History of a Founding Ideal* (New Haven: Yale University Press, 2003), 106–117.

99. Jessup, *Fifty-Three Years in Syria,* 2:522–524. See also Eugene Rogan, "Madness and Marginality: The Advent of the Psychiatric Asylum in Egypt and Lebanon," in Eugene Rogan, ed., *Outside In: On the Margins of the Modern Middle East* (London: I. B. Tauris, 2002), 104–126.

100. Richter, *A History of Protestant Missions in the Near East,* 192.

101. Jessup, *Fifty-three Years in Syria,* 2:744, 522.

102. Ibid., 1:27.

103. Smith, *Missionary Sermons,* 167; see also Ellen Fleischmann, "The Impact of American Protestant Missions in Lebanon on the Construction of Female Identity, c. 1860–1950," *Islam and Christian-Muslim Relations* 13 (2002): 411–426; for more on the gender ideology of American missionaries and how the liberation of Christian women from "Islam" did not mean equality with men, see Amanda Porterfield, *Mary Lyon and the Mount Holyoke Missionaries* (New York: Oxford University Press, 1997), 82–86.

104. Henry Harris Jessup, *Women of the Arabs,* ed. C. S. Robinson and Isaac Riley. (New York: Dodd & Mead, 1873); for more on the relationship between a rhetoric of the salvation of foreign women and late-nineteenth-century American ascendancy, see Joan Jacobs Brumberg, "Zenanas and Girlless Villages: The Ethnology of American Evangelical Women, 1870–1910," *Journal of American History* 69 (1982): 347–371; see also Louise Michele Newman, *White Women's Rights: The Racial Origins of Feminism in the United States* (New York: Oxford University Press, 1999), 22–55; see also Dana L. Robert, *American Women in Mission: A Social History of Their Thought and Practice* (Macon, Ga.: Mercer University Press, 1996), and Patricia Grimshaw, *Paths of Duty: American Missionary Wives in Nineteenth-Century Hawaii* (Honolulu: University of Hawaii Press, 1989), whose work studies the autonomy and empowerment of American Board missionary wives in Hawaii but also their implication and participation in a racial hierarchy there; for a more recent account of missionary women and the Orient, see Lisa Joy Pruitt, *A Looking-Glass for Ladies: American Protestant Women and the Orient in the Nineteenth Century* (Macon, Ga.: Mercer University Press, 2005). All these accounts privilege the perspective of the American women.

105. Jessup, *Women of the Arabs,* 136, 28, 139.

106. Thomas Laurie, *The Ely Volume; or, The Contributions of our Foreign Missions to Science and Human Well-Being* (Boston; ABCFM, 1885), 73. Robinson's book *Biblical Researches in Palestine, Mount Sinai, and Arabia Petraea* was published in 1838, a landmark study of biblical geography and

archaeology. See Bruce Kuklick, *Puritans in Babylon: The Ancient Near East and American Intellectual Life, 1880–1930* (Princeton: Princeton University Press, 1996), 20.

107. See, for instance, Henry Harris Jessup, *The Setting of the Crescent and the Rising of the Cross, or Kamil Abdul Messiah, A Syrian Convert from Islam to Christianity* (Philadelphia: Westminster Press, 1898).

108. Jessup, *Women of the Arabs,* 127.

109. Jessup, *Setting of the Crescent,* 5.

110. James L. Barton, *The Christian Approach to Islam* (Boston: Pilgrim Press, 1918), 309; for another view of American missionary idealism, see Hans-Lukas Kieser, "Some Remarks on Alevi Responses to the Missionaries in Eastern Antalolia (19th-20th centuries)" in Eleanor H. Tejirian and Reeva Spector Simon, eds., *Altruism and Imperialism: Western Cultural and Religious Missions in the Middle East* (New York: Middle East Institute, Columbia University, 2002), 120–142; for an elaboration of what Kieser describes as a utopian moment following the 1908 Young Turk Revolution, see also his "Muslim Heterodoxy and Protestant Utopia: The Interactions between Alevis and Missionaries in Ottoman Anatolia," *Die Welt des Islams* 41 (2001): 89–111.

111. Jessup, *Fifty-three Years in Syria,* 2:688. See also Hilton Obenzinger, *American Palestine: Melville, Twain, and the Holy Land Mania* (Princeton: Princeton University Press, 1999), and John Davis, *The Landscape of Belief: Encountering the Holy Land in Nineteenth-Century American Art and Culture* (Princeton: Princeton University Press, 1996), for more on American attitudes and representations of Palestine and the Ottoman Empire; for more on American attitudes toward the Jews of the Holy Land see Lester I. Vogel, *To See a Promised Land: Americans and the Holy Land in the Nineteenth Century* (University Park, Penn.: Pennsylvania State University Press, 1993), 226–233.

112. See type-set of a letter from Daniel Bliss to his brother [Fredrick?] Bliss, 30 August 1869, Box 4/Letters from Daniel Bliss to his family, 1852–1909, AA:2.3.1., Archives and Special Collections, Jafet Library, American University of Beirut (hereafter AUB Archives).

113. William R. Hutchison, *Errand to the World: American Protestant Thought and Foreign Missions* (Chicago: University of Chicago Press, 1987), 91–124. See also Ernest Lee, *Redeemer Nation: The Idea of America's Millennial Role* (Chicago: University of Chicago Press, 1968), 166–167; Wendy J. Deichmann Edwards, "Forging an Ideology for American Missions: Josiah Strong and Manifest Destiny," in Shenk, *North American Foreign Missions, 1810–1914,* 163–191.

114. Jessup, *Fifty-Three Years in Syria,* 1:361.

115. Ibid., 306; for descriptions and illustrations of the fair exhibits, see Marshall Everett, *The Book of the Fair* (Philadelphia: P. W. Ziegler, 1904).

116. Laurie, *The Ely Volume,* 453, 460.

117. Barton, *Daybreak in Turkey,* 88. For America, see Reginald Horsman, *Race and Manifest Destiny: The Origins of American Racial Anglo-Saxonism* (Cambridge: Harvard University Press, 1981), 184–186, 300–301; on the paradox of citizenship within the United States, see Rogers M. Smith, *Civic Ideals: Conflicting Visions of Citizenship in U.S. History* (New Haven: Yale University Press, 1997), 459–463.

118. Jessup, *Syrian Home Life,* 365.

119. Jessup, *Sermon,* 19.

120. See Henry Harris Jessup, *The Mohammedan Missionary Problem* (Philadelphia: Presbyterian Board of Publication, 1879), 78. See also Edward J. Blum, *Reforging the White Republic: Race, Religion, and American Nationalism, 1865–1898* (Baton Rouge: Louisiana State University Press, 2005).

121. Hutchison, *Errand to the World,* 92.

122. Daniel Bliss to unknown recipient [probably his family], 7 December 1859, AA:2.3.1, Box 4/Letters from Daniel Bliss to his family, 1852–1909, AUB Archives.

123. Jessup, *Sermon,* 12, 16–17.

124. William E. Strong, *The Story of the American Board* (Boston: Pilgrim Press, 1910), 492–493.

125. Hutchison, *Errand to the World*, 93.

126. Jessup, *Sermon*, 10.

127. Laurie, *The Ely Volume*, 457.

128. Jessup, *Fifty-Three Years in Syria*, 2:766; Jessup, *The Mohammedan Missionary Problem*, 14. In this regard, Jessup was unlike those missionaries in the United States who continued to grapple with the problem of saving Indians; see Higham, *Noble, Wretched, and Redeemable*, 187–209.

129. For more information on the U.S. missionary involvement in and representation of the Armenian question, see Jeremy Salt, *Imperialism, Evangelism, and the Ottoman Armenians, 1878–1896* (London: Frank Cass, 1993). See also Kieser, "Muslim Heterodoxy and Protestant Utopia," 102–103.

130. Earl of Cromer, *Modern Egypt*, 2 vols. (New York: Macmillan Company, 1908), 2:229.

7. The Vindication of As'ad Shidyaq

1. *Khabariyyat As'ad Shidyaq al-ladhi idtuhida li-ajl iqrarihi fi al-haqq* (Malta, 1833), British Library collection. Faris Shidyaq, *Al-saq 'ala al-saq fi ma huwa al-Farayaq aw ayyam wa shuhur wa a'wam fi 'ajm al-'arab wa al-a'jam* (1855; Beirut: Dar maktabat al-hayat, n.d.), 188.

2. Başbakanlık Devlet Arşivi, Istanbul (hereafter BBA), HR MKT 4/18 (1) and BBA, Cevdet Hariciye 4959.

3. BBA, Mesail-i Mühimme 967, 12 Ra. 1262 [15 April 1846].

4. Archives of the Maronite Patriarchate, Bkirke, Lebanon (hereafter AB), drawer of Yusuf Hubaysh, undated draft petition to Ottoman governor, presumably Selim Pasha from internal evidence. A Maronite petition was in fact made in 1841 and a favorable Ottoman reply received. See A. L. Tibawi, *American Interests in Syria: A Study of Educational, Literary, and Religious Work* (Oxford: Clarendon Press, 1966), 93–94; for a Greek Catholic petition, see BBA, HR MKT 25/49, Leff. 2 4 Ca 1265 [29 March 1849].

5. BBA, Mesail-i Mühimme, 967, 12 Ra. 1262 [15 April 1846].

6. Bruce Masters, *Christians and Jews in the Ottoman Arab World: The Roots of Sectarianism* (Cambridge: Cambridge University Press, 2001), 110–111; for the American interpretation of Ottoman recognition, see Papers of the American Board of Commissioners for Foreign Missions, deposited at Houghton Library, Harvard University (hereafter ABC), Near East, 1823–1860, Miscellaneous Letters, Documents, vol. 4, "Farewell Address; Presented by the American Missionaries, at Constantinople to the Lord Viscount Stratford de Redcliffe with the Reply of his Excellency."

7. The translation here is from an appendix in E. D. G. Prime, *Forty Years in the Turkish Empire; Or, Memoirs of the Rev. William Goodell*, 5th ed. (New York: Robert Carter and Brothers, 1878), 483–484; for almost identical Arabic and Ottoman versions of the proclamation, see Eli Smith's Arabic papers in ABC 50, Box 1. See also the National Archives, Kew, Foreign Office, Great Britain, Series 424/1, *Correspondence Respecting the Condition of Protestants in Turkey, 1841–1851*, Canning to Palmerston, 26 November 1850, enclosure 2 in no. 105, 137–138.

8. The phrase belongs to the American missionaries; see their memorial to Lord Cowley, 21 December 1847, enclosure 1 in Cowley to Palmerston, 29 December 1847, no. 99, in *Correspondence respecting the Condition of Protestants in Turkey, 1841–1851*, 126–127.

9. See Selim Deringil, "'There is no Compulsion in Religion': On Conversion and Apostasy in the Late Ottoman Empire, 1839–1856," *Comparative Studies in Society and History* 42 (2000): 547–575.

10. Hatt-i Hümayun of 1856, reproduced in J. C. Hurewitz, ed., *The Middle East and North Africa in World Politics: A Documentary Record*, vol. 1, *European Expansion, 1535–1914* (New Haven: Yale University Press, 1975), 315–318.

11. Archives du Ministère des Affaires Étrangères, Paris, AE MD/T ser., Mémoires et Documents, Turquie, 1840–1863, vol. 51, no. 9, "Memoire transmis à Londres et Paris par Aali Pacha," May 1855. See also Fuad Andic and Suphan Andic, *The Last of the Ottoman Grandees: The Life and the Political Testament of Ali Pasa* (Istanbul: Isis Press, 1996).

12. See Selim Deringil, *The Well-Protected Domains: Ideology and the Legitimation of Power in the Ottoman Empire, 1876–1909* (London: I. B. Tauris, 1999); see also Ussama Makdisi, "Ottoman Orientalism," *American Historical Review* 107 (2002): 768–796.

13. Tibawi, *American Interests*, 99. ABC 16.8.1, Syrian Mission, vol. 2, Wolcott to Anderson, 14 December 1840.

14. Jens Hanssen, *Fin-de-Siècle Beirut: The Making of an Ottoman Provincial Capital* (Oxford: Clarendon Press, 2005), 3–17. For Jessup, see chapter 6.

15. ABC 16.8.1, Syrian Mission, vol. 1, William Thomson's committee report on the results of the seminary, 6 April 1844.

16. Gregory M. Wortabet, *Syria and the Holy Land, Being a Course of Lectures*, rev. ed. (Halifax, 1856), 38.

17. Gregory M. Wortabet, *Syria and the Syrians: Or, Turkey in the Dependencies*, 2 vols. (London: James Madden, 1856), 1:7–8. See May Davie, *Beyrouth et ses Faubourgs, 1840–1940: Une integration inachevée* (Beirut: CERMOC, 1996), 35–37.

18. Edward Robinson, *Later Biblical Researches in Palestine and in the Adjacent Regions: A Journal of Travels in the Year 1852* (Boston: Crocker and Brewster, 1857), 25.

19. ABC 16.5, vol. 3, Near East, 1828–1842, Miscellaneous Letters, Wolcott to Anderson, 1 June 1842. See also Tibawi, *American Interests*, 96–100.

20. Tibawi, *American Interests*, 121.

21. A. L. Tibawi, *Arabic and Islamic Themes: Historical, Educational, and Literary Studies* (London: Luzac and Company, 1974), 261.

22. François Badour to Louis Allard, Beirut, 14 June 1852, reproduced in Sami Khuri, ed., *Une histoire du Liban à travers les archives des jésuites, 1846–1862* (Beirut: Dar el-Machreq, 1991), 350. As Wolcott explained, the mission at great expense had educated and housed several boys, almost all of whom were, following the British-led bombardment of Beirut in 1840 and the restoration of Ottoman rule, "lost to the mission" because they sought lucrative secular employment.

23. ABC 16.8.1, Syrian Mission, vol. 1, William Thomson's committee report on the results of the seminary, 6 April 1844.

24. Cited in Paul William Harris, *Nothing But Christ: Rufus Anderson and the Ideology of Protestant Foreign Missions* (New York: Oxford University Press, 1999), 75.

25. Cited ibid., 128.

26. ABCFM, *Report to the Prudential Committee of a Visit to the Missions in the Levant by Rufus Anderson* (Boston: T. R. Marvin, 1844), 25. Not surprisingly, an almost identical story played itself out in Istanbul among the Armenian converts to Protestantism. See Harris, *Nothing But Christ*, 127.

27. Wortabet, *Syria and the Holy Land*, 36. See Faris Shidyaq's letter to his brother Tannus from 11 May 1842, in Yusuf Ibrahim Yazbak, ed., *Awraq Lubnaniyya*, 3 vols. (Hazmiyya, Lebanon: Dar al-ra'id al-lubnani, 1983) 1:359–360.

28. Tibawi, *Arabic and Islamic Themes*, 262–263. A very similar story unfolded in Istanbul with Cyrus Hamlin's Bebek Seminary. See Harris, *Nothing But Christ*, 131–132.

29. ABC 30, Rufus Anderson Papers, vol. 10 (hereafter ABC 30.10), memoranda of discussions in meetings of missionaries during Anderson's visits to the Levant, 1843–44. This volume itself consists of three boxes. The notes of his conversation with the missionaries in Beirut is contained in the second and third boxes. Meeting at Mission House, 11 March 1844.

30. Harris, *Nothing But Christ*, 122.

31. See ABC 16.8.1, Syrian Mission, vol. 5, Van Dyck to Anderson, 17 August 1850, for Cornelius Van Dyck's severe private criticisms of his peers to Anderson in which he said that "an ungrounded want of confidence in pious natives has been a great stumbling block and hindrance to the success of the gospel in this land." For more details on Anderson and his interactions with the Syrian mission, see Habib Badr, "Mission to 'Nominal Christians': The Policy and Practice of the American Board of Commissioners for Foreign Missions and Its Missionaries Concerning Eastern Churches Which Led to the Organization of a Protestant Church in Beirut (1819–1848)" (Ph.D. diss., Princeton Theological Seminary, 1992).

32. ABC 30.10, meeting at Mission House, 21 March 1844.

33. See ABC 30.10 for various salary figures of American missionaries in Syria.

34. ABC 16.8.1, Syrian Mission, vol. 5, Smith to Anderson, 17 June 1851.

35. The words are those of Rufus Anderson. See his letter to Andrew Sommerville printed and circulated for the missionary stations in Turkey in ABC 2.1.1, Letters to Foreign Correspondents, vol. 26, Anderson to Sommerville, 4 June 1860. For the Arabic mission press, see Dagmar Glass, *Malta, Beirut, Leipzig, and Beirut Again: Eli Smith, the American Syria Mission, and the Spread of Arabic Typography in 19th Century Lebanon* (Beirut: Orient-Institut der Deutschen Morgenländischen Gesellschaft, 1998).

36. Yusuf Khuri, *Rajul sabiq li-ʿasrihi: al-muʿallim Butrus al-Bustani, 1819–1883* (Beirut: Bisan, 1995), 17.

37. Henry Diab and Lars Wahlin, "The Geography of Education in Syria in 1882 with a Translation of 'Education in Syria' by Shahin Makarius, 1883," *Geografiska Annaler,* ser. B, *Human Geography* 65 (1983): 105–128. See also ABC 16.8.1, Syrian Mission, vol. 5, Van Dyck to Anderson, 17 August 1850; and Yusuf Khuri, *Al-duktur Kurniliyus Fan Dik wa nahdat al-diyar al-shamiyya al-ʿilmiyya fi al-qarn al-tasiʿ ʿashar* ([Beirut]: Dar Suriyya li al-nashr), 106–149.

38. Edward E. Salisbury, "II. Syrian Society of Arts and Sciences," *Journal of the American Oriental Society* 3 (1853): 477–486; quotation is on 478. See also Yusuf Khuri, ed., *Al-jamʿiyya al-suriyya li al-ʿulum wa al-funun 1847–1852* (Beirut: Dar al-Hamraʾ, 1990).

39. Butrus al-Bustani, "Khitab fi taʿlim al-nisaʾ," in Khuri, *Al-Jamʿiyya al-suriyya.*

40. Bustani, "Khitab fi taʿlim al-nisaʾ," in Khuri, *Al-jamʿiyya al-suriyya,* 47.

41. *Missionary Herald* 40 (1844): 352.

42. *New York Morning Herald,* 19 May 1840, 1, 3, 4, in Yale Divinity School Library, Special Collections, Eli Smith Family Papers, RG 124, Box 3/2.

43. Salisbury, "II: Syrian Society of Arts and Sciences," 480.

44. This becomes particularly evident in Bustani's encyclopedia, *Kitab daiʾrat al-maʿarif,* of which he had completed six volumes by the time of his death in 1883. See Tibawi, *Arabic and Islamic Themes,* 249–250; also Fruma Zachs, *The Making of a Syrian Identity: Intellectuals and Merchants in Nineteenth-Century Beirut* (Leiden: Brill, 2005), 139–148.

45. Tibawi, *Arabic and Islamic Themes,* 251–252.

46. ABC 30.10(2), Meeting at Mission House, 20 March 1844. The words are Anderson's notes of Thomson's statement at the meeting.

47. Butrus al-Bustani, "Khutba fi adab al-ʿarab," Beirut, 15 February 1859, reproduced in Khuri, *Al-jamʿiyya al-suriyya,* 101.

48. Stephen Sheehi, *Foundation of Modern Arab Identity* (Gainesville: University Press of Florida, 2004), 28–32.

49. Bustani, "Khutba fi adab al-ʿarab," 117.

50. Ibid., 108–114.

51. Butrus al-Bustani, *Qissat Asʿad al-Shidyaq: Bakurat Suriyya* (Beirut: American Mission Press, 1860). All references are to the reprinted version redacted by Yusuf Khuri, *Qissat Asʿad al-Shidyaq: munazara wa hiwar multahib hawla hurriyat al-damir* (Beirut: Dar al-Hamraʾ, 1991). ABC 16.8.1, Syrian Mission, vol. 6, Report of the Beirut Station for the Year 1860, indicates that two

thousand copies of the "Life" of Asaad Shidiak were printed and priced at six piasters a copy. A reprint was issued in 1878.

52. ABC 16.8.1, Syrian Mission, vol. 6, Bustani to Anderson, 25 January 1860.

53. Bustani, *Qissat,* 9.

54. For more on Faris Shidyaq, see Mohammed Bakir Alwan, "Ahmad Faris ash-Shidyaq and the West" (Ph.D. diss., Indiana University, 1970). See also Yusuf Khuri and Yusuf Ibish, eds., *Mukhtarat min athar Ahmad Faris al-Shidyaq* (Beirut: al-mu'assasa al-sharqiyya lil-nashr wa al-tiba'a, 2001); and Geoffrey Roper, "Faris Shidyaq and the Transition from Scribal to Print Culture in the Middle East," in George N. Atiyeh, ed., *The Book in the Islamic World: The Written Word and Communication in the Middle East* (Albany: State University of New York Press, 1995), 209–231.

55. Bustani, *Qissat,* 39.

56. Tannus al-Shidyaq, *Kitab akhbar al-a'yan fi Jabal Lubnan,* ed. Fouad E. Boustany, 2 vols. (1859; Beirut: Publications de l'Université Libanaise, 1970); see also Kamal Salibi, *Maronite Historians of Medieval Lebanon* (1959; Beirut: Naufal, 1991), 161–233, for more on Tannus al-Shidyaq and his work.

57. Shidyaq, *Akhbar al-a'yan,* 1:119–120.

58. Ibid., 120.

59. Ibid., 2:479.

60. Ibid., 486–487.

61. See in this regard Sheehi, *Foundation of Modern Arab Identity,* 124–125, and Roper, "Faris Shidyaq and the Transition from Scribal to Print Culture in the Middle East," 209–231.

62. Bustani, *Qissat,* 11; for an excellent analysis of the missiological difference between Bustani and Isaac Bird's narrative of the Shidyaq affair, see David Kerr, "Maronites and Missionaries: A Critical Appraisal of the Affairs of As'ad al-Shidyaq (1825–1829)," in David Thomas, ed., *A Faithful Presence: Essays for Kenneth Cragg* (London: Melisende, 2003), 219–236.

63. Bustani, *Qissat,* 63. Emphasis added.

64. Compare Shidyaq, *Al-Saq,* 187–188, to Bustani, *Qissat,* 63–64.

65. Bustani, *Qissat,* 56–57, 59; see also Kerr, "Maronites and Missionaries," 233.

66. For a ferocious criticism of Bustani's narrative, see the apologetic manuscript by the Maronite Mansur al-Hattuni, *Hayat al-batriyark Yusuf Hubaysh* (The Life of Patriarch Yusuf Hubaysh), Microfilm A 000466, Special Collections and Archives, Jafet Library, American University of Beirut.

67. ABC 2.1, vol. 26, Andrew Somerville to Rufus Anderson, 5 October 1860, included in Anderson to Missionary Stations in Turkey, 1 November 1860.

68. Ussama Makdisi, *The Culture of Sectarianism: Community, History, and Violence in Nineteenth-Century Ottoman Lebanon* (Berkeley: University of California Press, 2000), 146–165.

69. This discussion of *Nafir Suriyya* is derived from Ussama Makdisi, "After 1860: Debating Religion, Reform, and Nationalism in the Ottoman Empire," *International Journal of Middle East Studies* 34 (2002): 601–617.

70. Butrus al-Bustani, *Nafir Suriyya,* ed. Yusuf Khuri (Beirut: Dar al-Hamra', 1990), no. 9, Beirut, 14 January 1861.

71. Recent critics of Bustani's writings such as Jens Hanssen have underscored Bustani's "bourgeois self-perception" because of his discourse on the civilizing project of a city. Hanssen, *Fin-de-Siècle Beirut,* 227. John Walter Jandoura, "Butrus al-Bustani: Ideas, Endeavors, and Influence" (Ph.D. diss., University of Chicago, 1981), asserts that Bustani's being "Christian" motivated his critical sentiments, which leaves the question of why thousands of other Christians did not express similar sentiments. See also Sheehi's analysis of Bustani's writings, *Foundation of Modern Arab Identity,* 15–45. None of these authors, however, analyzes Bustani's evangelical thought despite the enormous and obvious importance it had for all his writing, especially the relationship between a sense of evangelical "awakening" and a more secular national "awakening."

72. Khuri, *Rajul sabiq li-ʿasrihi,* 53–68; Albert Hourani, *Arabic Thought in the Liberal Age, 1798–1939* (1962; Cambridge: Cambridge University Press 1983), 99–102; Hanssen, *Fin-de-Siècle Beirut,* 164–169; Tibawi, *Arabic and Islamic Themes,* 242.

73. Loanza Benton, "The Diaries, Reminiscences, and Letters of Loanza Goulding Benton (Mrs. William Austin Benton) and William Benton, Missionaries to Syria, 1847–1869," 116. This diary is a facsimile of an unpublished typeset manuscript kindly put at my disposal by Marjorie Benton. Also cited in Hanssen, *Fin-de-Siècle Beirut,* 168, who provides a good comparative perspective of Bustani's work with other educational initiatives in the city in this period.

74. Khuri, *Rajul sabiq li-ʿasrihi,* 58. For Bustani's philosophy of education, see his *Daʾirat al-maʿarif,* vol. 6 (Beirut: Matbaʿat al-maʿarif, 1882), 86–88.

75. Tibawi, *Arabic and Islamic Themes,* 243; Jirji Zaydan, *Tarajim mashahir al-sharq fi al-qarn al-tasiʿ ʿashar,* 2 vols. (Cairo: Hilal, 1902), 2:26.

76. Benjamin C. Fortna, *Imperial Classroom: Islam, the State, and Education in the Late Ottoman Empire* (Oxford: Oxford University Press, 2000), 50–60.

77. Hanssen, *Fin-de-Siècle Beirut,* 169–178.

78. See Norbert J. Scholz, "Foreign Education and Indigenous Reaction in Late Ottoman Lebanon: Students and Teachers at the Syrian Protestant College in Beirut," 2 vols. (Ph.D. diss., Georgetown University, 1997), 1:97–98. The phrase that Rida used, "to distance Muslim male and female students from Islam through various satanic methods," can be found in Salah al-Din al-Munajjid and Yusuf Quzma Khuri, eds., *Fatawa al-imam Muhammad Rashid Rida,* vol. 6 (Beirut: Dar al-Kitab al-jadid, 1970), 2389. For Anderson's "denationalizing," see Tibawi, *Arabic and Islamic Themes,* 264; for more on Rashid Rida and Muslim reactions to the missionaries see Mahmoud Haddad, "Syrian Muslim Attitudes Towards Foreign Missionaries in the Late Nineteenth and Twentieth Centuries," in Eleanor H. Tejirian and Reeva Spector Simon, eds., *Altruism and Imperialism: Western Cultural and Religious Missions in the Middle East* (New York: The Middle East Institute, Columbia University, 2002), 253–274.

79. Daniel Bliss, *The Reminiscences of Daniel Bliss* (New York: Fleming H. Revell, 1920), 212–213.

80. Ibid., 198.

81. Daniel Bliss, *Letters from a New Campus* (Beirut: American University of Beirut Press, 1994), 254.

82. David Stuart Dodge to Daniel Bliss, 25 July 1865, Box 5, Correspondence with D. S. Dodge (1864–1883), AA: 2.3.1, Archives and Special Collections, Jafet Library, American University of Beirut.

83. For information about the Syrian Protestant College's racial policies and the crisis over teaching Darwin, see Shafik Jeha, *Darwin and the Crisis of 1882 in the Medical Department and the First Student Protest in the Arab World in the Syrian Protestant College,* trans. Sally Kaya, ed. Helen Khal (Beirut: American University of Beirut Press, 2004), 102–106; for the most complete account of the college's racial discrimination, see Scholz, "Foreign Education and Indigenous Reaction in Late Ottoman Lebanon," 2:311–332.

84. Cited in Zaydan, *Tarajim mashahir al-sharq,* 2:30.

Epilogue

1. Howard S. Bliss, *The Modern Missionary* (Beirut: Trustees of the Syrian Protestant College, 1920), 4–5. This was reproduced from an article originally published in the *Atlantic Monthly* in May 1920.

2. See Selim Deringil, "An Ottoman View of Missionary Activity in Hawaii," reproduced in *The Ottomans, the Turks, and World Power Politics* (Istanbul: Isis Press, 2000), 131–135; see also Jens Hanssen, *Fin-de-Siècle Beirut* (Oxford: Oxford University Press, 2005), which elaborates this point in terms of competing educational initiatives in the context of the modernization of Beirut.

3. The phrase comes from Mark Twain's ferocious criticism of missionaries and imperialism, "To the Person Sitting in Darkness," which first appeared in the *North American Review* in 1901 and is reproduced in Mark Twain, *Following the Equator and Anti-Imperialist Essays* (New York: Oxford University Press, 1996).

4. See Edward W. Said, "Clash of Definitions," reproduced in his *Reflections on Exile and Other Essays* (Cambridge: Harvard University Press, 2000), 569–590.

5. I am here also indebted to Ann Stoler's discussion of the "politics of comparison" found in her reading of U.S. historiography. See her essay "Tense and Tender Ties," in Ann Laura Stoler, ed., *Haunted by Empire: Geographies of Intimacy in North American History* (Durham: Duke University Press, 2006), 23–67. Bernard Lewis's work on the question of tolerance in the Middle East is the most obvious in this respect, a paradigm of misleading comparison between a putatively liberal West and a depraved modern Middle East; see, for instance, *The Jews of Islam* (Princeton: Princeton University Press, 1984) and the more recent *What Went Wrong? Western Impact and Middle Eastern Response* (New York: Oxford University Press, 2002). For an even more recent articulation of this paradigm, see Michael B. Oren, *Power, Faith, and Fantasy: America in the Middle East, 1776 to the Present* (New York: Norton, 2007). Edward Said's *Orientalism* (New York: Vintage, 1979), of course, remains utterly relevant in this regard.

6. Cited in Shafik Jeha, *Darwin and the Crisis of 1882 in the Medical Department and the First Student Protest in the Arab World in the Syrian Protestant College, Now the American University of Beirut,* trans. Sally Kaya, ed. Helen Khal (Beirut: American University of Beirut Press, 2004), 90.

7. John Waterbury, "Hate Your Policies, Love Your Institutions," *Foreign Affairs* 82 (2003): 58–68.

Index

Italic page numbers refer to figures.

Abbott, Peter, 89–90, 190
ʿAbd al-Munʿim, 44, 45
ʿAlma monastery, 82–84, 111–12, 114–18, 121–22
American Board of Commissioners of Foreign Missions (ABCFM): and American Indians, 11, 13, 30, 53, 56, 67–68, 142, 143, 145, 155, 212, 231n82, 242n53; and Asʿad Shidyaq as martyr, 150, 152, 154, 160; and benevolence, 64, 158, 193, 207, 211; Brainerd honored by, 54, 68; and China, 155, 162, 223n17; and competition among benevolent societies, 144–45; and deficiencies of native spirituality, 192–93; Eliot honored by, 19, 30, 53, 54, 68; and Hawaii, 62–63; history of, 12, 152, 154, 156, 158–59, 160; and interdenominational cooperation, 55; on Islam, 61, 62, 65–66; and lack of conversions in Syria, 190; and medical missionaries, 172; and Ottoman Empire, 63–64, 146–47, 155; and Puritan missionaries, 52–53, 54, 56; purpose of, 2, 51; and religious toleration, 171; and salvation of the heathen, 52, 53, 56, 57–58, 61, 154, 161, 162, 228n7; seal of, 3, 4, 54
American exceptionalism, 142, 155, 156, 172, 178, 180–81, 215

American Indians: and ABCFM, 11, 13, 30, 53, 56, 67–68, 142, 143, 145, 155, 212, 231n82, 242n53; and American expansion, 175, 178, 186; and American Protestant missionaries, 3, 4, 11, 20, 56, 111, 144, 176, 222n9, 246n128; assimilation of, 53–54, 145; and Brainerd, 3, 55, 56–57, 91; civilizing of, 22, 23, 24, 25, 26, 30, 31, 53, 54, 57, 68, 158; comparison to Ottoman Empire inhabitants, 12, 89; as dying race, 197; and Eliot, 3, 11, 19, 20, 21, 22, 23, 24–28, 29, 31, 54, 155; forced removal of, 142–43, 154, 162; and hierarchy of civilizations, 57, 64, 68, 176; Mather on, 20, 21–23, 26, 28, 29, 30, 42, 56, 57; and Puritan missionaries, 19, 23–27, 51, 52–53, 155, 177; Puritans' attitudes toward, 19, 20, 21–22, 28–29, 30, 34, 42, 56, 67–68, 93, 147, 158; resistance of, 27, 225n34; and settler colonialism, 11, 23–24, 26–27, 30, 31, 56, 57, 68, 158
American mission work: and American modernity, 169, 175, 178, 215, 216; and America's redemption, 11, 84, 118, 142, 143–44, 154–55, 158, 161; in biblical lands, 63, 64, 70; dialectic of failure and renewal of, 4; Jessup on, 166, 168, 169–76, 178, 181–82, 215; and lack of Arab Christian converts, 145–46; lack of success with

Italic page numbers refer to figures.

CPSIA information can be obtained
at www.ICGtesting.com
Printed in the USA
LVHW031716030119
602643LV00004B/311/P